RISK AND RESILIENCE

Adolescent Mothers and Their Children
Grow Up

RISK AND RESILIENCE

Adolescent Mothers and Their Children Grow Up

Edited by

John G. Borkowski,
Jaelyn R. Farris
Thomas L. Whitman
University of Notre Dame

Shannon S. Carothers
Georgetown University

Keri Weed
University of South Carolina, Aiken

Deborah A. Keogh
University of Notre Dame

 LAWRENCE ERLBAUM ASSOCIATES, PUBLISHERS
2007   Mahwah, New Jersey   London

Lawrence Erlbaum Associates, Inc., Publishers
10 Industrial Avenue
Mahwah, New Jersey 07430
www.erlbaum.com

Cover design by Tomai Maridou

Library of Congress Cataloging-in-Publication Data

Borkowski, John G
    Risk and Resilience: adolescent mothers and their children grow up /
    John G. Borokowski, Jaelyn R. Farris, and Thomas L. Whitman.
p.   cm.
    Includes bibliographical references and index.
    ISBN 978-0-8058-5054-6 — 0-8058-5054-6 (cloth)
    ISBN 978-0-8058-5055-4 — 0-8058-5055-4 (pbk.)
    ISBN 978-1-4106-1649-5 — 1-4106-1649-5 (e book)
        1. Teenage mothers—United States—Longitudinal. 2. Parent-moth-
    ers—United States—Longitudinal studies. I. Farris, Jaelyn Renee.
    II. Whitman, Thomas L. III. Title.

HQ759.4.B65 2007
306.874'32—dc22   2006026429
                                                                  CIP

Books published by Lawrence Erlbaum Associates are printed on
acid-free paper, and their bindings are chosen for strength and durability.

Printed in the United States of America
10 9 8 7 6 5 4 3 2 1

Contents

Foreword

This volume reports on a research project of enormous scientific, clinical, and policy significance. Teen mothers and their children have been studied, starting before the birth of the child and continuing for the next 14 years. The story told by this research offers many important lessons—about how lives unfold over time, how lives are linked across generations, and most profoundly, about risk and resilience in mothers and in their sons and daughters.

Furthermore, this volume offers an outstanding example of methodologically sophisticated, theory-driven, developmentally-informed, longitudinal research. Indeed, it is a model for other studies to emulate. There are many important methodological lessons—about how research aims evolve over time, about the interplay between inductive and deductive methods, and about how careful in-depth analysis can offer novel insights about risk and resilience and their predictors across time.

The story told is, in many respects, shocking. Although developmentally average at birth, these children began to show delays within the first year of life, and became increasingly impaired over time. Impairments were evident in the mother-child relationship, and in the child's social, adaptive, intellectual, and academic functioning. At age 8, the rate of mild mental retardation was five times what would be expected in the general population, but was often undiagnosed in this sample. Rates of maladaptive behavior (ADHD, Oppositional Defiant Disorder, and Conduct Disorder) were significantly elevated, and fully one-fifth of the children received therapy and/or psychopharmacological treatment for mental health problems. By most measures, only about a quarter of these children were functioning in the "normal" range. As adolescents, many experienced violence as well as abuse and neglect.

This is the risk side of the equation. But this volume also tells us much about resilience, defined as successful adaptation in the face of adversity. We learn about mothers who have not engaged in high-risk behaviors and who do not have psychiatric diagnoses. These mothers instead treated parenthood as a pathway to adulthood. We learn that maternal religiosity, rated as high in 45% of the sample, is a valuable resource that leads to less likelihood of child abuse and less maladaptive behavior in their children. We learn about how positive maternal capacities and parenting practices evident very early in the child's life can lead to improved child self-regulation and better adjustment and achievement during the school years through age 14.

In the face of the many risks described in this volume, it is notable that fully 30% of the children were considered to be resilient at age 14, based on competencies in the intellectual, academic, behavioral, and social domains. Father involvement is common, with over half of the 14-year olds in contact with their fathers. This is important because father involvement was associated with lower levels of behavior problems and better academic achievement.

Finally, this volume offers many implications for intervention. The research underscores the need for interventions that foster self-regulation skills in children (and their mothers). In addition, it speaks to the need for parenting education for pregnant mothers, as lack of knowledge about child development can foster abuse and neglect later in childhood, as well as lower levels of academic achievement and higher levels of behavior problems in their children. The volume elucidates models of prevention programming that are designed to target young mothers, and to provide early intervention for both mother and child. Of course, given that poverty is a pervasive force that erodes the quality of life of many of the sample members, the results also point to the need for anti-poverty interventions.

I personally have been following this study very closely for many years—nearly since its inception. I eagerly look forward to new publications and new opportunities to learn about the unfolding lives of the "adolescent" mothers who are now approaching midlife and their teenage children. What began as a study of early parenting has turned into a study of lifespan development that can inform us about risk and resilience in a unique but not rare population of concern to us all. I urge readers to relish the richness of this volume, and to savor the important new knowledge to be gained about pathways to a more resilient set of outcomes for us all.

—Marsha Seltzer

Preface

Although adolescent parenting is not a new phenomenon in the United States, the familial and cultural settings in which it is embedded have changed dramatically during the past several decades. In the first half of the 20th century, young single women who became pregnant often married or received emotional and financial supports from the fathers of their children. In other cases, families absorbed both the newborns and the young mothers into their supportive networks. Relatedly, it was relatively common for unmarried mothers to place their children for adoption.

In the 1960s, a new trend emerged in which teenage mothers increasingly rejected adoption as a viable option and, instead, raised their children as single parents, at times within the context of an extended family, but often on their own. Frequently, these mothers lived in poverty, surviving on welfare assistance and limited support from friends, partners, or families of origin. Although the birth rate for adolescents has declined drastically in the past decade, off-timed parenthood still remains a concern for many families, social agencies, and society at large.

With the occurrence of high rates of adolescent parenting in the 1970s and 1980s, public concern was raised about potentially adverse developmental outcomes for both teen mothers and their children. Although considerable research on adolescent parenting was conducted, it tended to be narrow in its scope of inquiry and generally was based on crossectional or short-term longitudinal designs. Minimal attention was given to investigating systematic, microgenetic changes in adolescent mothers and their children's psychological development over time, as influenced by both risk and protective factors. Also missing were answers to an important question: Why, and under what circumstances, do some teen mothers and some of their children fare better than others in terms of major life outcomes?

In 1984, a longitudinal study was launched to evaluate the social and psychological consequences of teenage parenting for both the mothers and their children. In contrast to previous research, mothers in the Notre Dame Adolescent Parenting Project (NDAPP), although poor, were not enmeshed in "deep poverty." At the inception of the study, the adolescents were, for the most part, in school or job training. Generally, their infants had normal birth weights and gestational ages, were without congenital anomalies, and showed little evidence of substance abuse. In contrast to teenage mothers in large urban settings, the Notre Dame sample appeared "more advantaged," and their infants were clearly healthier at birth.

In 2001, *Interwoven Lives: Adolescent Mothers and Their Children* was published by Lawrence Erlbaum Associates. The book described, in considerable detail, the development of adolescent mothers and their children across the first 8 years of life. Childhood delays were first noticed in their patterns of attachment at age 1, and in their IQ scores at age 3. School-related problems were observed in 70% of the children at age 8. In addition, mothers seldom remained in stable relationships, generally became trapped in low income jobs, had low self-esteem, and higher than expected rates of depression. With these data as the background, we now search in this company volume to *Interwoven Lives* (2001) for the processes that lead to resilience in some teen mothers and their children as well as major risk factors associated with long-term developmental delays that were repeatedly observed in a sizable proportion of participants in the NDAPP, especially the children involved.

The focus of this text is on tracing development at ages 8, 10, and 14, and identifying risk and protective factors associated with important life course trajectories during early adulthood for the mothers and early adolescence for the children. Its unique aspect is the identification of a range of relatively unexplored protective factors—such as religiosity, patterns of father involvement, and romantic relationships—that can positively influence developmental outcomes for both teenage mothers and their children as they move through major life transitions. This text also focuses on new approaches to design, methodology, and data analyses, as well as draws implications for future prevention and intervention programs.

In chapter 1, we describe the NDAPP, highlighting the nature of the sample and major findings through the first 5 years of life for both mothers and children. This chapter sets the stage for our analyses of developmental risks and resilient behaviors observed in mothers and children in multiple domains. Chapters 2, 3, and 4 present outcome data in intellectual, educational, and socioemotional domains for mothers and children when the former were between 27 and 31 years of age and the latter between 10 and 14 years. In chapters 5 and 6, we present the "dark side" of rearing children in poverty—focusing on child maltreatment and exposure to violence in children's lives and their adverse impact on development during late childhood and early adolescence. Chapters 7 and 8 discuss vulnerability in the face of multiple risks and identify protective factors that allow some children to "overcome the odds" and succeed in achieving the development tasks associated with early adolescents. Chapter 9 describes sophisticated design and analytic approaches to research on risk and resilience, with a specific focus on the analysis of longitudinal data. In chapter 10, we summarize the major outcomes in the NDAPP and develop a prototype prevention program that attempts to create and/or strengthen a variety of protective factors operating in the lives of teen mothers and their children. The prototype model draws on our knowledge of risk and resilience, based on insights from the NDAPP, in order to point the way for future research on the prevention of developmental delays among at-risk children.

ACKNOWLEDGMENTS

The Notre Dame Parenting Project and writing of this book has been generously funded by a series of grants from the Office of Adolescent Family Life (AR–000936) and the National Institute of Child Health and Development (HD–26456). Especially noteworthy is the history of support and assistance from the Mental Retardation and Developmental Disabilities Branch of NICHD.

There are many people to thank for their assistance in the development and execution of the Notre Dame Parenting Project. Without their help, there would be no data, and/or this book would never have been written. First, and most important, are the parents and children in the NDAPP for sharing their lives with us as well as the children's teachers who gave, and continue to give, so much of their time to make this project possible. Special thanks go to our valuable colleagues: Sebrina Tingley (our project manager who "stayed close" to the participants throughout the project) as well as a host of graduate research assistants who "labored in the field." Special appreciation is due several important individuals, including Cindy Schellenbach who helped formulate our original model of adolescent parenting, Scott Maxwell for his patient and competent statistical assistance, Virginia Colin for her assistance in scoring the Strange Situation assessments, and Jennifer Souders and Sarah Bassett for their considerable help in the preparation of this book. Finally, we would like to express our gratitude to our spouses, companions, and families by dedicating this book to them.

1

Adolescent Mothers and Their Children: Risks, Resilience, and Development

John G. Borkowski
Thomas L. Whitman
Jaelyn R. Farris

*The farther backward you can look, the farther forward
you are likely to see.*

—Winston Churchill

ADOLESCENT PARENTING IN THE NEW MILLENNIUM

Despite dramatic declines in the rate of adolescent childbearing in the United States since the early 1990s, teenage parenting continues to be a significant social problem. More than three quarters of

1

a million teens become pregnant each year, with more than one half of the pregnancies resulting in live births. Of these births, approximately 90% of the mothers choose to assume the responsibilities of parenting themselves rather than placing their children for adoption. A long line of research studies suggests that most teen mothers and/or their children are at risk for a variety of developmental problems (Furstenberg, Brooks-Gunn, & Morgan, 1987; Whitman, Borkowski, Keogh, & Weed, 2001). Life trajectories of adolescent mothers are highly variable, with perhaps only one third doing reasonably well as young adults (Furstenberg et al., 1987). From another perspective, more than 50% of their children typically experience academic difficulties during their early school years, usually attributable to early-appearing delays in intelligence, language, cognition, socioemotional adjustment, and social competence (Whitman et al., 2001). These problems often persist into late adolescence (Furstenberg et al., 1987).

This book describes the fate of a representative sample of teen mothers and their children—born in the late 1980s and early 1990s—across the first 14 years of their lives. We focus on identifying the risks associated with developmental delays and protective factors associated with resilience. Our goal is to understand the mechanisms and pathways through which risk and protective factors exert their influence on development during late childhood and early adolescence.

Using data from our longitudinal project that monitored the development of teen mothers and their children from pregnancy through early adolescence—the Notre Dame Adolescent Parenting Project (NDAPP)—we search for answers to the following questions: To what extent are teen mothers and their children at risk for developmental problems? Are the lives of teenage mothers and their children intimately "interwoven" or, instead, do they follow divergent developmental paths? What factors place them at risk for adverse outcomes? Conversely, what is the nature of pathways that lead to positive outcomes for both mothers and their children? In short, we investigate the correlates and causal mechanisms that influence development during late childhood and early adolescence and provide insights into the differences between resilient and vulnerable mothers and their children.

We seek answers to these questions in order to shed new light on the important phenomenon of teenage parenthood and the lifelong problems it poses for millions of children in the United States. It is important to understand the problems and issues associated with teenage parenting in order to inform social policies and to establish a more precise foundation for prevention and intervention programs. We believe this process should be guided by a careful analysis of risk and protective factors associated with teen parenting in order to allow mothers and children who are most vulnerable to be offered early intervention programs.

The Changing Nature of Adolescence

Perhaps the most dramatic recent change in the stages of human development is the prolongation of adolescence. One hundred years ago, adolescence, as marked by the onset of puberty and later by the assumption of adult roles, was relatively short, from 13–14 to 17–19. Within a century, the 5-year window that previously defined adolescence for hundreds of years has lengthened to about 15 years, from age 10 to age 25.

Both biological and cultural forces have been responsible for the expansion of adolescence as a critical stage of human development, marking the transition from childhood to adulthood. Physical-sexual maturation is occurring at much earlier ages, particularly among girls. In the United States, the average age of menarche was about 16 in the early 1800s. In contrast, a recent large study in the United States found that the average age of menarche in the mid-1990s was around 12, and that by age 10 the majority of European American girls had breast and/or pubic hair development; even more dramatically, 95% of African American girls had reached this same level of early puberty by age 10 (HermanGiddens et al., 1997).

The early appearance of puberty may create "maturational asynchronies" between the cognitive and affective systems, leading to prolonged delays in the emergence of self regulation (Dahl & Spear, 2004). In turn, deficits in regulation hinder planning and decision making in social, emotional, and academic domains, thus compromising the overall development of teenage mothers and their ability to assume adult roles, such as childrearing and stable employment. Recent imaging research supports the hypothesized delays in self-regulation associated with adolescence, showing that regions in the prefrontal cortex that mediate both cognitive and affect regulation continue to mature into the early 20s (Sowell & Jernegan, 1998).

From this perspective, the adolescent mothers followed in the NDAPP may well be different—especially in terms of their emotional regulation—from adolescent mothers sampled during the 1960s, such as those described by Furstenberg et al. (1987). Major changes in society have occurred in the past two decades that have further compromised parenting practices among adolescent mothers in the 1980s and 1990s. These include dramatic shifts in the welfare system that require early entrance into the workforce; less stable social support systems caused, in part, by greater mobility and volatility in extended families, including the presence of young grandmothers who are sometimes unable or unwilling to provide the same supports as in earlier generations; more violence among teenage girls in homes, schools, and neighborhoods; greater intimate partner, domestic, and dating violence; the easy availability of drugs and alcohol; and unresolved issues of depression and feelings of hopelessness. This is not to say that these same factors were not present in earlier generations of teen mothers to compromise their parenting practices, but rather that their prevalence and severity have increased. In short, we speculate that the changing nature of adolescence itself and the socialcultural factors encompassing the lives of the generation of teenage mothers studied in the NDAPP may have complicated their successful transition to adulthood and the assumption of the parenting role, providing obstacles to the healthy development of their children.

Trends in Teen Pregnancy and Early Childbearing

The teenage birth rate has declined continuously since 1991 and is at a historic low (Franzetta, Ikramullah, Manlove, Moore, & TerryHumen, 2005). Teens accounted for 50% of births to unwed mothers in 1970, but only 24% in 2004. In 2003, there were 42 births per 1,000 15- to 19-year-olds, a rate that is one third lower than the 1991 rate of 62 births per 1,000 and 18% lower than the 1985 rate of

51. African American teen birth rates declined by 45% between 1991 and 2003, whereas the teen birth rate declined 35% for European American teens and 22% for Latina teens. In 2003, birth rates continued to decline among both younger and older subgroups. The dramatic decline in birth rates to teenagers can be seen in Figure 1.1. It should be noted that the U.S. teen birth rate varies greatly by state, ranging from a low in New Hampshire of 20 births per 1,000 teens to a high in Mississippi of 65 births per 1,000.

Trends in declining adolescent birth rates have been accompanied by changes in sexual behaviors, number of first pregnancies, interpregnancy intervals, and abortion rate (Franzetta et al., 2005).

- There has been a decline since 1995 in the percentage of teens who have ever had sex. For instance, about 66% disagree or strongly disagree that it is acceptable for unmarried 16-year-olds to have sex.
- Among teens who had sex in 2002, compared with 1995, more reported that they used a contraceptive method at first sex, and more reported using a contraceptive method and dual contraceptive methods (e.g., hormonal and condom) on the most recent occasion.

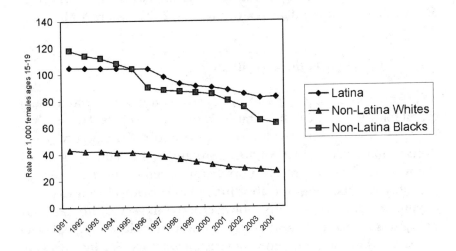

Figure 1.1.   U.S. teen birth rate by race/ethnicity, 1991–2004 (adapted from Franzetta et al., 2005).

- The proportion of adolescent Latina females who were sexually experienced dropped by nearly 33% between 1995 and 2002, representing the largest decline in sexual activity for any group.
- The number of pregnancies and the number of abortions declined, and the percentage of teen pregnancies that ended in abortion dropped dramatically: 40% of all teen pregnancies in the mid-1980s were terminated versus 29% in 2000.
- The decline in births to adolescent mothers needs to be interpreted in the context of the overall decline in total births in the United States.

Although these reductions in the U.S. teen birth rate are significant for individuals and society at large, there are important reasons to remain concerned about teenage childbearing in this country: A high proportion of teens are sexually experienced. Almost half of high school students have had sexual intercourse, and 1 in 5 teens has had sexual intercourse before age 15. An estimated 17% of current 15-year-old girls will give birth before age 20, and 1 in 5 teen births will be a repeat birth. What is most troublesome in these data is the fact that the youngest sexually active teenage girls are those most likely to have sex with an older man and experience nonvoluntary sex and higher rates of drug and alcohol use (Manlove, Moore, Liechty, Ikramullah, & Cottingham, 2005; Moore & Manlove, 2005).

Causes of Changes in the Teen Birth Rate

A variety of interest groups are quick to point out, and often claim credit for, the decline in birth rates among adolescents. Those advocating abstinence, more widespread and improved use of contraception, welfare reform, AIDS education, and right-to-life policies all claim some credit for recent population-based changes in teenage sexuality, childbearing, and abortion rates. The precise causes of the declining birth rate to teens, however, are unknown, although our best guess is that these decreases are not the result of any single factor, but rather the confluence of multiple factors. For instance, we know that more women now use condoms at first intercourse; contraceptive use is also increasing among adolescents, in part due to their fear of AIDS and sexually transmitted diseases (National Survey of Family Growth, 1997). New forms of contraception (e.g., "the patch") that are easier to use and more reliable have also played a role. From another perspective, teenagers well connected to their families—who are more open to discussions about moral values, peer pressures, and early sexuality—are less likely to begin sexual activity at an early age. More extensive demographic research is needed to identify the precise factors leading to the recent declines in teenage pregnancy and birth rates, especially the role of novel prevention programs (cf. Allen, Philliber, Herrling, & Kuperminc, 1997).

Cross-Cultural Comparisons in Sexual Activity and Birth Rates

Despite the decline in the birth rate to teens, the United States still leads the developed countries of the world in both early sexual behaviors and teen birth rates. For instance, teenagers in the United States are more likely to have had sexual intercourse prior to age 15 and more sexual relationships than teenagers in Great Britain, France, Canada, and Sweden. Figure 1.2 contrasts the U.S. birth and abortion rates with these four countries, revealing sizeable differences in both. These differences are due, in part, to the fact that only 55% of U.S. women under age 16 and 70% of women over age 19 use

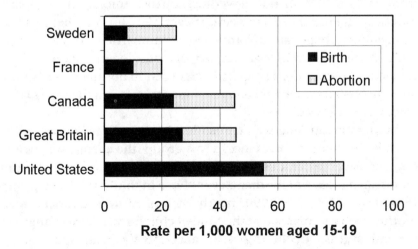

Figure 1.2. Birth and abortion rates for adolescents in five developed countries (adapted from Guttmacher Institute, 2006).

contraceptives at first sexual intercourse (Guttmacher Institute, 2006). It appears that teenagers in the United States lead the other industrialized countries in rates of pregnancy, childbearing, and abortions because they are less likely to use contraceptives, including longer-acting methods (e.g., hormonal) of birth control. In general, U.S. teenagers express ambivalence about contraceptive use, are often limited in their access to contraceptive methods, and appear to lack the self regulatory processes necessary to avoid unplanned pregnancies.

Changes in Marital Status Across Four Decades

An important demographic phenomenon affecting family structure, especially among teens, is the change in the number of out-of-wedlock births. In the early 1960s, it was relatively uncommon for adolescent girls to give birth outside of marriage (Elo, King, & Furstenberg, 1999). In contrast, by 1994 it was rare for younger European American teens—between 10 and 17—to be married at childbirth: Only about 20% in this age range were married, in contrast to about 70% in 1960. Within this broad age group, the biggest change from 1960 to 1990 occurred for those between 15 and 17, a shift from 15% to 75% in out-of-wedlock births. Among all European American teens, those between 18 and 19 showed the smallest change in marriage rates (from about 5% unmarried to 55%); nevertheless, this shift was sizable and of considerable social consequence. Although the last decade has seen major decreases in the teenage birth rate, similar changes in marital status at the time of first birth have not occurred.

Among African American teens, the rise in out-of-wedlock births has been even more dramatic. In this group, the change was nearly 60% across three decades. The sharp increase occurred for all African American adolescent mothers, even those in the 18 to 19 age group (Elo et al., 1999). By 1990, nearly 85% of African American teen mothers were unmarried at the time of childbirth. These changes in marital status—occurring over a relatively brief span of 30 years—have had major financial, emotional, and social implications for single mothers and their children. The lack of an adequate and stable financial base, together with fragile family structures, represent major obstacles for single mothers trying to become successful parents (McLanahan, 1999). The situation is likely even more problematic for unmarried teenage mothers, with their increasingly fragile support systems and dangerous neighborhood environments.

Fathers and Patterns of Childcare

The National Longitudinal Study of Adolescent Health has provided a comprehensive picture of the health-related behaviors of about 90,000 teenagers, both boys and girls. At a general level, the project found that African American youth (65%) were more likely to have intercourse than European American (33%) or Latino youth (41%) (Blum, Beuhring, & Rinehart, 2000). Interestingly, the risks for pregnancies caused by African American teenage males can be identified as early as age 8, with the major predisposing factor being a conduct disorder (a pattern of stable aggression) during the early school years (i.e., Grades 3 to 5) (Miller-Johnson, Winn, Coie, & Malone, 2004). The overall risk for impregnating a teen girl during middle and late adolescence is further enhanced by substance use and negative peer group involvement during early adolescence (Miller-Johnson et al., 2004).

Typically, the partner of a teenage mother is 2 to 4 years older than the mother, with a greater span occurring with younger teens (i.e., those 15 and under). Although there is a widely held belief that teenage fathers are generally nonsupportive of the mothers of their children, recent data suggest that father involvement, though somewhat sporadic, is typically maintained over the first few years of life. For instance, the Early Head Start Research and Evaluation Study reported that around 80% of fathers of 2-year-old children born to teen mothers had at least one contact in the previous month (Cabrera et al., 2004). Among Latinos, the frequency of paternal involvement is even higher (East & Felice, 1996). In this book, we identify factors that serve to enhance children's social and academic development, including father contact over the first 10 years of life (cf. chap. 8).

Repeat Pregnancies

Many teen mothers have a second child within 2 years after their first child. For instance, East and Felice (1996) found that 35% of the 200 adolescent mothers in their sample had a repeat pregnancy within 18 months after the first birth. The second pregnancy was often associated with a failure of the mother to return to school, thus deterring her ability to gain financial independence and economic security. It should be noted that women who bear their first children before age 20 have, on average, three children. In contrast, those who delay childbearing have, on average, two children during their lifetime (Furstenberg et al., 1987). Terry-Humen, Manlove, and Moore (2005) concluded their thorough review, *Playing Catch-Up*, with the observation that "teen pregnancy prevention programs need to delay childbearing not just by a few months or even into the late teens, but into the twenties, to enhance children's development" (p. 25).

An often-ignored factor that appears related to a repeat pregnancy is the degree of family support received by the teen mother while raising her first child. Apfel and Seitz (1999) reported that family support predicted subsequent childbearing: Both too much support (e.g., the grandmother provided total replacement care) or too little support (e.g., the adolescent received little or no help) were associated with a 42% rate of second pregnancies that occurred within 30 months, versus 24% among similar mothers who received moderate support, supplementary care, and coaching from family members, especially from the grandmother. A moderate amount of family support not only helps to prevent an immediate repeat pregnancy but also serves to help teen mothers from "dropping out" of their parenting roles and abandoning their commitments to their first-born children (cf. Apfel & Seitz, 1999).

LONGITUDINAL RESEARCH ON ADOLESCENT MOTHERS AND THEIR CHILDREN

Landmark Longitudinal Projects

In a widely cited project, Furstenberg et al. (1987) conducted a longitudinal study examining the fate of adolescent mothers and their children from early childhood through early adolescence. Primiparous mothers were recruited in Baltimore in the mid to late 1960s, a period of optimism for many in poverty, in part because of the promises and programs of the "Great Society." The adolescent mothers who were enrolled in this "Baltimore Project" experienced a variety of outcomes in the 17 years following their transition to parenthood. Although the project did not focus intensively on process variables—such as maternal depression, self-esteem, and stress—it did measure important maternal outcomes, such as income level, welfare status, and number of subsequent children.

More successful mothers were economically secure, or had modest incomes, compared with the "working poor" or welfare recipients; they also tended to limit further childbearing. The strongest predictor of welfare status at the time of the adult follow-up was the education level of the grandparents, independent of the teen mother's own educational status. Furstenberg et al. (1987) surmised that grandparents with more education had greater economic and social resources to assist their teenage daughters in becoming independent adults and more effective parents. Not surprisingly, the strongest predictor of fertility was the length of time before the second child was born. The success of some teens in delaying the second pregnancy and in limiting their total number of pregnancies was attributed, in part, to participation in school and community intervention programs, suggesting that these types of assistance may have compensated for limited family supports and personal resources.

A second major longitudinal project was initiated in New Haven at about the same time as the Baltimore Project (Horowitz, Klerman, Kuo, & Jekel, 1991). Follow-up data, collected nearly 20 years later, supported the general findings of the Baltimore project: 66% of teen mothers had completed high school; the majority had recently been on welfare; most had more than one but fewer than four children (Horowitz et al., 1991). It should be emphasized that it is difficult to tell whether these outcomes were due to off-timed births and/or to the factors that helped to produce the pregnancies in the first place.

East and Felice (1996) conducted a third important longitudinal project investigating the development of adolescent mothers and their children across the first 3 years of life. The San Diego project was unique in its assessments of parenting quality (every 6 months), use of medical care, repeat pregnancies, and the roles of fathers and grandmothers in parenting. The following factors emerged as predictors or correlates of maternal and parenting outcomes: (a) Older adolescents who had frequent prenatal medical visits and abstained from alcohol and other drugs showed more positive mother–child outcomes; (b) positive parenting and high confidence in parenting skills were associated with better social development in children, and low maternal stress was associated with fewer displays of aggression in children; (c) delayed repeat pregnancies were associated with less alcohol and drug use during the second pregnancy and, not surprisingly, resulted in better child outcomes; (d) Latina mothers and children were more at risk for developmental problems if they reported less mature parenting values (e.g., unrealistic expectations, less empathy, and greater use of punishment), less confidence in their parenting skills, and lower levels of child acceptance; (e) adolescents who had more favorable parenting attitudes and skills generally lived apart from their mothers but still received high amounts of child care and support; and (f) although 60% of the fathers were involved with their children at 3 years, only about 30% provided substantial financial supports. No clear associations were uncovered regarding father involvement and child outcomes. Although fathers rarely provided hands-on care, it is likely that the subgroup of more "involved fathers" provided at least a minimal protective mechanism, especially in the domains of social development and academic achievement (cf. Howard, Lefever, Borkowski, & Whitman, 2006).

INTERWOVEN LIVES: A NEW LOOK AT ADOLESCENT MOTHERS AND THEIR CHILDREN

A longitudinal study was launched at the University of Notre Dame in the mid-1980s to evaluate the social and psychological consequences of teen parenting for both mothers and their children. The NDAPP, supported by grants from the PHS (Office of Adolescent Family Life) and NICHD, has gathered data on teenage mothers and their children from pregnancy through the first 14 years of life. The first phase of this project was guided by a model of child development that featured social, psychological, and biological variables that were thought to predispose the infants of adolescent mothers to early developmental problems. The main focus of the second phase was on examining the emergence through age 5 of developmental delays in children of teen mothers, along with their maternal antecedents. The third phase followed the children of teen mothers as they reached 8 and 10 years, developmental periods during which many childhood impairments, such as mild retardation, learning disabilities, and conduct problems, began to be diagnosed.

The fourth phase involved collecting data when children reached age 14. In this phase, we had three major aims: (a) assess academic achievement during the middle school years as well as its major precursors; (b) measure socioemotional adjustment and involvement in risky behaviors during the early adolescent period and determine their antecedents; and (c) pinpoint the role of early maternal and child characteristics in explaining resilience, especially in the development of children's adjustment and self-regulatory capacities. Maternal and child development from pregnancy through age 8 was presented in *Interwoven Lives* (Whitman et al., 2001). This book focuses primarily on the development of mothers and children at 10 and 14 years of age.

A Model of At-Risk Parenting

Our project has been guided by a conceptual model of teen parenting that has a special focus on the variables that improve or restrict appropriate parenting practices (Borkowski, Ramey, & Bristol-Power, 2002; Whitman et al., 2001). The model provides a framework for examining the complex influences of antecedent variables on a variety of childhood developmental outcomes. The proposed model—presented in Figure 1.3—contains six major constructs central to at-risk parenting and successful childrearing. These include *maternal adjustment, child characteristics,* and *social support* (all proposed in Belsky's [1984] influential model of adult parenting), along with four unique constructs for at-risk mothers living in poverty—*cognitive readiness, learning ability, substance abuse, and past history of domestic violence, abuse, and/or neglect* (for simplicity, we have embedded substance abuse and his-

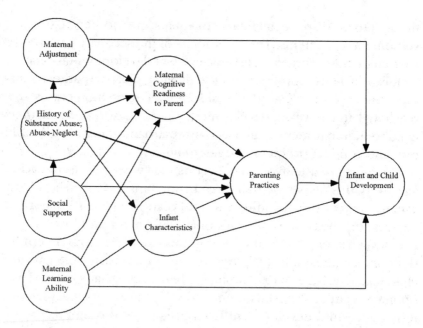

Figure 1.3.   A conceptual model of at-risk parenting (adapted from Whitman et al., 2001).

tories of abuse–neglect within a single construct; in fact, they are often causally related).

Although the model in Figure 1.3 postulates numerous direct and indirect influences on early parenting behaviors, the most important relationships can be summarized as follows: To parent effectively, an at-risk mother must be cognitively prepared. Cognitive readiness is related to a variety of maternal factors (personal adjustment, history of abuse, neglect, and learning ability) and social supports. These factors in turn influence maternal cognitive readiness to parent as well as early child characteristics. In conjunction, these sources of influence determine the nature and quality of parenting practices, including inconsistent parenting and child maltreatment. In addition, a mother's capacity to deal with the stressors associated with parenting depends on whether her child displays challenging characteristics (e.g., a difficult temperament) that can complicate the parenting task and tax her personal coping resources.

By the end of the 1st year of life, and during subsequent years, the quality of children's cognitive (e.g., attention and language) and socioemotional development (e.g., attachment and socioemotional functioning) are related to the combined influence of the factors represented in Figure 1.3, with cognitive readiness to parent (i.e., a mother's mental model of parenting) serving an important mediational role in explaining variability in the quality of parenting (including inconsistent and neglectful parenting), which in turn influences subsequent child development. We hypothesize that cognitive readiness to parent is the most amenable to change during the "critical window" of new parenting—shortly before, and immediately after the birth of the first child.

Characteristics of the NDAPP Sample

Recruitment, Attrition, and Sample Size. The adolescent mothers who participated in the NDAPP entered the study in small waves of four to five beginning in 1985 and continuing through 1991. A total of 281 adolescents were initially recruited: 233 from South Bend, Indiana, and 48 from Aiken, South Carolina. The highest attrition rate was from the time of the initial prenatal interviews to the 6-month postnatal assessments (25%). There was an additional attrition of about 8% from 6 months to 1 year. Thus of the 233 South Bend mothers who began Phase 1, 117 dyads remained in the project at 3 years of age and 110 dyads participated at 5 years. Of the 48 expectant mothers recruited in South Carolina, 27 participated at 3 years and 26 at 5 years. At age 8, we collected data on 110 participants, 105 at age 10, and 102 at age 14.

Major Maternal and Child Characteristics. The characteristics of our adolescent parent sample should allow meaningful generalizations to be made about the population of teen mothers in the United States, since it mirrors in many important respects their demographic characteristics. The average age of the mothers at the time of childbirth was 17.1 years. The sample was comprised of 62.5% African American, 33.2% European American, and 4.3% Latina mothers; 9% were married and about 20% were from small towns or rural areas. The mothers completed, on the average, 10.5 years of school. The average estimated IQ for the teen mother sample was 87, with 17% having IQs below 70 and few with IQs greater than 100. Intellectual ability was measured by the Vocabulary and Block Design subtests of the WAIS–R and WISC–R (the choice of test depended on the age of mother at time of entry to the program).

Relatively few of the infants (9%) had birth weights below 2,500 gm.; APGAR scores were not different from children of adult mothers; and 6-month Bayley IQs were 101.7. What is interesting here is that much like in the Abecedarian project (Borkowski & Ramey, 2002), infants at birth in the NDAPP were indistinguishable from infants of mothers in the general population, whereas teen mothers were reliably different from adult mothers on almost all constructs in the parenting model (e.g., cognitive readiness to parent, personal adjustments, social support, etc.). Shortly after birth, children started to display signs of developmental problems. The most notable signs in the first born children of adolescent mothers were the following: (a) at 6 months, about 67% of the infants were classified as having a difficult temperament; and (b) at 1 year, 62% of the sample was insecurely attached. These early appearing characteristics were precursors to a series of problems that emerged in the preschool years (Whitman et al., 2001). These developmental problems are reviewed later in this chapter.

Design and Methodology of the NDAPP. Measures of maternal and child functioning were taken prenatally and when children were 6 months, 1, 3, 5, 8, 10, and 14 years of age, with a focus on gathering proxy variables for later developing mental retardation, learning disabilities, and behavioral disorders (see Tables 1.1 and 1.2). As Table 1.1 shows, measures of maternal socioemotional adjustment and children's intelligence, adaptive behavior, socioemotional adjustment, and academic achievement were selected as the major criteria or outcome variables, whereas other measures (e.g., prenatal maternal cognitive functioning and postnatal maternal parenting practices) were selected as predictor variables during the first 10 years of the project.

Although the assessment scheme at age 14 contained many of the same outcomes, new measures of child (e.g., delinquency) and maternal (e.g., health and spirituality) outcomes were added (cf. Table 1.2). For instance, we focused more intently on social competence

TABLE 1.1

Assessments of Mothers Across a 10-Year Period

	During Pregnancy	6 months	1 yr.	3 & 5 yrs.	8 & 10 yrs.
Mother					
Intellectual	WISC/WAIS-R (short form)			WAIS-R (short form)	WAIS-R (short form)
Cognitive readiness	-Knowledge of child dev. -Parental style -Parenting attitudes				-Knowledge of child dev. -Parenting style -Parenting attitudes
Social support	Interview	Phone interview	Interview Inventory of parents and peer attachment	Interview Personal network	Family support scale Personal network
Socioemotional	YSR Social problem Solving skills		Child abuse potential (CAP) Self-esteem	CAP Beck depression Self-esteem State-trait anxiety (STAI)	CAP Beck depression Self-esteem STAI Self-efficacy
Parenting		MIS Parenting stress	MIS Mother–Child relationships	MIS Washington Home Scale Life stress	MIS Washington Home Scale
Child					
Intellectual	Bayley Scales of Infant Development	Bayley Scales of Infant Development	Stanford-Binet PPVT-R		WISC–III MFF20 PPVT–R
Self-Regulation					Teacher ratings of self-regulation Metamory Attributions for success and failure
Socioemotional		Carey Infant Temperament Questionnaire	Attachment Temperament	Temperament (BSQ) CBCL	Temperament (CBCL) Teacher report form CDI Cooper-Farran Behavior Rating Conners Teacher Report Index of Empathy Manifest anxiety General selfscale
Adaptive behavior		MIS	MIS	MIS Vineland Adaptive Behavior Scales	MIS Vineland Adaptive Behavior Scales
Achievement				PIAT (Math and reading)	PIAT–R School achievement

TABLE 1.2

The 14-year Assessment Protocol

Child		Mother	
Domain	Measures	Domain	Measures
Achievement (Math and Reading)	Standardized test scores[3] Grades[3] WIAT[1]	Demographic information	Life Circumstances Interview[2]
Intellectual competence	WISC–III[1]	Parenting	Quality of parenting[1] Stress Index for Parents[2] Self-efficacy for parenting[2]
Strategy knowledge	Index of Reading Awareness	Socio-emotional adjustmerit	CAPI[2] Beck Depression[2] Coopersmith Self-esteem State Trait Anxiety[2] Personal self-efficacy[2]
Attributional beliefs	Attribution Test[1] Possible selves[1]	Health and substance use	Stress and Health Questionnaire
Socio-emotional adjustment	Achenbach TRF[3] CDI[1] Coopersmith Self-esteem[1] YSR[1]	Social support	Support interview[2]
Social competence	Social support interview[1] Social skills rating system[2] Loneliness scale[1]	Spiritualality	Spiritual Experience Index[2] Kasl's Religious Index[2]
Risky behaviors	Delinquency[1] Drugs and alcohol use		
Protective factors	Spiritual Experience Index[1] Kasl's Religious Index[1]		

and risky behaviors. A particular strength of the study was its longitudinal and multidimensional approach to understanding the antecedents of developmental delays and resilience in both mothers and their children.

MAJOR FINDINGS FROM THE NDAPP

Maternal Functioning

Major results from the first two phases of the NDAPP were reported in our earlier Lawrence Erlbaum Associates book on *Interwoven Lives* (Whitman et al., 2001) and are only briefly summarized here. Adolescent mothers, during pregnancy, experienced a sequence of socioemotional and behavioral problems, problematic social supports, and were generally less prepared for parenting than adult parents. Three, 5, and 8 years after the birth of their first children, they tended to be undereducated, underemployed, and continued to have additional children (Whitman et al., 2001). As expected, however, there were considerable individual differences in maternal outcomes, with some mothers showing reasonably good adjustment, some showing generalized difficulties across multiple developmental domains, and some manifesting problems in only one specific area. Moreover, there was considerable instability in maternal functioning over time, particularly in the domain of personal adjustment (Whitman et al., 2001).

Six months after the birth of their first child, most mothers displayed less than optimal attitudes and knowledge about parenting and children (referred to in our model as cognitive readiness to parent), higher levels of stress, and more problematic parenting styles (Sommer, Whitman, Borkowski, Schellenbach, Maxwell, & Keogh, 1993; Whitman et al., 2001). Our research has emphasized the importance of these factors for early parenting practices and subsequent child development (Miller, Heysek, Whitman, & Borkowski, 1996; Wurtz-Passino et al., 1993). When children were 8 years of age, 38% of the mothers were depressed; more specifically, mild, moderate and severe depression were observed in 20.8%, 11.7% and 5.2% of our sample.

Many adolescent mothers also appeared to be at risk for practicing neglectful or abusive parenting (Dukewich, Borkowski, & Whitman, 1996; 1999), due, in part, to their inadequate readiness to parent. Early parenting brought with it unexpected conflicts between the mother's need to nurture her child and her own strong need for nurturance, often resulting in increased stress and a predisposition toward abusive–neglectful parenting practices. This tendency toward abuse and neglect was not originally hypothesized, but rather emerged as part of our analysis of inadequate parenting practices among adolescent mothers and now appears related to other maternal adjustment problems (Dukewich et al., 1996; 1999).

Young mothers, when interacting with their children, were found to be more intolerant, impatient, insensitive, more punitive, less accessible and less verbal than adult mothers (Sommer et al., 1993). Comparative analyses of videotaped social–play interactions revealed that adolescent mothers were significantly less verbal, less affectionate, less controlling, less flexible and more inappropriate in their stimulation of their children than adult mothers (Sommer et al., 1993). These parenting styles along with the other aforementioned maternal characteristics were related to later developmental delays in the children (Whitman et al., 2001).

Eighty-three percent of mothers were single at the time of the 8-year assessment; only 17% were married. However, 13% had been married previously but were currently divorced or separated. Another 13% were currently living with a boyfriend. Remarriage was not typical for this group; only 4 mothers (4.7% of total sample) reported multiple marriages. Fifty-seven percent were in contact with the biological fathers of their first children; roughly 80% reported that the fathers provided at least some type of support (e.g., financial, emotional, or help with child care). Most mothers were consistently living near or under the poverty line.

At the 8-year assessment, the majority of mothers (approximately 86%) reported having more than one child; percentages of mothers having two, three, and four children were 29.8%, 33.3%, and 20.2%, respectively. Roughly half (53.6%) of mothers reported being currently employed, and about 18% were attending school, most of them part time. The average number of years of education was 11.99 years; however, 82.3% said they wanted to or planned to go back to school.

The most frequently cited obstacles to continuing education were the cost of tuition as well as the availability and cost of child care.

Early Childhood Delays in the NDAPP

At the outset of the NDAPP, we noted that the infants of adolescent mothers were physically healthy at birth, as evidenced by their average gestational ages, birth weights, and APGAR scores, as well as low incidence of congenital problems. Even at 6 months and 1 year, Bayley IQ scores showed that the children were functioning mentally and physically within normal ranges. Moreover, comparative analyses failed to reveal behavioral differences in the responsivity and the general activity levels of the infants of teen and adult mothers.

Despite a generally optimistic profile of early development, problems emerged by the end of the 1st year of life. These developmental problems subsequently snowballed into more serious delays, with the children of adolescent mothers in the NDAPP manifesting an increasing array of problems at 1, 3, 5, 8 and 10 years of age. Among the more serious problems were insecure attachment, low IQs, language delays, visual–motor integration difficulties, internalizing and externalizing behaviors, and early-appearing school-related achievement problems.

The first developmental problem involved the relationship between mothers and children: A majority of the infants showed disorganized (41%) or other insecure (22%) patterns of attachment at 1 year of age, with only 37% of children classified as securely attached (versus 65% to 70% for children with adult mothers). The proportion of securely attached infants was lower than that typically observed, even in low SES samples (Vaughn, Egeland, Sroufe, & Waters, 1979) as well as in other studies with children of adolescent parents (Spieker & Bensley, 1994; Ward & Carlson, 1995). Additional evidence suggesting the early high-risk status of children in the Notre Dame sample can be seen in the fact that 66% of infants at 6 months of age were perceived by their mothers as having "difficult" temperaments (Whitman et al., 2001).

When the children reached 3 and 5 years of age, there was additional evidence of emerging developmental problems in four important domains: intellectual–linguistic, socioemotional, adaptive, and academic. A large percentage of children performed in the borderline and mentally retarded ranges of intellectual functioning: 45% at 3 years and 26% at 5 years, with only a small percentage scoring in the above average category. Even more troublesome, many children showed early signs of delayed language development and visual motor integration problems, with around 80% falling at or below the 10th percentile on the PPVT–R at both 3 and 5 years of age, while 57% were in this same range at 5 years of age on the Developmental Test of Visual Motor Integration. Academically, 50% and 34% of 5-year-old children were in the 10th percentile or below on the math and reading portions of the PIAT during kindergarten.

In many respects the results of our study paralleled the well-known Abecedarian project (Borkowski & Ramey, 2002): Children from low SES backgrounds, who are normal at birth, begin a gradual cognitive–behavioral decline, eventuating in major life crises for themselves and their parents. Data from the Abecedarian project showed children with borderline and low IQ mothers experienced a dramatic intellectual decline (20–30 IQ pts.), provided they did not receive intensive early intervention. Similarly, children in our sample displayed a decline from a mean IQ of 102 at 6 months of age to a mean IQ of 82 at age 3 (Whitman et. al., 2001). Moreover, the children were even more deficient in their receptive language abilities. On the Peabody Picture Vocabulary Test–Revised they had a mean score of 76 at 3 years of age, nearly 1½ SD below the expected mean of 100. Thus, children in our sample showed delays in receptive language as early as age 3 as well as declines in IQ; we hypothesize these "signs" were the major precursors of later learning problems that emerged during the elementary school years.

With respect to personal adjustment, a high percentage of children showed either internalizing (37% at age 3 and 24% at age 5) and/or externalizing (35% at age 3 and 14% at age 5) problems. Children also displayed adaptive behavior deficiencies. By age 5, average scores on the Vineland Adaptive Behavior Scales—which assess communication, daily living, socialization, and motor skills—had fallen to 1 SD below the population mean. Especially evident was the fact that children of adolescent mothers generally did not meet age-appropriate expectations for communication or daily living skills (cf. Whitman et al., 2001).

Perhaps the most revealing findings regarding major developmental outcomes were the number of children who displayed problems in multiple domains: intellectual, socioemotional, adaptive, and academic. At 3 years, 72% of the children had at least one developmental problem and 44% had more than one. Children at age 3 with multiple problems most commonly displayed cognitive deficiencies and signs of emotional dysfunction. By 5 years, 78% of the children had at least one problem whereas 48% had multiple problems. At 5 years, children with multiple problems most commonly exhibited deficiencies in cognitive and adaptive behavior domains, although comorbidity was also found with other combinations of developmental problems.

At 8 years of age, academic difficulties and adjustment problems surfaced when most children entered the second grade: 70% were experiencing academic difficulties, learning disabilities, or mild mental retardation. Nearly 40% met traditional criteria for LD or mild MR diagnoses. Despite these problems, the majority of children had not been identified as needing special services nor were they receiving special assistance in their classrooms. Early developmental problems, appearing as early as age 3, were preludes to more serious academic problems, observed in the second grade. Terry-Humen et al. (2005) found serious delays in reading and math skills in children of adolescent mothers beginning as early as age 4 and continuing through are 14. These delays were maintained even after maternal characteristics associated with age, such as SES, marital status, and educational attainment, were controlled. The off-timed pregnancy itself was a unique causal factor in children's academic problems.

In summary, the NDAPP involved a representative sample of high-risk mothers who themselves experienced a variety of socioemotional and cognitive problems (e.g., their average IQ as evaluated during their first pregnancy was 87) and who, in turn, raised children with risks early in life for later appearing academic and adjustment problems. The significance of our project lies in our attempt to unravel and identify the relative importance of multiple and changing risk factors that influence the lives of young mothers and their children, in particular those factors which effect development in intellectual, socioemotional, and school achievement domains.

RESILIENCE AND ADOLESCENT PARENTING

Although an examination of the lives of adolescent mothers and their children reveals that they are at risk for a variety of adverse developmental problems, it is also clear that not all individuals experience negative outcomes. Whereas some mothers manifested socioemotional problems and dysfunctional parenting styles, others did not. Similarly some children, but not all, experienced developmental problems such as mild mental retardation, academic problems, and/or conduct disorders. A primary focus of the NDAPP was to account for, and understand, the reasons for this wide range of individual differences in life outcomes, identifying why some but not all adolescent parents and their children displayed resilience despite exposure to significant challenges.

The Concept of Resilience

Resilience refers to successful adaptation despite exposure to risks or stressors (Masten, Best, & Garmezy, 1990). Three aspects of the definition are noteworthy: (a) resilience refers to a process or pattern of adaptation rather than a characteristic of a person per se; (b) the characterization of a person as resilient is based on inferences about adaptation in the face of adversity—in other words, in order to display resilience an individual has to be subjected to a clear risk or challenge; and, finally, (c) the person displaying resilience has to be judged as functioning adequately.

Resilience as a Process. As Masten and Powell (2003) have pointed out, resilience is not a trait. A person may be judged as resilient in one situation but not in another, at one point in time but not another, and in one domain of functioning (e.g., academic) but not in another (e.g., socioemotional). Commonly, resilience refers to a specific type of functioning in a specific situation at a specific point in time. As recommended in the literature (Luthar, Cicchetti, & Becker,

2000; Masten, 1994), we will use the term "resilience" in this book—rather than the term "resiliency"—to avoid implying that resilience is a personality trait.

Exposure to Adversity. To fully appreciate and understand an individual's degree of resilience, the adverse circumstances or risks to which a person is exposed must be examined. The term "risk" typically refers to circumstances or characteristics that increase the probability of maladaptation. In general, the best predictor of problem behaviors is not a single risk factor but rather an accumulation of adversities (Sameroff, Gutman, & Peck, 2003). In other words, maladaptive outcomes are more likely to occur when individuals are exposed to multiple risk factors over a long period of time. It is not uncommon for individuals to be exposed to more than one risk at any given time. In many cases, exposure to one risk factor is associated with exposure to other risk factors that encompass a series or sequence of negative experiences (Masten & Powell, 2003). For example, low socioeconomic status is often connected to an array of associated risks, including, poor living circumstances, violence, inferior education, and inadequate social service arrangements.

Insights into the processes underlying resilience can be derived through an examination of the protective factors surrounding a "successful" individual. Whereas risk factors are associated with an increased probability of an adverse outcome, protective factors and protective processes are associated with an increased probability of a positive outcome. Protective factors, such as having a good familial social support system, serve to moderate or buffer the adverse effects associated with risk factors. Protective processes, on the other hand, provide mediating pathways that aid individuals in overcoming the impact of risk.

There are several different characterizations of the relationships between risk and protection. One characterization is that some factors, such as intelligence, can serve as either risk or protective factors, depending on where a person lies on a continuum from low to high. Another suggests that some factors may be either risk factors—such as child abuse or neglect—or protective—such as religiosity—but not both. A third characterization is that some factors may be considered risks for one outcome but protection for a different outcome. The specific identification of a variable as risk or protection often depends on how it is conceptualized and measured, either categorically or on a continuum that encompasses its negative and positive features. A central question confronting researchers is how protective and risk factors combine to produce a specific developmental outcome. For example, can a strong social support system counterbalance the effects of a risk factor such as poverty, or can a high IQ or educational success buffer the effects of peer rejection on a child's socioemotional adjustment?

Successful Adaptation in the Face of Adversity.   Another question that has not yet been empirically resolved is the precise nature of resilience. If resilience refers to a specific type of adaptation, which occurs in the presence of adversity, what characterizes this process? Various answers to this question have been suggested in the literature (Luthar & Zelazo, 2003). For example, resilience has been used to describe a process whereby a person subjected to adversity temporarily demonstrates maladaptation but eventually recovers to function in an adaptive fashion. This process has sometimes been referred to as a "bounce-back" phenomenon. Resilience has also been used to describe a process in which an individual continues to function well during exposure to adversity. Such individuals have sometimes been described as invulnerable or immune to the effects of adversity. A third form of resilience refers to a process where the person not only is able to function well during exposure to adversity but actually shows an enhanced adaptive capacity; that is, they appear to thrive and grow stronger. Common to all of these conceptualizations is that an individual characterized as resilient must display positive adaptation to adversity and must function substantially better than what would be expected given exposure to the risk condition being studied (Luthar & Zelazo, 2003).

A Conceptual Model of Adolescent Parenting and Resilience

The research described in this book is directed primarily toward understanding resilience in children of adolescent mothers but also examines the resilience of the young mothers themselves. The research was initially guided by a model developed by Whitman, Borkowski, Schellenbach, and Nath (1987) and later revised by Whitman, Borkowski, Keogh, and Weed (2001); the basic model was reviewed earlier in this chapter (see Fig. 1.3). As described previously, this model includes seven constructs that are necessary to understand the development of children of adolescent parents: maternal socioemotional adjustment, maternal learning ability, maternal cognitive readiness, family social supports, history of abuse and violence, infant characteristics, and parenting characteristics. It was, and remains, our view that an understanding of the development of the children of adolescent parents as well the mothers themselves can flow from the systematic analyses of the interaction of these factors as they transpire over time.

Research has generally supported the validity of our model (Whitman et al., 2001). For example, structural modeling procedures were used to identify the direct and indirect paths that led to specific parenting skills and styles in a sample of 135 adolescent mothers and their infants (O'Callaghan, Borkowski, Whitman, Maxwell, & Keogh, 1999). Maternal intelligence and personal adjustment directly influenced cognitive readiness to parent which, in turn, was related to parenting as well as to child characteristics at 6 months of age. The model of adolescent and child development presented in Figure 1.3 and the research that flowed from it initially focused on understanding how adolescent motherhood, and the risks associated with it, adversely influenced parenting and children's development. Results of our research, however, indicated that a number of mothers and their children were functioning reasonably well, without significant developmental delays. As a consequence we became increasingly interested in understanding the factors and pathways that have led to resilient outcomes. The first step in understanding these processes is to extend the original model to encompass later childhood and adolescence, as well as to include domains of risk and protection that may influence resilience and/or vulnerability in young mothers and their children.

An Expanded Model of Parenting, Resilience, and Development

The model presented in Figure 1.3 provides a useful foundation for understanding the impact of early risks on children's development through infancy and early childhood. However, because this model was designed to describe early periods of life it does not fully account for additional variables that occur as children enter later childhood and adolescence. An expanded model of adolescent parenting and resilience is presented in Figure 1.4. The model begins where the previous model left off. Specifically, children's early development refers to their cognitive, behavioral, and socioemotional adjustment during infancy and early childhood and its impact on resilience during adolescence. Next, the model presents variables that act as additional risks or as protective factors during later childhood and adolescence. We focus on four constructs—maternal adjustment, father involvement, social support, and children's school experiences and classroom adjustment—that might serve as protective factors for at-risk children, especially during early adolescence. The model posits that these variables may have either direct effects on children's resilience or indirect effects that are mediated by parenting practices (e.g., monitoring, responsivity) during childhood and adolescence. In turn, the quality of parenting is assumed to be influenced by protective factors such as father involvement, social support from the family and community, and maternal adjustment, especially depression and uncontrolled aggression, as well as by the child's own history of development and maternal stress associated with childrearing.

In sum, the model of resilience begins where the previous model left off (cf. Fig. 1.3) and is based on the assumption that cognitive readiness to parent, parenting practices, and variables such as maternal depression, substance abuse, and family conflict pose a complex set of risks for children born to adolescent mothers. The extension of

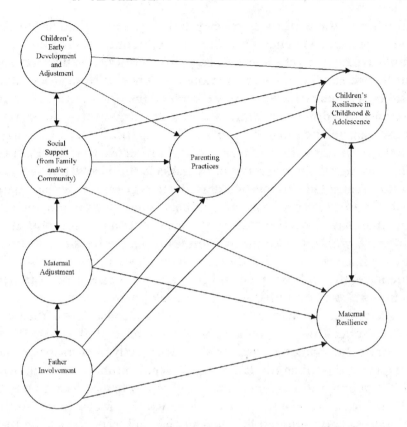

Figure 1.4.   An expanded model of adolescent parenting and resilience.

the model posits that protective factors during childhood or early adolescence play important roles in determining resilience or vulnerability during early adolescence for both mother and child. This expanded model of adolescent parenting and resilience is the framework that we have used to guide the NDAPP research that is presented in this book.

CONTRIBUTIONS OF THE PRESENT VOLUME

Past research examining resilience in the context of adversity has frequently focused on children who have been exposed to a wide variety of risk factors, including children of mentally ill, depressed, alcoholic, divorced, or deceased parents as well as children who grow up in the context of poverty and/or violence (Luthar, 2003). This research has generally attempted to identify salient child and family characteristics, as well as community resources, that serve as protective factors and that promote resilience. Investigators interested in resilience have typically examined the pathways that lead to adaptive functioning and normal development as well as elucidating those that lead to maladaptation. This perspective has been our guide to various studies of how risk and protective factors influence developmental outcomes for participants in the NDAPP through the first 14 years of life. In this book, we focus not only on the risks associated with adolescent parenting but also on understanding the factors that play protective roles in the lives of teen mothers and their children, who often confront significant daily adversities in their lives. A major focus is how these protective factors moderate the influence of the early prenatal and postnatal risks on socioemotional, behavioral, and cognitive/academic development.

The remaining chapters discuss important constructs in the field of resilience and use data collected as part of the NDAPP to illustrate the changing roles of risk and protective factors over time. Chapter 2 describes the fate of adolescent mothers as their own children enter adolescence, focusing on mothers who are able to overcome risks and who display resilience. The focus then shifts to resilience and vulnerability among the children born to young mothers. We describe the processes that facilitate resilience in four domains of functioning: intelligence, adaptation, psychopathology, and socioemotional functioning (chaps. 3 and 4). We turn then to a set of interrelated problems faced by many children growing up in poverty in the United States: maltreatment (chap. 5) and exposure to violence (chap. 6). Subsequent chapters approach developmental issues from a broader perspective, with a focus on the role of multiple risks (chap. 7) and an emphasis on protective factors and processes (chap. 8) that lead to favorable developmental outcomes. In order to study the emergence of resilience, it is essential to understand the complex issues related to design, methodology, and data analyses; the goal of chapter 9 is to provide a description of design and analytic approaches that are appropriate for the study of risk, protection, and resilience. The book concludes with a discussion of intervention and prevention programs that may contribute to the development of resilience among at-risk families (chap. 10).

Although the NDAPP is not an intervention project, our results provide a foundation from which others can develop empirically-based intervention and prevention programs to benefit at-risk children, youth, and their families. For instance, an awareness of risk and protective factors that operate early in a child's life allows interventions to be initiated earlier, with greater precision, and with better eventual success. Early childhood prevention programs are generally acknowledged to be more effective, as well as less costly, than interventions implemented during later childhood (Borkowski & Weaver, 2006). We maintain that research evaluating an early intervention curriculum not only serves to validate program effectiveness but also tests the underlying theory of resilience. The chapters that follow tell us more about risk and protective factors operating in the lives of adolescent mothers and their children.

REFERENCES

Allen, J. P., Philliber, S., Herrling, S., & Kuperminc, G. P. (1997). Preventing teen pregnancy and academic failure: Experimental evaluation of a developmentally-based approach. *Child Development, 64*, 729–742.

Apfel, N., & Seitz, V. (1999). *Support predicts teen mother's subsequent childbearing and parenting success.* Paper presented at the biennial meeting of the Society for Research in Child Development, Albuquerque, NM.

Belsky, J. (1984). The determinants of parenting: A process model. *Child Development, 55*, 83–96.

Blum, R. W., Beuhring, T., & Rinehart, P. M. (2000). *Protecting teens: Beyond race, income and family structure.* Minneapolis, MN: University of Minnesota Printing Services.

Borkowski, J. G., & Ramey, S. L. (2002). Parenting research: Implications for parenting practices and public policies. In J. G. Borkowski, S. L. Ramey, & M. Bristol-Power (Eds.), *Parenting and the child's world: Influences on intellectual, academic, and social-emotional development* (pp. 363–384). Mahwah, NJ: Lawrence Erlbaum Associates.

Borkowski, J. G., Ramey, S. L., & Bristol-Power, M. (Eds.) (2002). *Parenting and the child's world: Influences on intellectual, academic, and social-emotional development* (pp. 363–384). Mahwah, NJ: Lawrence Erlbaum Associates.

Borkowski, J. G., & Weaver, C. M. (2006). *Prevention: The science and art of promoting healthy child and adolescent development.* Baltimore: Brookes Publishing.

Cabrera, N. J., Ryan, R. M., Shannon, J. D., Brooks-Gunn, J., Vogel, C., Raikes, H., et al. (2004). Low-income fathers' involvement in their toddlers' lives: Biological fathers from the Early Head Start Research and Evaluation Study. *Fathering, 2,* 5–30.

East, P. L., & Felice, M. E. (1996). *Adolescent pregnancy and parenting: Findings from a racially diverse sample.* Hillsdale, NJ: Lawrence Erlbaum Associates.

Dahl, R. E., & Spear, L. P. (Eds.). (2004). *Adolescent brain development: Vulnerabilities and opportunities.* Annals of the New York Academy of Sciences, 1021.

Dukewich, T. L., Borkowski, J. G., & Whitman, T. L. (1996). Adolescent mothers and child abuse potential: An evaluation of risk factors. *Child Abuse and Neglect, 11,* 1031–1047.

Dukewich, T. L., Borkowski, J. G., & Whitman, T. L. (1999). A longitudinal analysis of maternal abuse potential and developmental delays in children of adolescent mothers. *Child Abuse and Neglect, 23,* 405–420.

Elo, I. T., King, R. B., & Furstenberg, F. F. (1999). Adolescent females: Their sexual partners and the fathers of their children. *Journal of Marriage and the Family, 61,* 4–84.

Franzetta, K., Ikramullah, E., Manlove, J., Moore, K. A., & Terry-Humen, E. (2005). *Facts at a glance.* Washington, DC: Child Trends.

Furstenberg, F. F., Brooks-Gunn, J., Morgan, S. P. (1987). *Adolescent mothers in later life.* Cambridge: Cambridge University Press.

Guttmacher Institute. (2006). *Facts in brief: Contraceptive use.* Washington, DC: Author.

Herman-Giddens, M. E., Slora, E. J., Wasserman, R. C., Bourdony, C. J., Bhapkar, M. V., Koch, G. G., et al. (1997). Secondary sexual characteristics and menses in young girls seen in office practice. *Pediatrics, 99,* 505–512.

Horowitz, S. M. Klerman, L. V., Kuo, H. S., & Jekel, J. F. (1991). Intergenerational transmission of school-age parenthood. *Family Planning Perspectives, 23,* 168–172.

Howard, K. S., Lefever, J. B., Borkowski, J. G., & Whitman, T. L. (2006). Fathers' influence in the lives of children with adolescent mothers. *Journal of Family Psychology, 20,* 468–476.

Luthar, S. S. (Ed.). (2003). *Resilience and vulnerability: Adaptation in the context of childhood adversities.* New York: Cambridge University Press.

Luthar, S. S., Cicchetti, D., & Becker, B. (2000). The construct of resilience: A critical evaluation and guidelines for future work. *Child Development, 71,* 543–562.

Luthar, S. S., & Zelazo, L. B. (2003). Research on resilience: An integrative review. In S. S. Luthar (Ed.), *Resilience and vulnerability: Adaptation in the context of childhood adversities* (pp. 510–549). New York: Cambridge University Press.

Manlove, J., Moore, K., Liechty, J., Ikramullah, E., & Cottingham, S. (2005). Sex between young teens and older individuals: A demographic portrait. *Child Trends Research Brief.*

Masten, A. S. (1994). Resilience in individual development: Successful adaptation despite risk and adversity. In M. C. Wang & E. W. Gordon (Eds.), *Educational resilience in inner-city America: Challenges and prospects* (pp. 3–25). Hillsdale, NJ: Lawrence Erlbaum Associates.

Masten, A. S., Best, K. M., & Garmezy, N. (1990). Resilience and development: Contributions from the study of children who overcome adversity. *Development and Psychopathology, 2,* 425–444.

Masten, A. S., & Powell, J. L. (2003). A resilience framework for research, policy and practice. In S. S. Luthar (Ed.), *Resilience and vulnerability: Adaptation in the context of childhood adversities* (pp. 1–25). New York: Cambridge University Press.

McLanahan, S. (1999). Father absence and the welfare of children. In E. M. Hetherington (Ed.), *Coping with divorce, single parenting, and remarriage: A risk and resiliency perspective* (pp. 117–145). Mahwah, NJ: Lawrence Erlbaum Associates.

Miller, C. L., Heysek, P. J., Whitman, T. L., & Borkowski, J. G. (1996). Cognitive readiness to parent and intellectual emotional development in children of adolescent mothers. *Developmental Psychology, 32,* 533–541.

Miller-Johnson, S., Winn, D. C., Coie, J. D., & Malone, P. S. (2004). Risk factors for adolescent pregnancy: Reports among African American males. *Journal of Research on Adolescence, 14,* 471–495.

Moore, K., & Manlove, J. (2005). *A demographic portrait of statutory rape.* Paper presented at the Conference on the Sexual Exploitation of Teens, Alexandria, VA.

National Survey of Family Growth. (1997). *Vital and health statistics: Fertility, family planning, and women's health* (Series 23: No. 19). Hyattsville, MD: Department of Health and Human Services.

O'Callaghan, M. F., Borkowski, J. G., Whitman, T. L., Maxwell, S. E., & Keogh, D. (1999). A model of adolescent parenting: The role of cognitive readiness to parent. *Journal of Research on Adolescence, 1,* 203–225.

Sameroff, A., Gutman, L. M., & Peck, C. (2003). Adaptation among youth facing multiple risks. *Resiliency and vulnerability: Adaptation in the context of childhood adversities* (pp. 364–391). Cambridge: Cambridge University Press.

Sommer, K., Whitman, T. L., Borkowski, J. G., Schellenbach, C. J., Maxwell, S. E., & Keogh, D. (1993). Cognitive readiness and adolescent parenting. *Developmental Psychology, 29,* 389–398.

Sowell, E. R., & Jernigan, T. L. (1998). Further MRI evidence of late brain maturation: Limbic volume increases and changing asymmetries during childhood and adolescence. *Developmental Neuropsychology, 14,* 599–617.

Spieker, S. J., & Bensley, L. (1994). Role of living arrangement and grandmother social support in adolescent mothering and infant attachment. *Developmental Psychology, 30,* 102–111.

Terry-Humen, E., Manlove, J., & Moore, K. (2005). *Playing catch-up: How children of teen mothers fare.* Washington, DC: National Campaign to Prevent Teen Pregnancy.

Vaughn, B., Egeland, B., Sroufe, L. A., & Waters, E. (1979). Individual differences in infant–mother attachment at twelve and eighteen months: Stability and change in families under stress. *Child Development, 50,* 971–975.

Ward, M. J., & Carlson, E. A. (1995). Associations among adult attachment, representations, maternal sensitivity, and infant–mother attachment in a sample of adolescent mothers. *Child Development, 66,* 69–79.

Whitman, T. L., Borkowski, J. G., Keogh D. A., & Weed, K. (2001). *Interwoven lives: Adolescent mothers and their children.* Mahwah, NJ: Lawrence Erlbaum Associates.

Whitman, T. L., Borkowski, J. G., Schellenbach, C. J., & Nath, P. S. (1987). Predicting and understanding developmental delays of adolescent mothers: A multidimensional approach. *American Journal of Mental Deficiency, 92,* 40–56.

Wurtz-Passino, A., Whitman, T. L., Borkowski, J. G., Schellenbach, C. J., Maxwell, S. E., Keogh, D., et al. (1993). Personal adjustment during pregnancy and adolescent parenting. *Adolescence, 28,* 97–122.

2

The Fate of Adolescent Mothers

Christine Willard Noria
Keri Weed
Deborah A. Keogh

I could not give her what I would like to have. I missed out on so much because I had to finish school. I had to work, I was a single mom. I was not ready. I really wasn't. There was a lot of things in life that I didn't experience yet. I had so much growing up to do ... I thought I knew everything. I wanted to prove everybody wrong. I didn't need anybody's help ... Emotionally I was not prepared and physically, I mean, you only have so much energy.

—Barbara, former teen mother

The transition from adolescence to adulthood is fraught with difficulty, even for the most resilient teenager. Adolescent mothers not only must negotiate the normal challenges associated with entering adulthood, such as economic self-sufficiency, but also accept the added responsibility of caring for their children. As many mothers, similar to Barbara, reflect back as adults on their adolescence, they realize how unprepared they were for parenthood. Adjusting to the new role as mother while still attempting to complete the developmental tasks of adolescence and coping with challenges imposed by the normative tasks associated with adulthood creates additional stress. Inadequate preparation for assuming these demanding responsibilities can portend serious developmental problems for both mothers and children.

Preparation for adulthood in the United States has been relegated primarily to institutions of higher learning, leaving non-college bound youth labeled "The Forgotten Half" (Haggerty, 1989). Neglecting the needs of this group, which includes adolescent mothers, costs individuals and society from an interpersonal, economic, and cultural perspective. With respect to adolescent mothers, the costs are doubled as they often involve both the mother and her children. Longitudinal research with teenage mothers, as they make the difficult transition from adolescence to adulthood, provides important sources of information regarding the resources needed and strengths available within individuals and families to facilitate successful development. Knowledge gained from these studies is important for social policy makers as they attempt to support adolescent mothers in making successful transitions to adulthood.

Much of our current knowledge about the lives of teen mothers during adulthood has come from the Baltimore study by Furstenberg, Brooks-Gunn, and Morgan (1987). Seventeen years after their first children were born, teen mothers in the Baltimore study were undereducated, unstable in their marital and close relationships, and less successful economically and vocationally, when compared with national averages for women in metropolitan areas who delayed childbirth until adulthood. Poor psychological adjustment, health problems, welfare dependence, poverty, and harsh parenting styles have also been associated with teenage motherhood (Coley & Chase-Lansdale, 1998).

In this chapter, we examine the impact of early childbearing on the development of adolescent mothers, more specifically family relationships, educational and vocational attainment, psychological adjustment, and parenting practices and skills. The main goal is to determine whether negative developmental outcomes persisted in the lives of teen mothers as they entered their early 30s. We also review relevant longitudinal research on risk and protective factors related to maternal development. Finally, we present new findings from the Notre Dame Adolescent Parenting Project (NDAPP), which has followed young women from the time of their pregnancies into their late 20s and early 30s, that search for predictors of maternal resilience and vulnerability.

TRANSITIONING TO ADULTHOOD

As teen mothers transition into adulthood they are faced with establishing economic self-sufficiency, maintaining psychological well-being, forming interpersonal relationships with their baby's fathers and/or intimate partners, and making critical decisions about subsequent fertility. In the midst of these challenges, teenage mothers are required to learn the skills necessary to become competent parents and cope with the demands and stress associated with parenting. The difficulties they experience navigating the paths to adulthood often lead to socioemotional problems, such as depression and anxiety, unless they develop adequate coping skills and establish strong social support systems. Parenting and psychological adjustment are often compromised by an early transition to adulthood, resulting in difficulties not only for the mothers but also for their children. Those who experience problems with psychological adjustment tend to have poor parenting skills and struggle to complete their education and achieve economic self-sufficiency.

In this section, we examine the literature on the relationships between teenage motherhood and family structure (i.e., marital status and fertility), economic and occupational attainment, psychological adjustment, and quality of parenting. This review serves as the background for our presentation of new findings on life adjustment among the mothers in the NDAPP as they entered their early 30s.

Family Structure: Fertility and Marital Status

Today, fewer families conform to the two-parent nuclear structure prevalent during the mid-1900s, and families headed by a single parent are on the rise (Simmons & O'Neill, 2001). Blended families, created by second and third marriages with children from each partner, have also become increasingly commonplace (Coleman, Ganong & Fine, 2000). Because a general understanding of recent trends in fertility and family stability in United States is important for gaining insights into the context in which adolescent parenting is situated, we review recent changes in fertility, marriage, and divorce rates in the United States. For teens, an off-timed transition to motherhood affects long-term fertility rates and the stability of intimate partner relationships, including marriage.

Fertility.   Age at first birth in the United States has been steadily increasing over the past 30 years, from 21.4 years in 1970 to almost 25 years in 2000 (Mathews & Hamilton, 2002). Although all races have evidenced similar trends, the mean age at first birth for African American and Latina women are typically several years younger than for European American women (22.3, 22.2, and 25.9 years old, respectively). This trend has been influenced by the need for extended education and career preparation and increased availability of contraception (Mathews & Hamilton, 2002).

The total number of births per woman has also been declining. According to data from the 2004 Current Population Survey, the average African American woman has 2 children by the age of 44, the average Latina woman has 2.3, and the average European American woman has 1.8 children (Dye, 2005). Despite the earlier age in starting their families, adolescent mothers do not have significantly more children than women who delay childbirth, when SES and race are taken into consideration (East & Felice, 1990; Furstenberg et al., 1987).

Individual differences in teen fertility rates may be explained by several factors. A longitudinal study found that 39% of its sample of African American and Puerto Rican inner-city adolescent mothers had a second pregnancy within 1 year following initial childbirth (Linares, Leadbeater, Jaffe, Kato, & Diaz, 1992). Delayed grade placement, poor reading achievement, and school absences were all predictive of repeat pregnancies, whereas the frequency of sexual activity and the method of contraception failed to predict additional pregnancies. It may be that teens who become pregnant a second time view parenting as a positive route for achieving adult status or, alternatively, place less value on educational and occupational achievement.

In the Baltimore Longitudinal Study (Furstenberg et al., 1987), the strongest predictor of fertility was the length of time before the second child was born. Relatedly, East and Felice (1996) found that teens were twice as likely to have a repeat pregnancy within 6 months if they had dropped out of school, received welfare, lived with their partner, and had mothers who frequently provided child care for their infants. These factors were associated with short inter-pregnancy intervals (Klerman, 2004).

Marital status.   Relationships with intimate partners are important not only in predicting increased subsequent childbearing but, when stable and long-term, are also markers of a successful transition to adulthood. Bramlett and Mosher (2002) reported that by the age of 30, 81% of European American, 77% of Latina, and 52% of African American women were married. However, one third of these couples experienced divorce or permanent separation after 10 years of marriage. Marriages of women under the age of 18 were twice as likely to end in divorce or separation after 10 years than those of women 25 years of age or older. Compared with young European American or Latina women, young African American women were more likely to experience divorce or separation and young Asian women less likely. Other risk factors identified as predictors of relationship instability included histories of sexual abuse, childbirth prior to marriage, anxiety, interracial marriage, high rates of community poverty, and low education levels (Bramlett & Mosher, 2002), whereas, protective factors included religiosity and stable nuclear families.

Consistent with these data, Furstenberg et al. (1987) found greater marital instability among early child bearers. Similarly, Hotz, McElroy, and Sanders (1997) noted that adolescent mothers spent more time unmarried in contrast with a comparison group of adolescents who had unintentional miscarriages, thereby delaying their entry into parenthood. Because teen mothers tend to experience more relationship instability in comparison with women who delayed childbearing until adulthood, they often face the demands of parenthood alone, as the primary caregiver of their multiple children. Since marriage has been positively associated with physical and mental health (Bramlett & Mosher, 2002), single-parent teenage mothers are at greater risk for poor psychological adjustment.

The Impact of Teen Motherhood on Education and Employment

Vocational and economic status in the United States is generally dependent on educational attainment (Newburger & Curry, 1999). To the extent that adolescent childbearing interrupts the education of teenagers, their subsequent vocational opportunities are restricted. Bearing additional children appears to increase the likelihood that young mothers will drop out of school, thereby impeding their ability to support their families (Seitz, 1996). Pregnant adolescents were more likely to be poor, undereducated, single, and had a higher likelihood of never receiving prenatal care (East & Felice, 1996). Their educational and economic outcomes were further compromised if they bore a second child within 18 months after the first birth. Former teenage mothers, matched with adult mothers on race, education, employment, income, family size and marital status when their children were 12 years old, were found to have lower levels of formal education than adult mothers (East & Felice, 1990). Somewhat surprisingly, former teen mothers did not differ significantly from the adult mothers in employment status and income level.

In addition to the major differences between teen and adult mothers in educational attainment, teen mothers typically complete fewer years of education relative to other teens their own age (Scott-Jones, 1991). There are also age-related differences in educational attainment among teen mothers themselves: Older teen mothers deviated more from the national norms for educational attainment than younger ones, especially among Latina and European American women (Scott-Jones, 1991). The difficulties that older teens faced in staying on grade level, relative to younger teen mothers, were likely due to the increased levels of familial support received by younger teens or compulsory school attendance requirements for children below the age of 16. Also, for older teen mothers, educational problems may have occurred prior to, and perhaps contributed to, their pregnancies and school drop-out (Scott-Jones, 1991).

Despite age-related differences among teenage mothers in educational attainment, school attendance for first-time mothers was related to positive development in multiple domains. African American and Puerto Rican American teenage mothers who remained in school were less likely to become pregnant again within the 1st year following birth, had fewer depressive symptoms, were on grade level, and were more academically successful as compared to teen mothers who dropped out of school (Linares, Leadbeater, Kato, & Jaffe, 1991). With respect to the long-term impact of early childbearing, Furstenberg et al. (1987) found only modest to moderate impact on career and economic outcomes for teen mothers 17 years after their children were born; the majority did not rely on public assistance. The strongest predictor of welfare status was the educational level of their parents. Furstenberg et al. (1987) surmised that parental education level influenced the extent to which parents were able to assist their teenage daughters in meeting their parenting obligations: Those grandparents with less education had fewer economic and social resources to offer their daughters. More generally, Hotz et al. (1997) argued that the adverse economic consequences accompanying teen parenting were more likely due to preexisting conditions, such as poverty during pregnancy and educational difficulties during middle school, than to the actual birth of the child.

Psychological Adjustment: Coping With Demands of Parenting

Teen mothers are often emotionally unprepared for the stressors associated with the demands of parenthood. They must cope with tasks related to adolescent development, including a search for self-identity, self-esteem, and peer acceptance, while simultaneously dealing with challenges of parenting. It is not surprising that depression, frustration, and aggression occur with higher frequency among pregnant adolescents than pregnant adults (Passino et al., 1993). Confusion about their status as an adult may disrupt or prolong the process of identity development among adolescent mothers.

McCrary and Weed (2005) compared identity formation in teen mothers to that of adult mothers, when both groups were in their early 20s. Teen mothers were more likely to indicate that they were still trying to figure out their beliefs and values (55%) or had adopted socially accepted beliefs without questioning them (25%), whereas adult mothers were more likely to indicate that their commitments to values and beliefs followed periods of doubt and questioning (65%). The amount of social support received at the time of the pregnancy predicted identity development for both adolescent and adult mothers (McCrary & Weed, 2005).

Teenage mothers also appear to struggle more than adult mothers with low self-esteem, anxiety, and depression (de Anda, Darroch, Davidson, Gilly, & Morejon, 1990; Whitman et al., 2001). Chronically depressed teenage mothers tend to live alone, move more frequently, and experience more stressful life events. In addition, depression has been related to low rates of graduation, repeat childbearing, and welfare involvement. Not only was the ability to cope with stressful life events impaired by depression but also chronic depression was associated with a rejection of the parenting role (Leadbeater & Linares, 1992). Interestingly, grandmothers' acceptance of their daughters and encouragement of their independence were related to fewer depressive symptoms at 6 months, 1 year, and 3 years postpartum (Leadbeater & Linares, 1992).

In one of the few studies that examined the long-term socioemotional costs of early parenthood, Kalil and Kunz (2002) used data collected from the National Longitudinal Survey of Youth to test the relative contribution of age and marital status at first birth to depression between the ages of 27 and 29. Marital status was more important than age in predicting depressive symptoms in young adulthood, with socioemotional adjustment of married adolescent mothers being comparable to that of married adult mothers. Support from mother and spouse appeared to be critical to the maintenance of psychological well-being in young mothers following an off-timed birth. In turn, psychological well-being was an important precursor of educational and occupational attainment.

Quality of Parenting Among Adolescent Mothers

The transition to parenthood is considered by many as an important marker of adulthood. To the extent that this transition occurs for mothers and fathers who are physically and cognitively prepared to assume their new roles, parenthood brings opportunities for personal growth. When the transition to parenthood occurs earlier than the other developmental markers of adulthood and when parents are unprepared for these new challenges, the developmental consequences for mothers and children are often serious.

Adolescent mothers often lack adequate preparation for parenting, have imprecise knowledge concerning infant and child development, and report negative attitudes about parenting (Sommer et al., 1993). In infancy, the lack of preparedness for parenting has been reflected in the quality of interactions between the teen mother and her baby (Whitman et al., 2001). In contrast to adult mothers, teens generally interacted less with their babies, were less emotionally and verbally responsive, offered positive support infrequently, and were not as attuned to their infants' emotional cues during free play (Whitman et al., 2001).

Early childbearing not only places teen mothers at risk for insensitive and ineffective parenting, but the demands of parenting and the associated stress place many at risk for child abuse and neglect (Wolfe, 1985). For instance, Bolton (1990) found that 36% to 51% of all abused children were raised by adolescent mothers, though only 20% of children are born to adolescent mothers. Relatedly, Connelly and Straus (1992) found that maternal age at first birth was a significant predictor of physical abuse, even when race, income, and education were controlled.

A study presented in *Interwoven Lives* (Whitman et al., 2001) focused on relationships among maternal prenatal resources, early perceptions of parenting, and developmental outcomes as teens transitioned into their 20s (Mylod, Whitman & Borkowski, 1997). Pregnant adolescents with more cognitive resources fared better than pregnant adolescents with more limited resources. More specifically, teen mothers with higher prenatal IQs and better cognitive preparation for parenting had higher self-esteem, lower anxiety, fewer depressive symptoms, more responsive interactional styles with their children, and a lower potential for child abuse at 3 years postpartum. Additionally, parenting stress mediated the relationship between prenatal cognitive resources and parent–child interactions at 3 years, suggesting that mothers who were less cognitively prepared for parenting perceived their parenting roles as more stressful; these perceptions, in turn, were associated with less optimal parenting behaviors (Mylod et al., 1997).

A review of more than 100 studies examining development in adolescent mothers indicated that the struggles of adolescent mothers in a single domain of development, such as immature affective regulation or hostile interactions with peers or family members, often exerted a synergistic effect on other areas of maternal development (Trad, 1995). Such chains of events in turn often led to maternal adjustment problems that adversely affected the emerging relationships between adolescent mothers and their infants.

TRANSITIONING TO ADULTHOOD: CONTRIBUTIONS FROM THE NDAPP

The NDAPP differs from previous longitudinal studies in several important ways. First, the face of poverty in the United States has changed drastically between 1966—the start of the Furstenberg et al. study (1987)—and 1986, when the NDAPP was launched. Welfare reforms have made an impact on how teen mothers continued their education and entered the workforce at an earlier age in order to support their families. In contrast to the mothers in the Furstenberg et al. study (1987), some mothers in the NDAPP cohort were expected to enter the workforce due to time limits for receiving public assistance.

Second, the NDAPP study included more frequent measurements of critical outcomes than previous longitudinal research, allowing for a better understanding of fluctuations in maternal psychological adjustment, parenting, and educational and occupational attainment as participants completed the developmental tasks of adolescence and began their transitions to adulthood. Mothers were seen every 2 to 4 years, with interviews occurring more frequently toward the beginning of their involvement in the project (during pregnancy to 5 years) when developmental changes were more rapid. Finally, the NDAPP assessed multiple domains of development, resulting in longitudinally-based information about changes in maternal educational attainment and economic success as well as changes in psychological adjustment and parenting practices, data which were overlooked in past longitudinal studies of teenage mothers.

In the following sections, studies from the NDAPP are presented, examining how early risk and protective factors influenced successful adaptation to the developmental tasks of adulthood in the domains of fertility, marital status, economic and educational attainment, psychological adjustment, and parenting. The relationships among three of these descriptive outcomes—educational attainment, employment, and adjustment—are further analyzed with respect to maternal resilience and its stability from the early 20s through age 30. Lastly, relationships among prenatal protective and risk factors and resilience during the third decade of life are presented to identify maternal characteristics that may lay the foundations for successful transitions to adulthood.

TEENAGE MOTHERS IN EARLY ADULTHOOD

The remainder of this chapter examines teenage mothers as they approach and enter their 30s. Specific examination of variables within the domains of fertility, family structure, educational and occupational attainment, maternal adjustment, and parenting are presented in order to provide comprehensive descriptive information about how teenage mothers fare as young adults, a stage of development at which there is a dearth of information in the existing literature. Next, we created a maternal resiliency index, which allowed an examination of whether and how mothers attained multiple markers of adult status: education, employment, and maternal adjustment. Maternal resilience and vulnerability was then assessed across time, starting in their early 20s and ending in their 30s. Finally, we examined predictors of maternal resilience at age 30, in order to determine the contextual factors and personal characteristics that served as precursors of successful transitions to adulthood.

Fertility and Marital Status at 30

As adolescent mothers entered their 20s, 49% had delayed having a second child (Whitman et al., 2001). During their late 20s, 14.5% had only one child, 26.6% two children, 29.8% three children, 25% four children, and 4% five or more children (Noria, 2005). Figure 2.1 shows the distribution of family size as the adolescent mothers in the

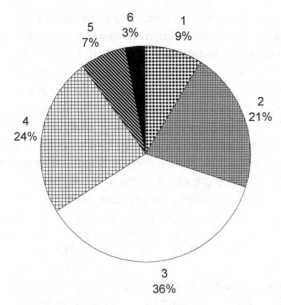

Figure 2.1. Number of children as mothers turn 30.

NDAPP entered their 30s; approximately 91% had additional children, with 70% having a total of 3 or more children. Compared to a national sample of women in their early 30s (Dye, 2005), teen mothers had almost twice as many children (3.1 versus 1.6 children); only 13.4% of the normative sample had four or more children, compared to 34.4% of the adolescent mothers in the NDAPP.

In contrast to prior longitudinal research (Furstenberg et al., 1987), mothers in the NDAPP not only started their families at younger ages than normative samples but also had more children. For instance, in the Baltimore study at the 17-year follow-up, 21% had no additional children (vs. 9% in the NDAPP); 41% had a total of two children (vs. 21%); 26% three children (vs. 36%); 12% four or more children (vs. 34.4%). In short, mothers in the more recent NDAPP cohort had larger families than mothers in the Baltimore study. One possible explanation for the difference in the two samples is that when mothers enrolled in the Baltimore study, abortion was not legal in the United States (Furstenberg et al., 1987). As a result, some mothers in the Baltimore study may have not have wished to carry the initial pregnancy to term, but did, and, consequently, may also have had more negative attitudes about parenting and repeat pregnancies. In contrast, mothers in the NDAPP had abortion as an option and chose to carry their children to term. It might be inferred that children in the NDAPP were more "wanted" and that mothers were more open to having larger families.

Interbirth intervals in the NDAPP were related to fertility and SES: Mothers who did not have additional children within 2 years of their first had higher SES and had smaller family sizes as they reached their late 20s (Noria, 2005). Results of stepwise regression analyses were consistent with past research findings (Furstenberg et al., 1987; Noria, 2005), indicating that shorter interbirth intervals following initial births were significantly correlated with the total number of children at age 30, accounting for approximately 41% of the variance: Mothers who became pregnant shortly after the birth of their first children had larger family sizes than those who delayed a second pregnancy.

In the NDAPP, 83.6% of the mothers were single as they entered their 20s. By the middle to late 20s, 54% remained single, 37% had been married at least once, and 7.4% married twice (Noria, 2005). As the sample transitioned into their 30s, the percentage of women who had never married dropped to 27%. Figure 2.2 shows relationship history of the mothers as they reached age 30: More than 50% of the sample demonstrated relationship stability in that they had never married or were currently married to their first husband.

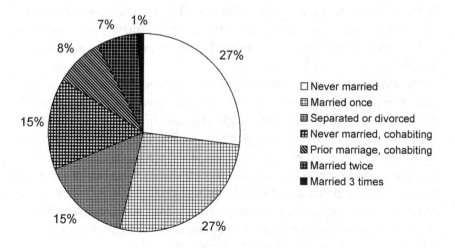

Figure 2.2.   Maternal relationships as mothers turn 30.

Marital status varied by racial background. For European Americans, most mothers had been or were at one time married (67%) or were currently cohabiting (33%). In contrast, only 56.5% of African Americans had either married (32.5%) or were currently cohabiting (24%). African Americans were less likely to have married when compared to European Americans, and only 6.5% of African American women had divorced, in contrast to 22% of European American women. European Americans were also more likely to have experienced a second or third marriage (45% of those married) or to cohabit following a failed marriage (22% of those cohabiting) than were African Americans (8% and 0%, respectively). The percentage of both European American and African American teen mothers who married by age 30 was somewhat lower than in a nationally representative sample in which 81% of European American and 52% of African American mothers were married (Bramlett & Mosher, 2002).

In recent years, cohabitation has become an acceptable alternative to marriage for individuals in the United States (Simmons & O'Connell, 2003). In the NDAPP, the majority (54.3%) reported cohabiting with only one partner while their children were young. Between 8 and 14 years postpartum, 45% of early cohabiting mothers were engaged in stable relationships; the average length of time mothers were involved with the intimate partner was 4.8 years. Close to 30% reported cohabiting with two intimate partners, and only 8.5% reported three intimate partners. Although close to 25% were able to sustain a long-term committed relationship during their children's early years, the more general trend was toward relationship instability.

In summary, mothers in the NDAPP had larger family sizes by the time their first-born children were 14 than those who delayed childbearing until adulthood; they also had more children than cohorts of teen mothers in adulthood from previous longitudinal research (Furstenberg et al., 1987). In addition, mothers whose children were born in close succession also had larger families. One half of mothers were stable in marital status, having either never married or were currently married to their first husbands. Thus, most mothers in the NDAPP approached age 30 as single parents, having primary responsibilities for financially supporting their families.

Impact of Adolescent Motherhood on Labor Force Participation

Resilience implies success in meeting societal expectations (Luthar & Zigler, 1991). For many young women in the United States, these expectations center on educational attainment, economic self-sufficiency, and career success. As with analyses of fertility and marital status, these demographic variables were examined within the NDAPP sample of teen mothers as they entered their 30s.

By their early 20s, 65% of the mothers from the NDAPP had graduated with a high school diploma or received a GED, and by their late 20s 85% had received one of these degrees. Some of these high school graduates furthered their education; by their early 30s, 24% had attended college, and an additional 5% graduated from college. Fourteen percent indicated they were continuing their education at age 30.

Stepwise regression analyses revealed that maternal intelligence accounted for approximately 15% of the variance in educational attainment while delayed grade placement explained an additional 5%. Graduation rates in the NDAPP sample were comparable to those of national samples (Greene & Winters, 2005; Newburger & Curry, 1999). In addition, a predictable disparity existed between European American, African American, and Latina women, with close to 89% of European American teens receiving a high school diploma or GED, in contrast to 75% of African American and 80% of Latina mothers.

As mothers approached their 20s, 41% were working at least part time; during their early 20s, the percentage rose to 49.6% (Whitman et al., 2001). During their late 20s, however, only 37% were employed. Considerable instability in employment status was noted since approximately 90% of the sample had been employed at least part of the time during the previous 2 years. As women transitioned into their 30s, approximately 66% were working. Of those, 34.5% were at their current job for less than 1 year, resulting in 55% of the total sample either not working or having worked at their current job for less than 1 year. In contrast, 46.6% of those who were employed had held their current job 3 years or more. Stepwise regression analysis of length of time at current job suggested that only delayed grade placement accounted for significant variance in this outcome (7%). Labor force participation of the NDAPP sample was comparable to the 55% rate found in a national sample (Dye, 2005).

Both educational attainment and work status are considered in the determination of socioeconomic status (SES). The average Hollingshead score was 55.5 (SD = 11.66; Range 22—73), indicating that mothers had low SES as they entered their 30s. Regression analyses of SES were consistent with prior analyses and indicated that delayed grade placement was the only significant predictor, accounting for close to 13% of the variance in SES.

Approximately two thirds of families in the NDAPP received some form of public assistance (e.g., housing allowance, Medicaid, food stamps) while mothers were in their early 20s. As they turned 30, the majority still relied on the financial support of others to meet the needs of their families, with more than one half receiving financial assistance in the form of child support or from family members. The most frequent form of governmental assistance was medical, with 63% of the sample relying on Medicaid for children's healthcare. Nearly half (47%) of the families also depended on food stamps to make ends meet, but only 18% received Temporary Assistance for Needy Families (TANF) funds. Only 32.2% of mothers in the NDAPP had received no form of government assistance.

In sum, teen mothers continued to experience difficulties in supporting their families. Although the majority had completed high school, only a small percentage had finished college. Despite increases in the number of mothers employed as they entered their 30s, mothers continued to experience underemployment and rely on public assistance to support their families. Teen mothers who remained dependent on government assistance as they turned 30 also tended to have more symptoms of depression and anxiety and lower self-esteem, suggesting that poor maternal psychological adjustment may be a barrier to economic self-sufficiency.

Psychological Adjustment as Mothers Turn 30

Adolescent mothers displayed lower self-esteem, increased depressive symptoms, and greater anxiety, when compared to normative samples as they entered their 20s (Whitman et al., 2001). During their late 20s, socioemotional difficulties continued for many, particularly because 20% were experiencing clinical levels of depression (Noria, 2005). Table 2.1 presents data on maternal depression, anxiety and self-esteem between the ages of 20 and 31. All three measures showed general improvements in maternal adjustment from late adolescence to their 30s; trend analyses confirmed that the average levels of anxiety and depression declined over time, whereas self-esteem improved slightly.

Twenty-four percent of the NDAPP sample evidenced symptoms of clinical levels of depression on the Beck Depression Inventory (BDI; Beck, 1987). The majority had scores in the mild range, but close to 5.5% reported moderately high levels of depression. Maternal anxiety, as assessed with the Trait Subscale of the State-Trait Anxiety Inventory (Spielberger, 1983), decreased over time: Mothers had trait anxiety scores at the 72nd percentile and the 65th percentile at ages 20 and 22, respectively, suggesting above average levels of anxiety; however, by age 25, the average scores dropped to the 59th percentile, and then declined to the 54th percentile after age 30. Self-esteem was measured using the Coopersmith Self-Esteem Inventory (CSI; Coopersmith, 1981). Scores from the CSI improved over time, with levels of self-esteem at age 30 falling at the 50th percentile.

In order to understand the characteristics that place some mothers at risk for poor psychological adjustment in adulthood, a

TABLE 2.1

Descriptive Statistics for Three Measures of Maternal Adjustment During Early Adulthood: Depression, Self-esteem and Anxiety

Age	Depression[a]		Self-esteem		Anxiety	
	M	SD	M	SD	M	SD
20	10.16	7.74	16.32	4.62	40.68	10.24
22	9.34	8.00	16.47	4.58	38.28	10.43
25	9.33	7.46	17.21	4.24	36.24	10.92
27	7.14	7.53	17.65	4.67	34.55	10.77
31	6.74	5.38	18.55	3.94	35.49	9.41

Note. [a]Clinical cut offs: 0-9 normal, 9-16 mild, 17-29 moderate, 30-36 severe.

variety of prenatal characteristics were used to predict depression, anxiety and self-esteem. Three prenatal risk factors accounted for approximately 26% of the variance in depression scores as mothers entered their 30s. Levels of anxiety and depression, as assessed by the Youth Self-Report (YSR; Achenbach, 1991) during pregnancy, explained close to 18% of the variance in depressive symptomatology at 30. Socioeconomic status during pregnancy accounted for 4.4% of the variance in depression, and histories of sexual abuse accounted for an additional 3.8% of the variance. Those who reported more symptoms of depression had experienced greater depression and anxiety as pregnant teenagers, tended to be from lower socioeconomic backgrounds, and had histories of sexual abuse.

Only prenatal anxiety and depression explained significant variance in trait anxiety for 30-year-old mothers, about 14.4% of the variance, indicating that mothers who reported more symptoms of depression and anxiety during their pregnancies also were more likely to report symptoms of anxiety 14 years later. Adjustment problems measured prenatally accounted for 17.6% of the variance in self-esteem. As expected, problems with anxiety and depression were associated with lower self-esteem. However, problems associated with aggression and delinquency were, somewhat surprisingly, associated with higher levels of self-esteem, suggesting that mothers with high self-esteem may have more confidence in asserting themselves, but tended to express their assertiveness in aggressive ways.

In summary, compared to normative samples of women in their early 30s, the majority of adolescent mothers appeared to be functioning within normal ranges. Although some mothers experienced problems with depression, anxiety and self-esteem, trend analyses indicated that trait anxiety and depressive symptoms generally declined, and self-esteem improved. The NDAPP data may overestimate the strength of these trends due to some selective attrition in the sample. More specifically, in comparison to participants who dropped out, those who remained in the study were more depressed at 3 years postpartum, reported more anxiety when their children were 5, and had somewhat lower self-esteem.

Parenting Skills From Adolescence Through Adulthood

In the NDAPP, teen mothers were less cognitively prepared for parenting when compared to adult mothers, as reflected by their rigid attitudes toward parenting, inadequate knowledge of infant development, unrealistic expectations of their children, and punitive parenting styles (Sommer et al., 1993). Less prepared teen mothers experienced greater parenting stress and were less responsive to their children. They also were less attentive and interactive as well as less flexible, less verbal, and less positive when observed playing with their 6-month-old infants. Prenatal cognitive readiness for parenting was associated with more skillful interactions with infants at 6 months and was found to play a central role in predicting future parenting (Whitman et al., 2001).

Developmental Changes in Parenting. As the children of teen mothers from the NDAPP grew from infancy through early childhood, their mothers acquired extensive parenting experience, with many young mothers demonstrating stability in parenting. Mothers were videotaped while interacting with their children at 6 months, 3 years and 5 years of age (Whitman et al., 2001). At each time point, interactions were scored on items reflecting verbal encouragement and responsiveness. Assessments of the quality of maternal interactions when infants were 6 months old were moderately correlated with similar assessments taken at 5 years, indicating stability in interactional styles.

In addition, mothers' use of verbal encouragement and responsiveness increased over time during early childhood (Weed, Keogh, Borkowski, & Whitman, 2005). Larger increases in verbal encouragement were observed in mothers who were more intelligent and who had infants with more advanced mental skills (Bayley) at 6 months, whereas increases in responsiveness were seen in mothers who rated their babies as having "easy temperaments." In contrast, mothers who perceived their infants to have "difficult temperaments" tended to become less responsive over time. Results from the NDAPP are consistent with the notion that teen mothers as a group acquire more effective parenting skills over time as children's communication skills improve (Luster & Mittelstaedt, 1993).

Parenting at 30-something.   As children become teenagers, parents sometimes struggle with trying to maintain close relationships while supporting their children's emerging autonomy (Sroufe, 2002). For some mothers in the NDAPP, these challenges surfaced as the mothers themselves entered into their 30s. Quality of parenting, 14 years after the birth of their first children, was assessed; specifically, items measuring monitoring, supervision, warmth, democratic parenting and shared activities were examined. These items were first developed for use in the National Longitudinal Study of Adolescent Health (Add Health; Harris & Ryan, 1999), and allowed for comparisons to be made between NDAPP mothers and those in a nationally representative sample.

Adolescents reported that their parents monitored their activities in several areas, including choice of friends, clothing, bed time, TV viewing, and weekend curfews. Over one half of the mothers in the NDAPP (55.2%) were reported to be home always or most of the time when children returned from school, compared with only 48.9% of mothers in the Add Health data set. Mothers from the NDAPP also tended to monitor curfews (74.4%) and bedtimes (46.1%) somewhat more frequently than mothers in the Add Health project (65% and 34%, respectively). In addition teens from the NDAPP reported that mothers supervised their outside of school activities most of the time.

The majority of adolescents in the NDAPP agreed that they were satisfied with their communication with their mothers (79.8%), their overall relationship (86.5%), and felt close to their mothers (84.3%); percentages were similar to teens from the Add Health project. Mothers also participated in an average of two different activities per week with their teens, such as attending church, playing sports, going shopping or helping with a school project. Slightly fewer than 50% of teens reported attending church with their mothers within the past 4 weeks, compared to only 37.64% of teens from the Add Health study. Furthermore, 33.7% reported that they had worked on a project for school with their mothers, compared to only 13.21% of Add Health teens. Thus, in many respects, mothers in the NDAPP sample were similar to mothers in the Add Health study.

In summary, mothers in the NDAPP appear to have made considerable positive gains in parenting practices. In infancy, early mother–child interactions reflected poorly developed parenting skills in teen mothers when compared to adult mothers. However, both encouragement and responsiveness in mother–child interactions improved as children became toddlers. By age 14, mothers were as involved as, and in some cases more so, than mothers from a national sample in terms of monitoring and supervising their teens' activities. Children of teen mothers also reported satisfaction in their relationships with their mothers regarding closeness, communication and their overall relationships.

RESILIENCE OF TEEN MOTHERS IN ADULTHOOD

Many mothers in the NDAPP experienced positive growth during their transition to adulthood, including educational attainment, workforce participation, psychological adjustment, and effective parenting practices. In the following section, we examine how three important markers of adulthood—education, employment, and adjustment—defined resilient mothers and how resiliency changed over time. Additionally, prenatal risk and protective factors were used to predict maternal resilience and vulnerability from early to middle adulthood.

Maternal Resilience and Vulnerability in Their Early 20s

Adolescent mothers from the NDAPP were categorized as resilient or vulnerable in their early 20s based on an index of the quality of maternal functioning (Weed, Keogh, & Borkowski, 2000). The index was based on work by Luthar and Zigler (1991) who suggested resilience should be assessed through social competence, that is, meeting both societal expectations and furthering personal development. Four important social outcomes (i.e., high school graduation, continued education, work history, and current job status) and three psychological outcomes (positive self-esteem, low depression, and low anxiety) were included in the index (Weed et al., 2000). Mothers received one point for achieving each of the seven outcomes, resulting in scores ranging from 0 to 7. The resiliency index was viewed as a continuum, with higher scores indicative of maternal resilience and lower scores indicating vulnerability. Mothers were considered resilient if they had scores of 5 or greater and vulnerable if they scored 3 or less; those with scores of 4 were considered neutral because they had neither successful nor problematic outcomes.

The construction of the maternal resiliency index reflected variability in possible pathways to success. For instance, employment or continued schooling may be equally important pathways, but doing both while parenting may prove counterproductive. Similarly, psychological factors may be related to the potential to meet vocational or educational expectations, with depression, anxiety, and low self-esteem acting as barriers to holding down a job or applying knowledge gained through education to everyday life situations (Weed et al., 2000). However, personal strengths in two of these areas may compensate for weaknesses. For example, high self-esteem and the absence of depressive symptoms may attenuate the negative effects associated with high anxiety. For these reasons, the resiliency index included multiple measures of valued social outcomes as well as multiple measures of psychological adjustment, reflecting the overall configuration of the mothers' lives at 5 years postpartum.

Interestingly, fewer than 40% of the adolescent mothers in the NDAPP were classified as resilient at 5 years. The majority of resilient mothers (83%) had positive adjustment and had completed high school; they varied in amount of time spent working since first becoming a mother and whether they were currently employed or in school. Adolescent mothers who were resilient during their early 20s had completed more schooling at the time of the teenage pregnancy, were younger, had more support from friends and siblings, and espoused empathetic parenting attitudes. Younger teens, who were nonetheless on grade level for their age, may have been more likely to stay in school than older teens, who were often below grade level and may have been more likely to drop out when faced with an unexpected pregnancy (Weed et al., 2000).

These findings demonstrated the difficulties that teen mothers faced in successfully transitioning to adulthood in their early 20s. Less than 40% were able to finish school and enter the workforce successfully while remaining well-adjusted. However, as mothers aged and had more time to complete the tasks of adulthood, they made progress toward attaining these goals despite lack of clarity regarding the processes through which they achieved resilience. In the next study we examined the stability of maternal resilience over a 5-year time frame as mothers progressed through their third decade of life.

Teen Mothers in Their Late 20s

Few studies on resilience in teen mothers have employed a longitudinal design across multiple domains of development. This type of design not only allows for an examination of the stability of resilience or vulnerability but also enables the prediction of which mothers may become resilient in later life. Using the same maternal resiliency index as Weed et al. (2000), Noria (2005) investigated the stability of maternal resilience from the early to the late 20s to describe how mothers attained the developmental tasks of adulthood. Resilience was viewed not as a static characteristic, but rather as a dynamic process that could change given the contexts in which mothers developed.

Participants were classified as resilient, vulnerable, or neutral at 5, 8, and 10 years postpartum. When analyzed cross-sectionally, similar percentages of resilient and vulnerable mothers were found: about 45% of the sample was classified as vulnerable at each time point, about 35% resilient at 5 and 8 years, and 43% resilient at 10 years. However, when the classifications were examined longitudinally, only 38.2% of the sample evidenced stability in their classifications, with 18.3% exhibiting resilience, 2.3% neutral status, and 17.6% vulnerability at all three measurement occasions. The remainder improved from vulnerable to neutral or resilient status (25.2%), declined from resilient to vulnerable or neutral status (19.9%), or demonstrated an unclear pattern of instability (16.7%), fluctuating among the three categories across time.

Because the context of development sets the stage for future outcomes, maternal prenatal characteristics, such as cognitive resources, maternal adjustment, and school involvement, were used to predict maternal resilience at 5 and 10 years postpartum. Both cognitive resources and school involvement were related to resilience at 5, but only school involvement was related to resilience at 10. Mothers who had higher IQ scores, were more cognitively prepared for parenting, and who completed more years of schooling at the time of pregnancy were resilient at 5 years postpartum. In contrast, mothers who reported high GPA, were on grade level and exhibited social competence in school were resilient at both 5 and 10. However, maternal life stress, internalizing, and externalizing problems were unrelated to resiliency status at either time point, suggesting that psychological maladjustment during pregnancy did not interfere with the attainment of the markers of adult status in early adulthood.

Noria (2005) hypothesized that if protective factors were in place during pregnancy, such as positive adjustment, cognitive readiness for parenting, and school success, mothers would more quickly attain developmental tasks of adulthood, which in turn would set the stage for positive developmental outcomes in their late 20s in terms of subsequent fertility, educational completion, positive parenting attitudes, and psychological adjustment. To address this issue, early resilience was examined as a mediator between prenatal maternal risk and protective factors and later child abuse potential (Noria, 2005), as measured by the Child Abuse Potential Inventory (Milner, 1986).

Testing a mediational model requires three steps: (a) regress the mediating variable onto the independent variable, (b) regress the dependent variable of interest onto the independent variable, and (c) simultaneously regress the dependent variable onto the independent and mediating variables, resulting in a significant decrease in the strength of the relationship between the independent and dependent variables due to the presence of the mediating variable (Baron & Kenny, 1986). Two models were tested in which 5-year resilience was examined as a mediator between prenatal cognitive resources and 10-year abuse potential, and prenatal school involvement and abuse potential.

As required by the first step in testing a mediational model, both school involvement and cognitive resources independently predicted maternal resilience at 5 years, such that mothers who had greater cognitive resources and were more successful and involved in school were resilient. To complete the second step, abuse potential scores at age 10 were regressed onto cognitive resources and school involvement. Cognitive resources predicted child abuse potential, such that mothers who had higher IQs, were more cognitively prepared for school and had completed more education at pregnancy had lower potential to abuse. In addition, school involvement was a significant predictor of abuse potential, such that mothers on grade level with higher GPAs and greater social competence at school exhibited less potential to abuse their children.

The final step in testing mediation was carried out by simultaneously regressing abuse potential onto prenatal school involvement and resilience. Being resilient 5 years following the birth of the first child mediated the relationship between school involvement and child abuse potential: Maternal abilities to complete schooling, enter the workforce, and be psychologically well-adjusted were the pathways through which prenatal school involvement influenced child abuse potential. However, when cognitive resources and 5-year resilience were used to simultaneously predict abuse potential, resilience did not serve as a mediator, suggesting that successfully making the transition to adulthood in the early 20s does not guarantee that maternal functioning is adequate in all domains of development in later adulthood. In the next project, we continued to examine maternal resilience in the domains of educational attainment, employment, and psychological adjustment, as first-born children, now 14, dealt with the developmental tasks of their own adolescence.

Maternal Resilience at 30: Education, Employment and Adjustment

As mothers entered their fourth decade of life, patterns of education, employment, and adjustment were analyzed again using the resilience index from prior NDAPP investigations (Noria, 2005; Weed et al., 2000) Similar to findings from past research with teenage mothers in later life (Furstenberg et al. 1987; Horwitz, Klerman, Kuo, & Jekel, 1991), we expected that a greater number of mothers would experience success in attaining these three tasks of adulthood. We also examined how resiliency status changed from early the 20s to the 30s, identifying whether some mothers were consistently vulnerable or resilient. Finally, we determined whether early risk and protective factors played a role in maternal resilience and vulnerability as teen mothers entered their 30s.

The majority of mothers (57.9%) were classified as resilient, indicating that most had either successfully completed their education or entered the workforce, and were psychologically well-adjusted. However, almost a quarter (23.7%), were classified as vulnerable; they continued to experience psychological, educational and employment difficulties. The remaining 18.4% were classified as neutral, achieving some success in one or two areas functioning but still having difficulties in economic self-sufficiency or adjustment.

Table 2.2 shows the number of mothers who were classified as resilient, neutral, or vulnerable during their early 20s and again in their 30s. This classification scheme helps to clarify the stability of resilience during early adulthood. Consistency in classifications from the 20s to the 30s was observed for 58% of the sample. Stability was achieved at both ends of the spectrum, with 21% rated as vulnerable and 37% rated as resilient both in their early 20s and in their 30s. Positive growth was observed in 33%, and negative growth in only 7%, suggesting that most mothers who changed status continued to make advances in education and employment while improving their psychological adjustment.

In order to identify the precursors of the successful transition to adulthood, risk and protective factors were used to predict resilience as mothers entered their 30s. Potential risk factors included low SES in the families of origin, histories of physical and sexual abuse, adjustment problems during adolescence, age and educational levels during pregnancy, grade repetition, and short inter-birth intervals. Potential protective factors included prenatal cognitive readiness for parenting, maternal intelligence, and social

TABLE 2.2
Consistency in Resiliency Status During the Early 20s and Early 30s

Status at 20	Status at 30			
	Vulnerable	Neutral	Resilient	Total
Vulnerable	16	9	8	33
Neutral	1	2	8	11
Resilient	1	3	28	32
Total	18	14	44	76

competence. Stepwise regression analyses were used to identify risk and protective factors associated with resiliency status.

In contrast to findings earlier in adulthood (Noria, 2005; Weed et al, 2000), the only variable that accounted for significant unique variance (7.3%) in resiliency was prenatal cognitive readiness. Pregnant adolescents with more optimal parenting attitudes and styles, and with more accurate knowledge and expectations about infant and child development, were more likely to be resilient as they turned 30. Perhaps as more mothers were able to complete their education and enter the workforce, early maternal characteristics were less important in distinguishing among those who were successful in transitioning to adulthood and those who were not.

Mothers at 30: Major Contributions of the NDAPP

Although there was considerable interindividual variability in the developmental trajectories of teenage mothers, data from the NDAPP, as well as previous research, have demonstrated that maternal development improves with the transition to adulthood. For instance, we found that 57.9% of mothers in the NDAPP were resilient in their early 30s: Most had finished high school, entered the workforce, and were psychologically well-adjusted. However, some mothers continued to experience stress and adversity as they entered their 30s:

- Almost 24% of former teen mothers were classified as vulnerable at age 30, failing to complete their education, enter the workforce, or achieve healthy psychological functioning.
- Although 66.7% were working in their early 30s, on average, they reported major financial problems; relatedly, 65% in the NDAPP at age 30 were single parents.
- The majority of teen mothers (68%) received some level of public assistance in their early 30s; of those who did not, more than one half received child support or financial support from family members.
- Teen mothers generally had more children than the national average by age 30 and were less likely to be married; a rapid repeat pregnancy following the first birth was the strongest predictor

of fertility, with mothers bearing a second child within 12 to 18 months having more total number of children.

- Although trends in psychological adjustment (e.g., depression and anxiety) improved from the early 20s to the early 30s, 24% of the sample evidenced clinical levels of depression at age 30.

These findings contribute to the extant literature by providing an in-depth perspective on teen mothers in their early 30s, some 14 years after first becoming mothers. Previous longitudinal research has indicated that by midlife, most former teenage mothers can be classified as resilient, becoming economically self-sufficient, completing high school, gaining employment, and limiting their fertility (Furstenberg et al., 1987; Horwitz et al., 1991, Werner & Smith, 2001). Our findings suggest that mothers in the NDAPP, regardless of their apparent educational success, were underemployed and unable to support their growing families. This problem was further compounded by their choices regarding additional children, resulting in a fertility rate that exceeded that of women who delayed childbearing until adulthood. Although teen motherhood was a risk factor for low educational and economic attainment, poor psychological adjustment, and difficulties limiting family size, cognitive readiness for parenting during pregnancy emerged as a protective factor and predicted the successful transition to adulthood for many teen mothers.

RESILIENCE AND VULNERABILITY AMONG ADOLESCENT MOTHERS

The findings in the NDAPP on the transition to adulthood are similar to those reported by Oxford et al. (2005). In this study, three profiles, or types of mothers, based on information collected between pregnancy and middle childhood, emerged: *problem-prone* mothers (15%) engaged in high-risk behaviors; *psychologically vulnerable* mothers (42%) tended to be depressed and viewed motherhood as compensatory for negative feelings about themselves; and *normative* mothers (43%) saw motherhood as an alternate route to adulthood.

As teen mothers neared 30, the problem-prone group demonstrated the poorest psychological functioning, similar to vulnerable mothers in the NDAPP. The psychologically vulnerable group was similar to neutral mothers in the NDAPP; they continued to report more personal problems and poorer mental health, even though they had completed their education, were employed, and had attained financial independence. In contrast, resilient mothers in the NDAPP as well as the normative group in the Oxford et al. (2005) study were not without adjustment problems; as a whole, however, they demonstrated better personal adjustment and greater economic self-sufficiency than other teen mothers. In general, they were achieving the tasks associated with early adulthood.

The issue of whether or not maternal adjustment during early adulthood can be attributed to adolescent childbearing itself, as opposed to correlated or background factors such as poverty, dropping out of school, and delinquency, is difficult to resolve. The profiles discussed by Oxford et al. (2005) suggested that teen mothers may have preexisting problems that led not only to their adolescent pregnancy but were, in part, responsible for difficulties encountered in their transition to adulthood. Off-timed pregnancy, with its complex and challenging transitions, thrusts many adolescents into the parenting role without adequate preparation. For many, this transformation creates multiple challenges and setbacks, disrupting developmental trajectories that were in place prior to their pregnancies. Fortunately, the process of resilience enabled a majority of mothers in the NDAPP to eventually reestablish pathways to personal and family success during early adulthood. As the NDAPP data have shown, however, a sizeable number of mothers (24%) encountered major life adjustment problems, especially if they were not adequately prepared to assume their parenting roles prior to childbirth.

In a review of literature on the socioeconomic consequences of adolescent pregnancy, Bissell (2000) concluded that educational and vocational disadvantages were not the direct consequences of early childbearing but rather correlated with it due to family backgrounds and cultural expectations. Bissell's (2000) review, similar to conclusions reached by Furstenberg et al. (1987), suggested that simply delaying pregnancy until adulthood does little to ameliorate low educational attainment or improve the level of an initially poor occupational status. Although teen pregnancy has been shown to be a risk factor, in its own right, for low educational attainment, poverty and dependence upon public assistance (Maynard, 1997), the precise causal role of background factors (e.g., poverty, crime, and poor education) versus off-timed pregnancies in the successful transition to adulthood remain unresolved. Clearly, more research is needed on how the personal and environmental factors that place teens at risk for negative developmental outcomes, such as academic failure and aggression, interact with teen pregnancy itself and early childrearing in order to better understand the processes of risk and resilience operating in the lives of former adolescent mothers and their adolescent children as they grow up together.

REFERENCES

Achenbach, T. M. (1991). *Manual for the youth self-report and 1991 profile*. Burlington, VT: University of Vermont Department of Psychiatry.

Baron, R. M., & Kenny, D. A. (1986). The moderator–mediator variable distinction in social psychological research: Conceptual, strategic, and statistical considerations. *Journal of Personality and Social Psychology, 51*, 1173–1182.

Beck, A. T. (1987). *Beck depression inventory*. San Antonio, TX: The Psychological Corporation.

Bissell, M. (2000). Socioeconomic outcomes of teen pregnancy and parenthood: A review of the literature. *The Canadian Journal of Human Sexuality, 9*, 191–204.

Bolton, F. G., Jr. (1990). The risk of child maltreatment in adolescent parenting. In A. R. Stiffman & R. A. Feldman (Eds.), *Contraception, pregnancy, and parenting.* (pp. 223–237). Oxford, England: Jessica Kingsley Publishers.

Bramlett, M. D., & Mosher, W. D. (2002). *Cohabitation, marriage, divorce, and remarriage in the United States.* National Center for Health Statistics. Vital Health Stat 23(22).

Coleman, M., Ganong, L., & Fine, M. (2000). Reinvestigating remarriage: Another decade of progress. *Journal of Marriage and the Family, 62*, 1288–1307.

Coley, R. L., & Chase-Lansdale, P. L. (1998). Adolescent pregnancy and parenthood: Recent evidence and future directions. *American Psychologist, 53*, 152–166.

Connelly, C. D., & Straus, M. A. (1992). Mother's age and risk for physical abuse. *Child Abuse and Neglect, 16,* 709–718.

Coopersmith, S. (1981). *Self-esteem inventories.* Palo Alto, CA: Consulting Psychologists Press.

de Anda, D., Darroch, P., Davidson, M., Gilly, J., & Morejon, A. (1990). Stress management for pregnant adolescents and adolescent mothers: A pilot study. *Child and Adolescent Social Work, 7,* 53–67.

Dye, J. L. (2005). *Fertility of American women: June 2004.* Current Population Reports. Washington, DC: U.S. Census Bureau.

East, P. L., & Felice, M. E. (1990). Outcomes and parent–child relationships of former adolescent mothers and their 12-year-old children. *Developmental and Behavioral Pediatrics, 11,* 175–183.

East, P. L., & Felice, M. E. (1996). *Adolescent pregnancy and parenting: Findings from a racially diverse sample.* Hillsdale, NJ: Lawrence Erlbaum Associates.

Furstenberg, F. F., Brooks-Gunn, J., & Morgan, S. P. (1987). *Adolescent mothers in later life.* New York: Cambridge University Press.

Greene, J. P., & Winters, M. A. (2005). *Public high school graduation and college-readiness rates: 1991–2002.* Manhattan Institute for Policy Research: Education Working Paper (8).

Haggerty, R. J. (1989). Youth and America's future: The forgotten half. *Journal of Developmental and Behavioral Pediatrics, 10,* 321–325.

Harris, K. M., & Ryan, S. (1999, August). *Parenting and adolescent risk behavior and health outcomes: The adolescent health study.* Presented at the conference Parenting and the Child's World: Multiple Influences on Intellectual and Social–Emotional Development, Bethesda, MD.

Horwitz, S. M., Klerman, L. V., Kuo, H. S., & Jekel, J. F. (1991). School-age mothers: Predictors of long-term educational and economic outcomes. *Pediatrics, 87,* 862–868.

Hotz, V. J., McElroy, S. W., & Sanders, S. G. (1997). The impacts of teenage childbearing on the mothers and the consequences of those impacts for government. In R. A. Maynard (Ed.), *Kids having kids: Economic costs and social consequences of teen pregnancy* (pp. 54–94). Washington, DC: The Urban Institute Press.

Kalil, A., & Kunz, J. (2002). Teenage childbearing, marital status, and depressive symptoms in later life. *Child Development, 73,* 1748–1760.

Klerman, L. V. (2004). *Another chance: Preventing addiction births to teen mothers.* Washington, DC: National Campaign to Prevent Teen Pregnancy.

Leadbeater, B. J., & Linares, L. O. (1992). Depressive symptoms in Black and Puerto Rican adolescent mothers in the first three years post-partum. *Development and Psychopathology, 4,* 451–468.

Linares, L. O., Leadbeater, B. J., Jaffe, L., Kato, P. M., & Diaz, A. (1992). Predictors of repeat pregnancy outcomes among Black and Puerto Rican adolescent mothers. *Developmental and Behavioral Pediatrics, 13,* 89–94.

Linares, L. O., Leadbeater, B. J., Kato, P. M., & Jaffe, L. (1991). Predicting school outcomes for minority group adolescent mothers: Can subgroups be identified? *Journal of Research on Adolescence, 1*, 379–400.

Luster, T., & Mittelstaedt, M. (1993). Adolescent mothers. In T. Luster & L. Okagaki (Eds.), *Parenting: An ecological perspective* (pp. 69–99). Hillsdale, NJ: Lawrence Erlbaum Associates.

Luthar, S. S., & Zigler, E. (1991). Vulnerability and competence: A review of research on resilience in childhood. *American Journal of Orthopsychiatry, 61*, 6–22.

Mathews, T. J., & Hamilton, B. E. (2002). *Mean age of mother, 1970–2000.* National vital statistics reports: 51(1). Hyattsville, Maryland: National Center for Health Statistics.

Maynard, R. A. (Ed.). (1997). *Kids having kids: Economic costs and social consequences of teen pregnancy.* Washington, DC: The Urban Institute Press.

McCrary, M. M., & Weed, K. (2005, March). *Age at first pregnancy, formal operational thought and social support as predictors of identity formation of young mothers.* Poster presented at the Society for Research in Adolescence Annual Meeting, San Francisco, CA.

Milner, J. S. (1986). *The child abuse potential inventory* (2nd ed.). Webster, NC: Psytec.

Mylod, D. E., Whitman, T. L., & Borkowski, J. G. (1997). Predicting adolescent mothers' transition to adulthood. *Journal of Research in Adolescence, 7*, 457–478.

Newburger, E. C., & Curry, A. (1999). *Educational attainment in the United States: March 1999.* Current Population Reports. Atlanta, GA: U.S. Census Bureau

Noria, C. W. (2005). *Teenage mothers become "twenty-something:" Paths to self-sufficiency.* Unpublished doctoral dissertation, University of Notre Dame.

Oxford, M., Gilchrist, L., Lohr, M., Gillmore, M., Morrison, D., & Spieker, S. (2005). Life course heterogeneity in the transition from adolescence to adulthood among adolescent mothers. *Journal of Research on Adolescence, 15*, 479–504.

Passino, A., Whitman, T. L., Borkowski, J. G., Schellenbach, C. J., Maxwell, S. E., Keogh, D. A., et al. (1993). Personal adjustment during pregnancy and adolescent parenting. *Adolescence, 28*, 97–122.

Scott-Jones, D. (1991) Educational levels of adolescent child bearers at first and second births. *American Journal of Education, 99*, 461–480.

Seitz, V. (1996). Adolescent pregnancy and parenting. In Zigler, E. F., Kagan, S. L., & Hall, N. F. (Eds.), *Children, families, and government: Preparing for the twenty-first century* (pp. 268–287). New York, NY: Cambridge University Press.

Simmons, T., & O'Connell, M. (2003). *Married-couple and unmarried-partner households: 2000.* Census 2000 Brief. Washington, DC: U.S. Census Bureau.

Simmons, T., & O'Neill, G. (2001). *Households and families: 2000.* Census 2000 Brief. Washington, DC: U.S. Census Bureau.

Sommer, K. S., Whitman, T. L., Borkowski, J. G., Schellenbach, C. J., Maxwell, S. E., & Keogh, D. A. (1993). Cognitive readiness and adolescent parenting. *Developmental Psychology, 29,* 389–398.

Spielberger, C. D. (1983). *Manual for the state trait anxiety inventory.* Palo Alto, CA: Consulting Psychologists Press.

Sroufe, L. A. (2002). From infant attachment to promotion of adolescent autonomy: Prospective, longitudinal data on the role of parents in development. In J. G. Borkowski, S. Ramey, & M. Bristol-Power, (Eds.), *Parenting and the child's world: Influences on intellectual, academic, and social-emotional development* (pp 187–202). Mahwah, NJ: Lawrence Erlbaum Associates.

Trad, P. V. (1995). Mental health of adolescent mothers. *Journal of the American Academy of Child and Adolescent Psychiatry, 34,* 130–142.

Weed, K., Keogh, D., & Borkowski, J. (2000). Predictors of resiliency in adolescent mothers. *Journal of Applied Developmental Psychology, 21,* 207–231.

Weed, K., Keogh, D., Borkowski, J., & Whitman, T. (April, 2005). *Adolescent mothers' interactions with their children from 6-months through 5-years of age.* Poster presented at the Society for Research in Child Development's Biennial Conference, Atlanta, GA.

Werner, E. E., & Smith, R. S. (2001). *Journeys from childhood to midlife: Risk, resilience, and recovery.* Cornell University Press: Ithaca, NY.

Whitman, T. L., Borkowski, J. G., Keogh, D. A., & Weed, K. (2001). *Interwoven lives: Adolescent mothers and their children.* Mahwah, NJ: Lawrence Erlbaum Associates.

Wolfe, D. A. (1985). Child-abusive parents: An empirical review and analysis. *Psychological-Bulletin, 97,* 462–482.

3

Children's Uncertain Futures: Problems in School

Jennifer Burke Lefever
Jody S. Nicholson
Christine Willard Noria

"I know that mothers are the first teachers that children know."

—Maya Angelou

Although children born to adolescent mothers tend to be virtually indistinguishable from their peers during infancy in intelligence and language, their developmental paths diverge rapidly as they become toddlers and preschoolers (Whitman, Borkowski, Keogh, & Weed, 2001). The failure to encourage optimal development in home and preschool environments often contributes to this divergence, leaving at-risk children vulnerable to academic problems as they enter elementary school; they often lack the necessary cognitive, language, and academic skills to achieve at grade level during their first years of formal education. Although we have learned much about early-appearing deficits associated with adolescent parenting (Whitman et al., 2001), few studies have tracked at-risk children from childhood through adolescence, systematically examining the antecedents of academic and intellectual delays.

In this chapter, we briefly summarize what we know from major longitudinal studies about the intellectual and language development, as well as academic success and failure, of children born to adolescent mothers. With this review as a backdrop, we present a detailed description of development of children in the Notre Dame Adolescent Parenting Project (NDAPP), highlighting their intellectual and academic development during childhood and early adolescence. Finally, we focus on a critical predictor of academic competence—the ability to regulate one's own behavior.

RISKS FOR INTELLECTUAL AND ACADEMIC DELAYS

Children of adolescent mothers are at risk for cognitive delays and school-related problems (Broman, 1981; Furstenberg, Brooks–Gunn, & Morgan, 1987; Whitman et al., 2001). These problems are not only related to maternal age, but also linked to a myriad of sociodemographic risks commonly found among teen-mother-led households, such as low educational attainment, low incomes, and limited healthcare options. Several major longitudinal studies have observed development in at-risk children through middle childhood, describing the impact of specific risk factors on intellectual development and academic achievement. In the following section, we briefly describe three landmark studies, highlighting major findings of risks associated with adolescent parenting.

National Collaborative Perinatal Project

One of the largest projects to explore the development of mothers and their children is the National Collaborative Perinatal Project (NCPP; Turkheimer, Haley, Waldron, D'Onofrio, & Gottesman,

2003). The NCPP evaluated the link between pre- and peri-natal risks and impaired childhood mental, neurological, and physical abilities. More than 100,000 women and children were followed from pregnancy through the first 8 years of the child's life, with information gathered at birth, 8 months, 1, 4, and 7 years. Racial minorities and impoverished families represented a high proportion of the overall sample (Turkheimer et al., 2003). Extensive data were collected from the 1950s to the 1970s at multiple sites throughout the US (Piquero & Buka, 2002; Turkheimer et al., 2003). The following review examines risks for children's intellectual and academic delays.

Several studies focused exclusively on adolescent mothers in the NCPP and illuminated the consequences of multiple risk factors on child development (Broman, 1981; Camp, Broman, Nichols, & Leff, 1998). One study described how the developmental paths of children from adult and teen mothers diverged over time (Broman, 1981). The children of adolescent mothers scored significantly higher than children of adult mothers on tests of intelligence at 8 months; but, by age 4, children of teen mothers scored significantly lower than peers born to adult mothers. Most striking was the rate of mental retardation in African American children of teen mothers (9.5%), which was almost double that of children of adult African American mothers (5%). At 7 years, the children also differed on rates of delay in mathematics achievement, and for the African American children, delays in reading and spelling achievement. Risk factors for later-appearing retardation included young maternal age, low SES, lack of formal education (less than 9 years of school), multiple births (twins and triplets), seizures during pregnancy, and low maternal intelligence (Camp et al., 1998).

National Longitudinal Survey of Youth

Although the National Longitudinal Survey of Youth (NLSY) was originally designed to evaluate factors that influenced labor force participation, supplemental data collection on mothers and children in this sample has contributed to our general understanding of development in at-risk children. In the NLSY, data were collected on more than 12,000 youth born in the late 1950s and early 1960s. Racial and ethnic minorities and economically disadvantaged European American youth were over-represented (Martin & Burchinal, 1992). Extensive data were collected on mothers and their children including standardized tests of intellectual and academic outcomes and assessment of the home environment. This review focuses on studies of the cognitive attainment and academic achievement of the children of adolescent mothers in the NLSY.

In the first-born children of young African American and European American mothers in the NLSY, maternal intelligence and intellectual and emotional supports available in the home were better predictors of child cognitive attainment than mother's age at childbirth or maternal educational attainment (Moore & Snyder, 1991). Mothers with higher IQs, who provided warm and stimulating environments, had children with higher IQ scores in preschool and early elementary school. The home environment was the primary predictor of cognitive attainment for the children of Latina mothers. In a separate study, including data from all children who were over the age of 5, children of teen mothers had lower cognitive attainment than children born to young adult mothers (Levine, Pollack, & Comfort, 2001). The relationship between young maternal age and poor child cognitive attainment was almost completely accounted for by race, family size, and maternal intelligence.

Two studies in the NLSY observed the influence of socio-demographic risks and environmental factors on academic achievement of children of young mothers (Cooksey, 1997; Levine et al., 2001). In the first study, children of adolescent mothers had significantly poorer reading recognition and comprehension than children born to young adult mothers; however, effects were attenuated when factors such as maternal intelligence, family income, and intellectual stimulation were controlled (Cooksey, 1997). In the second study, the strength of the relationship between maternal age and achievement was reduced when factors such as race, gender, family size, and maternal intelligence were considered (Levine et al., 2001).

The Baltimore Project

The first major research project to focus primarily on adolescent mothers began in Baltimore in the mid-1960s to evaluate a comprehensive care program (Brooks–Gunn, Guo, & Furstenberg, 1993).

The sample was comprised of African American adolescent mothers from disadvantaged backgrounds; most mothers grew up in homes led by teenage mothers. Developmental outcomes for both mothers and children were observed at five time points across a 20-year period: 1, 3, 5, 17, and 20 years after an initial prenatal interview. The school-related outcomes of the children as well as their predictors are presented here.

Children in the Baltimore project were generally on track academically before they entered school, with scores in the expected range on the Caldwell Preschool Inventory at ages 3 and 5. The children scored lower than peers born to higher resource adult mothers, but comparable to most African American urban preschoolers (Furstenberg et al., 1987). Risk factors for low scores included living in a single-parent household, lack of father involvement, maternal unemployment, and no preschool attendance.

Despite academic readiness scores in the normal range at school entry, the Baltimore children had high rates of academic problems by adolescence. Of the 92% still enrolled in school at age 17, half had repeated at least one grade during their school career. Although most of the sample attended general level classes, 17% were enrolled in remedial classes, and only 12% attended advanced classes. Male participants had poorer academic outcomes than females; they were more likely to have been held back and twice as likely to be enrolled in remedial classes. Two thirds as many males as females attended advanced classes (Furstenberg et al., 1987). At the 20-year assessment, 10% were still attending high school, 33% had dropped out, 6% attained a GED, 36% had completed high school only, and 15% had completed high school and were currently enrolled in higher education classes. Overall, slightly more than 40% of the sample repeated a grade as adolescents, with males being more likely to repeat a grade as well as to drop out of high school (Brooks–Gunn et al., 1993).

The Baltimore children were at high risk for adverse academic outcomes, including a high likelihood of grade repetition and school drop out. These problems were linked to a lack of social support, poor parenting practices, and poverty (Furstenberg, Hughes, & Brooks–Gunn, 1992). The probability of obtaining a high school education depended on factors such as prenatal maternal educational aspirations, maternal attendance at a special program for pregnant teenagers, and father presence in middle childhood and young adulthood. Further educational attainment was predicted by preschool attendance, general abilities during early childhood, and maternal welfare status (Brooks–Gunn et al., 1993).

The NCPP, NLSY, and the Baltimore study have provided a solid foundation of knowledge about the cognitive and academic development of at-risk children. Children born to adolescent mothers tend to be within the average range of intelligence and academic readiness during infancy, but show signs of developmental delay by preschool (Broman, 1981; Cooksey, 1997; Whitman et al., 2001) and elevated rates of school failure and drop-out during adolescence (Brooks–Gunn et al., 1993; Furstenberg et al., 1987). To learn more about how at-risk children change over time, we turn now to a discussion of the NDAPP data set. A strength of the NDAPP dataset is the repeated measurement of development from early childhood through adolescence, that allowed the tracking of children's cognitive and academic outcomes from 3 to 14 years. The following sections present data on cognitive and academic development from preschool to early adolescence and a potential mechanism for achieving academic success for high-risk children—self-regulation.

CONTRIBUTIONS OF THE NDAPP

The NDAPP was based on a theoretical model of off-time parenting (cf. chap. 1), which included many of the risk factors identified in our literature review including low levels of maternal intelligence and language, immature parenting skills, poor personal adjustment, and inadequate social supports. In the NDAPP, a broad array of information was gathered from both mothers and children over a span of 14 years in order to: (a) observe changes over time at both the individual and group level, (b) identify precursors of cognitive delays such as mild mental retardation, and (c) pinpoint potential mechanisms associated with more optimal developmental outcomes.

Mental Development and Behavioral Adaptation

The first question of interest centers on how three core skills, necessary for academic success (intelligence, receptive language, and adaptive behaviors), changed from 3 to 14 years. Data were collected at ages 3, 5, 8, 10, and 14 years through standardized testing and maternal interview. Children's intelligence was measured at 3 and 5 years using the Stanford–Binet Form LM (Terman & Merrill, 1973) and at ages 8, 10, and 14 years using the Wechsler Intelligence Scales for Children–III (WISC–III; Wechsler, 1991). Receptive language was measured at ages 3, 5, 8, and 10 years, using the Peabody Picture Vocabulary Test–Revised (PPVT–R; Dunn & Dunn, 1981). The Vineland Adaptive Behavior Scales (VABS; Sparrow, Ball, & Cicchetti, 1984) was included at the same time points to provide additional information about the children's risks for mild mental retardation. It should be noted that all but one of the measures were standardized with a mean of 100 ($SD = 15$); the exception was the Stanford–Binet Form LM, which has the same mean but a standard deviation of 16.

Changes in Intelligence, Receptive Language, and Adaptive Behavior. Figure 3.1 shows average scores for intelligence, receptive language, and adaptive behavior from 3 to 14 years of age. The top half of the figure represents the low average range (from the standardized mean to $-1 SD$), while the bottom half represents a range of

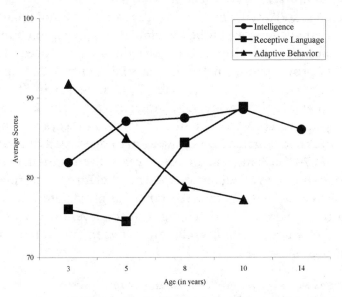

Figure 3.1.   Intelligence, receptive language, and adaptive behavior from 3 to 14 years.

lower functioning (1 to 2 *SD* below the mean). An initial inspection of Figure 3.1 suggests that children's language skills improved dramatically from 3 to 10 years, adaptive behaviors declined from 3 to 10, and intelligence changed minimally from 3 to 14.

Changes in Intelligence From 3 to 14 Years. We expected that the level of intelligence for children in the NDAPP sample would be within the normal range within the 1st year but would decline significantly over time (Broman, 1981; Whitman et al., 2001). In fact, this is what occurred from 6 months ($M = 101.79$; $SD = 17.61$) to 3 years ($M = 81.85$, $SD = 13.02$) (Whitman et al., 2001). However, as can be seen in Figure 3.1, intelligence remained fairly stable over time with some signs of improvement. Children's intelligence scores fluctuated by about ½ *SD* from 3 to 14 years, from 81.85 to 88.52, remaining around 1 *SD* below normal. The percentage of children with IQs lower than the cutoff for mild developmental delays (75) declined from a high of 30% at 3 years to a low of 16% at 10 years. The average intercorrelation of intelligence scores from one assessment period to the next showed reasonable stability ($M = .74$).

Changes in Receptive Language from 3 to 10 Years. As receptive language and intelligence are so intertwined, we anticipated that receptive language would follow a similar trajectory. In contrast to intelligence, the children's receptive language scores showed marked improvement from 3 to 10 years (cf. Figure 3.1). Children's scores were well below the expected level at ages 3 and 5, but increased to within the low average range at ages 8 and 10. The percentage of children with evidence of delays in receptive language (with scores more than 1 *SD* below normal) decreased dramatically, from about 70% at 3 and 5 to 40% at 10 years. Even with dramatic improvement the rates of delay remained high relative to a normal sample, in which there is an expected rate of approximately 16%. Even though there were dramatic changes in the level of receptive language, the average intercorrelation between measurements remained high ($M = .68$).

Changes in Adaptive Behavior From 3 to 10 Years. Little is known about longitudinal changes in adaptive behavior in at-risk samples. In the NDAPP, children's average scores declined with each consecutive measurement period, as can be seen in Figure 3.1. At ages 3 and 5, the children's adaptive behavior scores were within the low normal range, but by ages 8 and 10 they were well below normal. In fact, by age 10 years, nearly 80% of the sample showed evidence of mild delays, with scores more than 1 *SD* below the mean. Deficits in adaptive behavior, combined with below average intelligence and receptive language, do not bode well for the children's ability to achieve in reading and math during middle and high school.

Reading and Mathematics Achievement

A second question of interest concerned how children's reading and mathematics achievement scores changed from ages 5 to 14 years. Academic achievement was measured at age 5 using the Peabody Individual Achievement Test (PIAT; Dunn & Markwardt, 1970), at 8 and 10 using the revised version of the PIAT (PIAT–R; Markwardt, 1989) and at 14 years using the Wechsler Individual Achievement Test (WIAT; Wechsler, 1992). Figure 3.2 shows the average reading recognition and math achievement scores at ages 5, 8, 10, and 14 years.

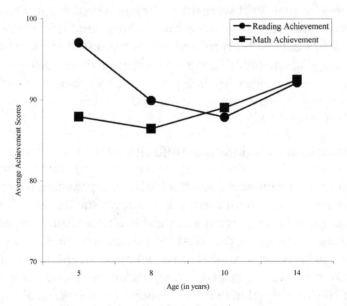

Figure 3.2   Academic achievement from 5 to 14 years.

These measures were also standardized with a mean of 100 (SD = 15). The top half of the figure represents the low average range and the bottom half represents below average performance.

Changes in Academic Achievement From 5 to 14 Years. We expected that the NDAPP sample's pattern of academic achievement scores would be similar to that of other at-risk children, with evidence of delays by kindergarten (Leadbeater & Bishop, 1994; Moore & Snyder, 1991; Whitman et al., 2001) and declines throughout the early school years (Pungello, Kupersmidt, Burchinal, & Patterson, 1996). Figure 3.2 shows that contrary to expectations, the NDAPP sample's average math achievement scores remained approximately 1 SD below normal from 5 to 10, ranging from 86.40 (SD = 17.36) to 88.97 (SD = 16.98), but improved slightly by 14 years (M = 92.41, SD = 14.56). However, it can also be seen in Figure 3.2 that reading achievement declined markedly from 5 to 10 years. Scores were near the standardized mean at age 5, in the low average range at age 8, and nearly 1 SD below the standardized mean at age 10. There was some evidence of recovery by 14 years as the sample had an average score (M = 92.04, SD = 15.23) in the low normal range. At age 5 the reading scores from the PIAT were primarily based on the ability to recognize letters and, at that age, scores neared the standardized mean. By age 8, the children's ability to read words was tested; the low average scores at ages 8 and older offered evidence that their reading abilities were not keeping pace with their peers. The correlations for achievement measures across time were high (M = .60 for mathematics and M = .79 for reading).

Classification of School-Related Difficulties

To better understand the joint effect of IQ, receptive language, adaptive behavior, and achievement on children's success in school, we examined children's performance and behavior within the context of the classroom. Using the NDAPP's measures of intelligence, standardized achievement, and adaptive behavior, all children at ages 5, 8, and 10 years were grouped in one of four diagnostic categories to identify those struggling in the classroom: (a) average achievement; (b) low achievement; (c) risk for learning disability, as defined by an average intelligence and an achievement–aptitude discrepancy; and (d) risk for mild mental retardation, as defined by low intelligence, low achievement, and adaptive behavior deficits. These classifications were then compared to data gathered from the teachers concerning the children's classroom performance and special services offered to individual children. Discrepancies between the teachers' reports of service referrals and the diagnostic classifications indicated children who were "falling through the cracks" in the school system and not receiving auxiliary services necessary to help them achieve to their highest potential.

Classification of Students.   Children were considered average in academic performance if their standard scores for receptive language, reading, and math achievement were all 85 or greater; conversely, low achievement was defined as having a score below 85 on one or more of the achievement measures. Students with LD showed a discrepancy of 21 or more points between either achievement measure and intelligence, after accounting for regression toward the mean. Finally, those with mild MR were defined as having an IQ less than 75 and adaptive behavior deficits in two or more subscales of the Vineland Adaptive Behavior Scales. At 14 years the children were classified into the first three of these four categories using the measures as described above, with the exception that receptive language was not measured. We were unable to make the fourth classification as adaptive behavior was not assessed at 14 years.

Summary of Classification Data.   Table 3.1 presents the percentage of children in each diagnostic category at ages 5, 8, 10, and 14 years. An examination of these data reveals three interesting findings: (a) The percentage of children with signs of mild MR is strikingly high at 8 years (17%), 5 times what would be expected in a normal population; (b) the children performed better over time, with the percentage with average school performance increasing markedly (from 21% to 58%) and the percentage with low achievement declining (from 67% to 40%); and (3) despite this improvement, on average about half of the sample had low levels of achievement.

TABLE 3.1

Classification of Children into Four Educational Categories Based
on Measures of Intelligence, Achievement, and Adaptive Behavior

Diagnostic Category	5 years	8 years	10 years	14 years
	(n=144)	(n=113)	(n=119)	(n=85)
Average School Performance	20.8%	25.7%	36.1%	57.6%
Low Achievement	66.7%	46.9%	45.4%	40.0%
Learning Disabilities	3.5%	10.6%	7.6%	2.4%
Mild Mental Retardation	9.0%	16.8%	10.9%	NA

Teacher Reports of Classroom Behavior. The Teacher Report
Form of the Achenbach Child Behavior Checklist (Achenbach, 1991)
was gathered from the NDAPP children's primary teachers at ages 8
and 10 years to learn more about children's performance and behavior in the classroom. According to these reports, 8.4% of the sample
had been in special education, 12.2% had repeated a grade, and
nearly half (47.4%) had been referred for special services. In the
NDAPP sample, nearly 75% of the children experienced school-related difficulties as early as the second grade; yet, only half had ever
been referred for any form of special services.

Diagnostic classifications and teacher reports provide important
sources of information about achievement-related problems, referrals for special services, and participation in special education programs for children of teen mothers. This information, however, does
little to elucidate how specific changes in academic success and failure occur. Four recent projects from the NDAPP offer insights about
how children changed over time and identified factors that predicted
academic delays. In the first project, developmental trajectories for
intelligence, receptive language, adaptive behavior, and achievement were analyzed from ages 3 to 10 years, with prenatal maternal
risks predicting both developmental outcomes and rates of change.
The next three studies provide an in-depth analysis of children's
self-regulation, and its role in explaining reading comprehension
and classroom performance. These projects point to a potential approach for fostering resilience in at-risk children: comprehensive
teaching of self-regulation skills in both home and school settings.

Trajectories of Development From 3 to 10 Years

Children of adolescent mothers have alarmingly high rates of mild MR, school failures, and cognitive delays (Broman, 1981; Furstenberg et al., 1987; Whitman at al., 2001). These delays often increase over time, as early risks set children on the course for later adverse developmental outcomes, often limiting both the extent to which they can achieve and their ability to change positively over time. Our next analytical goal is to track change in the children from 3 to 10 years as well as to determine the factors that predicted major changes in children's development. We first turn to a study that utilized the longitudinal, repeated-measure design of the NDAPP to model both individual and group trajectories, assessing the impact of prenatal maternal risks on the children's development over a 10-year period.

Hierarchical Linear Modeling was used to estimate outcomes at age 10 and to describe change between 3 and 10 years. Although this analysis is conceptually similar to the analysis presented earlier in the chapter (cf. Fig. 3.1 and 3.2), it allows for stronger assertions about developmental changes and their relationships to prenatal predictors. See chapter 9 for a more complete discussion of the usefulness of growth curve modeling for understanding changes in risk and resilience over time. Due to the high intercorrelations among the repeated measures of intelligence, receptive language, adaptive behavior, and academic achievement from 3 to 14 years, it might be inferred that development was stable over time. However, correlational analyses can only inform us about how children changed relative to other children in the NDAPP sample, not how they changed as individuals. Using Hierarchical Linear Modeling, we analyzed information from up to 159 dyads in our sample rather than being limited to the 88 dyads who had complete information.

Children's growth trajectories for intelligence, receptive language, and adaptive behavior were modeled from age 3 to 10 years and achievement in reading and mathematics was modeled from age 5 to 10 years (Lefever, Borkowski, & Whitman, 2006). Data from the 14-year assessments were not included due to changes in measurement (receptive language and adaptive behavior were not measured and a new measure for academic achievement was used). Second, developmental trajectories were predicted by prenatal factors including maternal intelligence, cognitive readiness to parent, and depression, informing us about the role of early risk in later development.

Intellectual and Academic Outcomes at 10 Years

Figure 3.3 presents the estimated trajectories for children's intelligence, receptive language, and adaptive behavior from 3 to 10 years, and achievement from 5 to 10 years. Estimated average outcomes at age 10 are shown by the final point in Figure 3.3. Average outcome scores for the children in the domains of intelligence, receptive language, and achievement in reading and mathematics were approximately 1 *SD* below normal, with scores ranging from 86.52 for achievement in reading to 88.86 for intelligence. Adaptive behavior scores were the most problematic with an estimated score (*M* = 76.08) nearly 2 *SD*s below the mean.

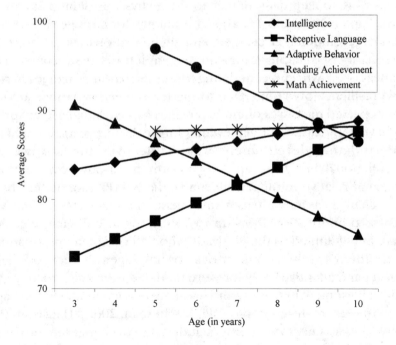

Figure 3.3   Estimated trajectories of intellectual and academic development from 3 to 10 years.

Changes in Intelligence, Language, and Behavioral Skills

Children improved in the areas of intelligence and receptive language from 3 to 10 years, with scores increasing significantly at a rate of 1 point per year for intelligence and 2 points per year for receptive language (Lefever et al., 2006). Achievement in mathematics remained stable from 5 to 10 years; the estimated slope of 1/10 of 1 point increase per year was not significantly different from 0. In contrast, the trajectories for both reading achievement and adaptive behavior declined significantly at a rate of approximately 2 points per year, a drop of nearly 1 *SD* in each case. When three domains of adaptive behavior were examined independently (daily living, socialization, and communication skills), communication showed the greatest decline. During middle childhood, the communication domain relied heavily on skills in written communication.

For the domains of intelligence and receptive language, children improved from age 3 to 10 years until they were, on average, in the low normal range of functioning. For achievement in mathematics, the children started within the normal range and remained relatively stable around 1 *SD* below normal. Both reading recognition and adaptive behavior declined over time, with reading achievement falling from a point near the mean to about 1 *SD* below normal. Adaptive behavior declined from the low average range to more than 1½ standard deviations below normal. Children showed the greatest declines in reading and writing, skills that are essential components for academic success.

Prenatal Maternal Risk and Children's Developmental Trajectories

To observe the influence of early risk on development, prenatal maternal risk factors were entered into the models to predict both developmental outcomes and rates of change. The following prenatal variables were selected from the NDAPP model for their theoretical importance: maternal intelligence, cognitive readiness to parent, and depression. To gauge the magnitude of the impact of risk factors on the trajectories, the percentage of reduction of parameter variance (*PRV*) was calculated. This calculation is conceptually similar to R^2, used in regression to estimate effect sizes.

Early risk had a greater impact on the children's outcomes at age 10 than on changes over time. For the estimated outcomes, the reduction in variance associated with the risk factors ranged from 9% to 26%. For changes over time the percentage of reduction in variance ranged from 0% to 32%. Maternal intelligence and cognitive readiness to parent played the most significant roles in predicting children's intellectual and academic development: Mothers who were more intelligent and cognitively prepared for parenting had children with the most successful outcomes at age 10. Cognitive readiness played the most significant role in predicting change; higher cognitive readiness was linked to either improvement or a slower decline in reading achievement. The following two figures visually depict the association of prenatal maternal risk and children's trajectories in intelligence and reading achievement.

Figure 3.4 shows how prenatal maternal intelligence, the only significant predictor, was associated with children's intelligence from 3 to 10 years. The middle line represents the trajectory for children whose mothers scored at the sample mean level of intelligence. The top trajectory represents children with mothers with normal levels

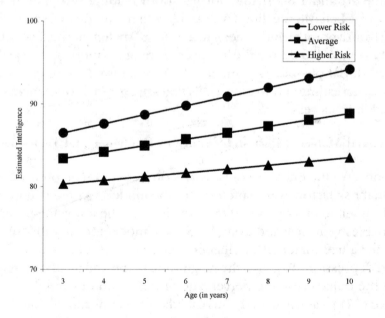

Figure 3.4.   Early risk and child intelligence from 3 to 10 years.

of intelligence and the bottom trajectory represents children of mothers with low intelligence. The association between prenatal maternal intelligence and children's outcomes can be easily seen as their estimated scores at age 10 differ by about 1 *SD*, with the lower-risk children having a score near the standardized mean and the higher-risk children with a score more than 1 SD below the mean. The association of maternal risk and the rate of change is more subtle, with the lower-risk children increasing about 1 point per year more rapidly than the higher-risk child.

Figure 3.5 shows the role of early risks in the development of reading skills. The top trajectory represents children in the lower-risk group (mothers with normal IQs and adequate cognitive readiness to parent) and the bottom trajectory represents those in the higher-risk group (mothers with low IQs and poor cognitive readiness to parent). It is evident in Figure 3.5 that the slopes from 3 to 10 years are quite different, with the higher-risk group of children declining at a rate 2 points per year faster than the children in the lower-risk group. By age 10, their reading scores differed by slightly more than 1 *SD* .

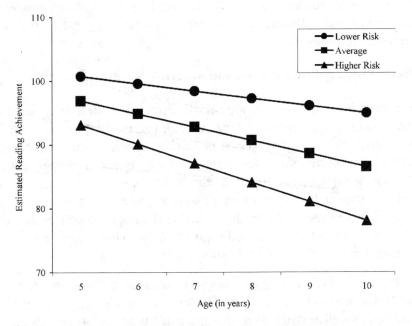

Figure 3.5.   Early risk and child reading achievement from 5 to 10 years.

From estimated trajectories, we can conclude that children in the NDAPP were either stable or improving over time in terms of intelligence, receptive language, and achievement in mathematics, but declined in domains that required skills in reading and writing. On average they performed at the lower end of the normal range at age 10, with the exception of adaptive behavior, where there were delays characteristic of diagnosable disabilities. In the next section we focus on a possible mechanism, self-regulation, which might account for some of the declines in reading and writing.

SELF-REGULATION IN THE CLASSROOM

The ability to regulate emotions, social behaviors, and information processing is critical for success in the classroom (Gottman, Katz, & Hooven, 1997; Martinez-Pons, 1996; Rydell, Berlin, & Bohlin, 2003). Regulation affects children's abilities to attend to new information, complete tasks, and constructively engage teachers and peers (Lengua & Sandler, 1996; Martinez-Pons, 1996) and is a potential link between early risk and poor classroom performance. The following three studies from the NDAPP explore connections between early maternal risks and poor academic performance during the elementary school years.

Early Risks, Self-Regulation, and Academic Readiness

Children learn to self-regulate socially through modeling by parents and peers (Zimmerman, 1998). As children become more skilled, regulation becomes an internal, cognitive process. Rudimentary regulation skills are often developed as early as age 3 (Kopp, 2002; Murray & Kochanska, 2002). In the first project, the emergence of self-regulation in the context of at-risk parenting was explored. Schatz, Borkowski, Whitman, Smith, and Keogh (2005) evaluated the mediational role of self-regulation between early risk and preacademic and behavioral skills at age 5.

Design.   Early maternal risks were measured through prenatal and 6-month maternal reports of parenting knowledge, style, and attitudes, as well as child abuse potential at 1 year. Child cognitive and emotional regulation was measured at age 3 by observational ratings of mother–child interactions in a free-play situation and items from a maternal report of daily child behaviors (Child Behavior Check-list/2–3; Achenbach, 1992). Academic and adaptive skills were measured at age 5 using standardized testing (PIAT–R) and maternal interview (VABS and CBCL/4–18; Achenbach, 1991).

Results and Implications.   Structural equation modeling (SEM) was used to test the relationship among the constructs of early maternal risk, children's regulation, and cognitive and behavioral outcomes at age 5. The overall fit of the model was assessed using indexes such as the Comparative Fit Index (CFI), Root Mean Square Error of Approximation (RMSEA), c^2, and the c^2 over degrees of freedom ratio. A CFI close to 1 (Bentler, 1990), an RMSEA equal to or less than .08 (Browne & Cudek, 1993), and a nonsignificant c^2 would offer evidence of a good fit of the data. However, as the c^2 statistic can be influenced by sample size, the ratio of c^2 over the degrees of freedom was also considered. This ratio should be less than 3 for an acceptable fit (Carmines & McIver, 1981).

Figure 3.6 shows a simplified version of the mediational model. The model was a satisfactory fit to the data with a CFI = .83, RMSEA = 0.07, and RMSEA 90% CI = .05–.09. Although the chi-square was significant, c^2 [81, N = 169] = 144.50, p < .001, the discrepancy ratio

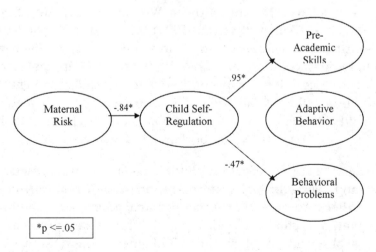

Figure 3.6.   Self-regulation as a mediator of the relationship between early maternal risk and children's preacademic skills.

was acceptable, $c^2/df = 1.78$. The paths among the constructs and the standardized estimates of the strength and direction of the relationships can be seen in Figure 3.6. Early maternal risk had a significant relationship with children's regulation: Higher risk predicted poorer regulatory skills in children. Regulation was significantly associated with preacademic skills and adjustment at age 5; stronger regulators had more advanced prereading skills and fewer behavioral problems. Early risk did not directly predict any of the children's outcomes; therefore, regulation mediated the association of early maternal risk and children's school readiness (Schatz et al., 2005). In summary, immature and rigid parenting practices led to poor regulation which, in turn, left many children unprepared to enter school. Inadequate cognitive and emotion regulation during preschool sets the stage for poor performance within the classroom, putting children at a disadvantage from the outset of their educational journey.

Self-Regulation and School Functioning

The construct of self-regulation includes a variety of motivational, behavioral, and meta-cognitive processes critical for academic success (Zimmerman, 1996) such as task orientation and controlling one's own behavior (Magnus, Cowen, Wyman, Fagen, & Work, 1999; Cowen, Work, Wyman, & Jarrell, 1994), as well as self-monitoring, goal-setting, and self-evaluation (Fantuzzo, Rhorbeck & Hightower, 1989). In the second project exploring the role of self-regulation in academic success, it was hypothesized that self-regulation in middle childhood would mediate the relationship between early maternal and child characteristics and educational outcomes for the children at ages 8 and 10 years (Noria, Borkowski, & Whitman, 2005).

Design.   Early maternal and child characteristics were assessed at ages 3 and 5 years through maternal report of abuse potential, cognitive readiness to parent, maternal personal adjustment, child temperament, and child internalizing and externalizing problems, as well as observations of mother–child interactions (Noria et al., 2005). Children's self-regulation was measured at ages 8 and 10 through teacher report of skills used in the classroom

(Teacher–Child Rating Scale (T–CRS); Hightower, Spinell, & Lotyczewski, 1989). Achievement and classroom adjustment measures were collected at ages 8 and 10 through standardized testing, mother-report, and teacher-report. Mediation was tested through a series of multiple regression equations following commonly accepted guidelines (Baron & Kenny, 1986).

Results and Implications.   Early parenting, as well as maternal and child adjustment, were predictive of academic achievement and classroom behavior, jointly accounting for 9.4% and 7.7% of the variance respectively. More positive parenting practices, such as greater cognitive preparedness, better interactional styles, and less abuse potential, as well as better maternal and child adjustment were associated with higher achievement and more positive classroom behaviors. When children's self-regulation was included in the models, the percentage of variance explained increased to 30.4% for achievement and 47.8% for classroom behavior. Self-regulation was a significant individual predictor for achievement, accounting for 21% of the variance. Both self-regulation and the children's adjustment were significant individual contributors to classroom behavior with self-regulation accounting for 40.2% of the variance and adjustment contributing 3.3%. Children with good early adjustment and adequate regulation, including a greater task orientation, had better classroom behavior, as well as reading and math achievement scores within the expected range. The mediational role of self-regulation between early characteristics and academic outcomes could not be established as early mother and child characteristics did not predict self-regulation.

Although self-regulation was not a mediator of parenting and early characteristics on classroom success, there were direct and independent relationships from early characteristics and self-regulation to academic performance (Noria et al., 2005). In particular, cognitive readiness to parent emerged as a significant individual predictor of achievement, uniquely explaining 6.2% of the variance. For math achievement, two aspects of the parenting construct (child abuse potential and knowledge of child development) as well as children's abilities to self-regulate, were each significant predictors, accounting for 4.1%, 9.1%, and 13% of the variation in math skills. Maternal knowledge of child development and children's self-regulation were also unique predictors of reading achievement, accounting for 11.2% and 14.8% of the variance. Children's regulatory abilities were critical in predicting a broad range of indicators of academic success, more so than early parenting practices and children's adjustment.

When these results are viewed through the lens of social–cognitive learning theory, several reasons for the lack of a direct relationship between early maternal characteristics and self-regulation emerge. First, it may be that most teen mothers have not developed consistent regulation skills themselves and, hence, are unable to teach and to model these skills to their children. Second, in some instances caregivers or preschool teachers may help to create a stable, structured, and enriched learning environment necessary for the emergence of children's regulation. These two likely circumstances explain, in part, why there were inconsistencies in the relationship between early parenting and children's self-regulation.

Self-regulation and Reading Competence

Self-regulation is a potential explanatory mechanism for problems in reading achievement as it is essential for the advanced learning and complex thinking underlying reading competence and comprehension (Paris & Paris, 2001; Thiede, Anderson, & Therriault, 2003). Smith, Akai, and Borkowski (2006) tested a theoretical model of reading development observing the relationship between reading readiness at age 5 and later reading competence at age 14. In this study the mediational role of self-regulation between preacademic reading skills, such as receptive language and letter recognition, and reading achievement during adolescence was examined.

Design.　Reading readiness was measured at age 5 through standardized testing using the PIAT, PPVT–R, and Developmental Test of Visual Motor Integration (Beery, 1989) and maternal interview (the Communication domain of the VABS). Regulation was measured at age 10, through teacher and maternal report of the child's behavior using items from the Teacher–Child Rating Scale and the Achenbach Child Behavior Checklist/4–18. Reading competence at age 14 was measured via standardized testing (WIAT) and child self-report on the Index of Reading Awareness (IRA; Jacobs & Paris, 1987). Structural equation modeling was used to test the model, taking advantage of multiple measures of each construct and accounting for missing data.

Results and Implications.   To test the mediational relationship, the appropriateness of two structural models was examined. The first tested the role of self-regulation as an indirect link between reading readiness and reading competency; the only path between reading readiness and competence was through self-regulation. In this model, self-regulation completely mediated the relationship between reading readiness and later reading competency. The second included both a direct pathway between reading readiness and competency and an indirect pathway through self-regulation. In this model self-regulation acts as a partial mediator. The overall fit of each model was evaluated using the indexes described previously.

The first model tested the impact of reading readiness on reading competence with self-regulation as a mediator (see Fig. 3.7). This model had the best overall fit—with a nonsignificant c^2 (c^2 (25) = 19.82, p = .76), a discrepancy ratio less than 3 (c^2/df = .79), a RMSEA

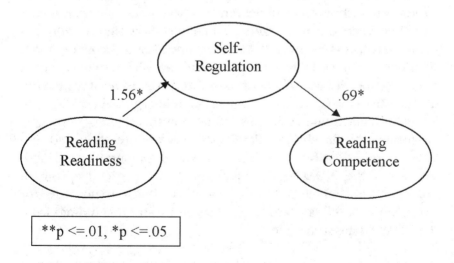

**p <=.01, *p <=.05

Figure 3.7.   Self-regulation as a mediator of the relationship between prereading skills and reading comprehension.

less than .08 (RMSEA = .000), and a CFI equal to 1.00—and the paths between the constructs were significant. The model in Figure 3.7 explained 67% of the variance in reading competence, whereas the model including both the direct and indirect paths between reading readiness and reading competence explained a smaller portion of variance (50%). Thus, the best-fitting and most parsimonious model suggested that self-regulation mediated the relationship between early reading readiness and reading competence during adolescence.

Since self-regulation contributed to the stability of reading performance during elementary school, gains in self-regulation could also disrupt downward reading trajectories and improve reading achievement. It is possible to identify children with deficits in prereading skills and strengthen their self-regulation skills to prevent later reading difficulties. In high-risk samples, students need explicit training in cognitive and emotional self-regulation (Smith et al., 2006), in addition to instruction on reading-specific metacognitive strategies (Keer, 2004).

Summing Up: Contributions From the NDAPP

We know that children of adolescent mothers tend to develop on par with their peers during infancy, but begin to show signs of developmental problems as early as the preschool years (Broman, 1981; Whitman et al., 2001). By late adolescence at-risk youth have higher rates of school failure, school drop out, and other school-related difficulties (Brooks-Gunn et al., 1993; Furstenberg et al., 1987). The NDAPP filled in some of the missing links in this chain of events, by describing how the children developed between preschool and adolescence and identifying risk factors for developmental delays. Findings from the NDAPP also highlighted the protective role of self-regulation, which influenced whether children succeeded or struggled in the classroom. Some of the more striking findings from the NDAPP dataset include:

- Children had unusually high rates of undiagnosed mild mental retardation (17%) and learning disabilities (11%) at age 8; approximately 25% of those who needed additional educational supports had not been referred for special services.

- From ages 3 to 10 years, children showed improvement in intelligence and receptive language, remained stable in math achievement, but declined dramatically in reading skills and adaptive behaviors.
- Despite gains in two intellectual domains (intelligence and receptive language), children still performed in the low-average range in these domains at ages 10 and 14 years.
- Self-regulation predicted academic performance from preschool to adolescence.
- Self-regulation mediated the effects of early maternal risks on school readiness at age 5 as well as the relationship between reading readiness at age 5 and reading competency at age 14.

Clearly, the most problematic areas of development for children in the NDAPP were reading and writing competencies. Similar delays have been found in the other samples of children of adolescent mothers (Cooksey, 1997; Levine et al, 2001) as well as disadvantaged children in the United States (U.S. Department of Education, 2004). The lack of formal language skills and reading competency in later childhood and adolescence was not surprising given that most at-risk mothers fail to use appropriate verbal stimulation, speaking to their children less often than mothers with more resources, using more negative words and simpler phrases (Hann, Osofsky, & Culp, 1996; Hart & Risley, 1992; Luster & Vandenbelt, 1999). This lack of language enrichment has a cascading and, most likely, cumulative negative influence across the lifespan. Without the tools that language provides, children enter school unprepared to learn in classroom settings, curtailing their advancement in reading and writing. They generally are unable to compete academically with their peers, thus limiting their vocational prospects and future earning potential.

CONCLUSION: TEACHING SELF-REGULATION

Cognitive and emotional regulation skills are critical for academic success. The data presented in this chapter highlighted the pervasive impact of self-regulation throughout childhood on academic achievement, predicting preacademic skills (Schatz et al., 2005), classroom performance during middle-childhood (Noria et al., 2005), and reading competencies in adolescence (Smith et al., 2006). Development of regulation skills, such as the ability to attend to new information and control impulsive behaviors, could forestall the emergence of the academic problems that are prevalent in this population.

Factors present in both home and school settings independently influence the development of regulation, thereby enhancing school performance and classroom behavior (Brody, Dorsey, Forehand, & Armistead, 2002; Noria et al., 2005). Fostering regulation skills in both environments has the potential to counter the impact of failures in either setting. For example, a highly organized classroom, with clear rules, and active student involvement may counter the influence of emotionally distant caregivers on children's abilities to regulate their own behaviors. Conversely, children with involved caregivers, who actively model regulation, may successfully develop regulation skills despite disorganized classrooms.

The prospect of teaching children and adolescents skills that improve performance across contexts and domains makes self-regulation an important focus for classroom interventions. For example, as few as six hour-long sessions which focused on training students to use the metacognitive strategies of goal setting, explicit strategy use, and reflection improved the regulation skills of eighth graders (Perels, Gurtler, & Schmitz, 2005). In another school-based intervention, training teachers to implement strategies that promoted regulation (planning approaches to problems and reflecting on their resolution, as well as scaffolding the students' abilities to integrate new material with prior knowledge) was also effective in enhancing motivation and information processing skills during late adolescence (Rozendaal, Minnaert, & Boekaerts, 2005). Although children's self-regulation is not specifically targeted in most home-based interventions, advanced forms of regulation are likely a product of programs where warm and flexible parenting is taught and encouraged.

Cognitive and emotional regulation offers the promise of encouraging intellectual, social, and academic competence in at-risk children on a broad scale. School-based interventions have the capacity to reach large numbers of children and could be enriched by complementary caregiver training in techniques that encourage and induce regulation. Self-regulation can be intentionally fostered through direct interventions that model meta-cognitive skills, train caregivers to support emerging regulatory abilities (Martinez-Pons, 1996), and motivate teachers to encourage their students' use of regulation in multiple contexts (Pressley, et al., 2001; Rozendaal et al., 2005). Vulnerable children can acquire skills in cognitive and emotional regulation, leading to increased intellectual and academic attainment, heightened motivation, and enhanced interpersonal relationships. These attributes help the children face the challenges imposed by their risky environments, leading to more resilient educational, occupational, and personal outcomes.

REFERENCES

Achenbach, T. (1991). *Manual for the Child Behavior Checklist/4–18 and 1991 profile.* Burlington, VT: University of Vermont Department of Psychiatry.

Achenbach, T. (1992). *Manual for the Child Behavior Checklist/2–3 and 1992 profile.* Burlington, VT: University of Vermont Department of Psychiatry.

Baron, R. M., & Kenny, D. A. (1986). The moderator–mediator variable distinction in social psychological research: Conceptual, strategic, and statistical considerations. *Journal of Personality and Social Psychology, 31,* 1173–1182.

Beery, K. (1989). *The administration, scoring, and teaching manual for the development test of visual–motor integration* (3rd Rev. ed.). Cleveland: Modern Curriculum Press.

Bentler, P. M. (1990). Fit indexes, Lagrange multipliers, constraint changes and incomplete data in structural models. *Multivariate Behavioral Research, 25,* 163–172.

Brody, G. H., Dorsey, S., Forehand, R., & Armistead, L. (2002). Unique and protective contributions of parenting and classroom processes to the adjustment of African American children living in single-parent families. *Child Development, 73,* 274–286.

Broman, S. H. (1981). Long-term development of children born to teenagers. In K. G. Scott, T. Field, & E. G. Robertson (Eds.), *Teenage parents and their offspring* (pp. 195–224). New York: Grune & Stratton.

Brooks-Gunn, J., Guo, G., & Furstenberg, F. F., Jr. (1993). Who drops out of and who continues beyond high school? A 20-year follow-up of Black urban youth. *Journal of Research on Adolescence, 3*, 271–294.

Browne, M. W., & Cudek, R. (1993). Alternative ways of assessing model fit. In K. A. Bollen & J. S. Long (Eds.), *Testing structural equation models* (pp. 136–162). Newbury Park, CA: Sage.

Camp, B. W., Broman, S. H., Nichols, P. L., & Leff, M. (1998). Maternal and neonatal risk factors for mental retardation: Defining the 'at-risk' child. *Early Human Development, 50*, 159–173.

Carmines, E. G., & McIver, J. P. (1981). Analyzing models with unobserved variables: Analysis of covariance structures. In G. W. Bohrnstedt & E. F. Borgatta, (Eds.), *Social Measurement: Current Issues.* Beverly Hills, CA: Sage.

Cooksey, E. C. (1997). Consequences of young mothers' marital histories for children's cognitive development. *Journal of Marriage and the Family, 59*, 245–261.

Cowen, E. L., Work, W. C., Wyman, P. A., & Jarrell, D. D. (1994). Relationships between retrospective parent reports of developmental milestones and school adjustment at ages 10 to 12 years. *Journal of the American Academy of Child and Adolescent Psychiatry, 33*, 400–406.

Dunn, L., & Dunn, L. (1981). *Peabody Picture Vocabulary Test–Revised.* Circle Pines, MN: American Guidance Service.

Dunn, L. M., & Markwardt, F. C. (1970). *Peabody Individual Achievement Test.* Circle Pines, MN: American Guidance Service.

Fantuzzo, J. W., Rohrbeck, C. A., & Hightower, A. D. (1989). A teacher assessment of self-controlling skills and their relationship to self-control and adjustment ratings. *Journal of School Psychology, 27*, 35–45.

Furstenberg, F., Brooks-Gunn, J., & Morgan, S. P. (1987). *Adolescent mothers in later life.* Cambridge: Cambridge University Press.

Furstenberg, F. F., Jr., Hughes, M. E., & Brooks-Gunn, J. (1992). The next generation: The children of teen mothers grow up. In M. K. Rosenheim & M. F. Testa (Eds.), *Early parenthood and coming of age in the 1990s* (pp. 113–135). New Brunswick, NJ: Rutgers University Press.

Gottman, J. M., Katz, L. F., & Hooven, C. (1997). *Meta-emotion: How families communicate emotionally.* Mahwah, NJ: Lawrence Erlbaum Associates.

Hann, D. M., Osofsky, J. D., & Culp, A. M. (1996). Relating the adolescent mother–child relationship to preschool outcomes. *Infant Mental Health Journal, 17*, 302–309.

Hart, B., & Risley, T. R. (1992). American parenting of language-learning children: Persisting differences in family–child interactions observed in natural home environments. *Developmental Psychology, 28*, 1096–1105.

Hightower, A. D., Spinell, A., & Lotyczewki, B. S. (1989). *Teacher–Child Rating Scale (T–CRS) guidelines.* Rochester, NY: Primary Mental Health Project, Inc.

Jacobs, J. E., & Paris, S. G. (1987). Children's metacognition about reading: Issues in definition, measurement, and instruction. *Educational Psychologist, 22,* 255–278.

Keer, H. V. (2004). Fostering reading comprehension in fifth grade by explicit instruction in reading strategies and peer tutoring. *British Journal of Educational Psychology, 74,* 37–70.

Kopp, C. (2002). Commentary: The codevelopments of attention and emotion regulation. *Infancy, 3,* 199–208.

Leadbeater, B. J., & Bishop, S. J. (1994). Predictors of behavior problems in preschool children of inner-city Afro-American and Puerto Rican adolescent mothers. *Child Development, 65,* 638–648.

Lefever, J. B., Borkowski, J. G., & Whitman, T. L. (2006). *The cognitive and academic development of children of adolescent mothers.* Manuscript submitted for publication.

Lengua, L. J., & Sandler, I. N. (1996). Self-regulation as a moderator of the relation between coping and symptomatology in children of divorce. *Journal of Abnormal Child Psychology, 24,* 681–702.

Levine, J. A., Pollack, H., & Comfort, M. E. (2001). Academic and behavioral outcomes among the children of young mothers. *Journal of Marriage and the Family, 63,* 355–369.

Luster, T., & Vandenbelt, M. (1999). Caregiving by low-income adolescent mothers and the language abilities of their 30-month-old children. *Infant Mental Health Journal, 20,* 148–165.

Magnus, K. B., Cowen, E. L., Wyman, P. A., Fagen, D. B., & Work, W. C. (1999). Parent–child relationship qualities and child adjustment in highly stressed urban black and white families. *Journal of Community Psychology, 27,* 55–71.

Markwardt, F. C., Jr. (1989). *Peabody Individual Achievement Test–Revised Manual.* Circle Pines, MN: American Guidance Service.

Martin, S. L., & Burchinal, M. R. (1992). Young women's antisocial behavior and the later emotional and behavioral health of their children. *American Journal of Public Health, 82,* 1007–1010.

Martinez-Pons, M. (1996). Test of a model of parental inducement of academic self regulation. *Journal of Experimental Education, 64,* 213–227.

Moore, K. A., & Snyder, N. O. (1991). Cognitive attainment among firstborn children of adolescent mothers. *American Sociological Review, 56,* 612–624.

Murray, K. T., & Kochanska, G. (2002). Effortful control: Factor structure and relation to externalizing and internalizing behaviors. *Journal of Abnormal Child Psychology, 30,* 503–514.

Noria, C. W., Borkowski, J. G., & Whitman, T. L. (2005). *Self-regulation, school achievement, and classroom adjustment in children of adolescent mothers.* Manuscript submitted for publication.

Paris, S. G., & Paris, A. H. (2001). Classroom applications of research on self-regulated learning. *Educational Psychologist, 36,* 89–101.

Perels, F., Gurtler, T., & Schmitz, B. (2005). Training of self-regulatory and problem-solving competence. *Learning and Instruction, 15,* 123–139.

Piquero, A. R., & Buka, S. L. (2002). Linking juvenile and adult patterns of criminal activity in the Providence cohort of the National Collaborative Perinatal Project. *Journal of Criminal Justice, 30,* 259–272.

Pressley, M., Wharton-McDonald, R., Allington, R., Block, C. C., Morrow, L., Tracey, D., et al. (2001). Strategy instruction for elementary students searching informational text. *Scientific Studies of Reading, 5,* 1088–8438.

Pungello, E. P., Kupersmidt, J. B., Burchinal, M. R., & Patterson, C. J. (1996). Environmental risk factors and children's achievement from middle childhood to early adolescence. *Developmental Psychology, 32,* 755–767.

Rozendaal, J. S., Minnaert, A., & Boekaerts, M. (2005). The influence of teacher perceived administration of self-regulated learning on students' motivation and information-processing. *Learning and Instruction, 15,* 141–160.

Rydell, A. M., Berlin, L, & Bohlin, G. (2003). Emotionality, emotion regulation, and adaptation among 5- to 8-year-old children. *Emotion, 3,* 30–47.

Schatz, J. N., Borkowski, J. G., Whitman, T. L, Smith, L. E., & Keogh, D. A. (2005). *Maltreatment, self-regulation, and developmental delays in at-risk children.* Manuscript submitted for publication.

Smith, L. E., Akai, C. E., & Borkowski, J. G. (2006, March). *From reading readiness to reading competence: The role of self-regulation in at-risk children.* Poster session presented at the Gatlinburg Conference, San Diego, CA.

Sparrow, S. S., Balla, D. A., & Cichetti, D. V. (1984). *Vineland Adaptive Behavior Scales.* Circle Pines, MN: American Guidance Service.

Terman, L. M., & Merrill, M. A. (1973). *Stanford-Binet Intelligence Scale, 1972 Norms Edition.* Boston: Houghton Mifflin.

Thiede, K. W., Anderson, M. C. M., & Therriault, D. (2003). Accuracy of metacognitive monitoring affects learning of texts. *Journal of Educational Psychology, 95,* 66–73.

Turkheimer, E., Haley, A., Waldron, M., D'Onofrio, B., & Gottesman, I. I. (2003). Socioeconomic status modifies heritability of IQ in young children. *Psychological Science, 14,* 623–628.

U.S. Department of Education (2004). *FY 2004 performance and accountability report.* Retrieved February 6, 2005, from http://www.ed.gov/reports/annual/2004report/report.pdf

Wechsler, D. (1991). *Manual for the Wechsler Intelligence Scale for Children (3rd ed.)*. San Antonio, TX: The Psychological Corporation.

Wechsler, D. (1992). *Wechsler Individual Achievement Test: Manual*. San Antonio, TX: The Psychological Corporation.

Whitman, T. L., Borkowski, J. G., Keogh, D. A., & Weed, K. (2001). *Interwoven lives: Adolescent mothers and their children*. Mahwah, NJ: Lawrence Erlbaum Associates.

Zimmerman, B. J. (1996). Enhancing student academic and health functioning: A self-regulatory perspective. *School Psychology Quarterly, 11,* 47–66.

Zimmerman, B. J. (1998). Academic studying and the development of personal skill: A self-regulatory perspective. *Educational Psychologist, 33,* 73–86.

4

Children's Uncertain Futures: Socioemotional Delays and Psychopathologies

Jody S. Nicholson
Jaelyn R. Farris

Our greatest glory is not in never falling, but in rising every time we fall.

—Confucius (551–479 BC)

T he high rates of adolescent psychopathologies in the United States result in substantial costs to families, schools, agencies, and society at large. Nearly 10% of teenagers in 2003 and 2004 experienced symptoms consistent with severe depression (Office of Applied Studies [OAS], 2005), and approximately 8% of children between the ages of 4 and 17 were diagnosed with Attention-Deficit/Hyperactivity Disorder (ADHD; Visser & Lesesne, 2005). Unfortunately, misdiagnosis and inappropriate treatment of childhood disorders are commonplace. For instance, depression is often underacknowledged during adolescence, with more than half of teenagers with symptomatology of major depression receiving neither a clinical diagnosis nor appropriate treatment for their problems (OAS, 2005). In contrast, 56% of U.S. children diagnosed with ADHD received medication to alleviate symptomatology in 2004, but often without corresponding behavioral therapy (Visser & Lesesne, 2005). Misdiagnosis and inadequate treatments lead to inefficient use of healthcare resources, and limit the potential of children, whose mental health needs are typically not met.

The misdiagnosis and inadequate treatment of youth psychopathologies stem, in part, from a lack of general knowledge about the onset and progression of psychological disorders in children and adolescents. In particular, little is known about psychopathologies in children who have not been referred for clinical treatment and about the relationship between adolescent parenting and specific clinical disorders in children. Given the multitude of risk factors to which children of adolescent mothers are often exposed, it seems likely that their rates of socioemotional problems and psychopathology would be higher than in a typical population. For example, the available research suggests that children born to young mothers are at increased risk for Conduct Disorder (Wakschlag et al., 2000). Most studies of youth psychopathologies, however, utilize samples of clinic-referred boys. Our ability to generalize these findings to community-based samples consisting of both boys and girls is, therefore, limited.

The NDAPP dataset provides unique research opportunities because it examines in a prospective fashion the development of a nonclinical sample of both boys and girls who reside in a community setting. Research using NDAPP data has shed light on early internalizing and externalizing problems in at-risk children, as well as the onset and progression of internalizing— and externalizing—related psychopathologies such as Depression, Anxiety, ADHD, Oppositional Defiant Disorder (ODD), and Conduct Disorder (CD). In this chapter, we begin by examining the empirical literature on internalizing and externalizing problems and their relationship to specific psychopathologies. Next, we describe findings on the socioemotional development of children born to adolescent mothers, including a summary of previous findings from the NDAPP. Finally, we present data on the prevalence of internalizing and externalizing disorders from ages 5 through 14, with a focus on the prevalence of Depression, Anxiety, ADHD, ODD, and CD.

SOCIOEMOTIONAL DEVELOPMENT AND PSYCHOPATHOLOGY

Ego resilience and ego control are two important forms of behavioral regulation (Cicchetti, Rogosch, Lynch, & Holt, 1993). Ego resilience refers to flexibility and persistence in approaching complex tasks, whereas ego control is the capacity to adapt impulses and emotions during problem solving. The over-regulation of ego-control is found in various forms of internalizing behaviors, such as loneliness, anxiety, shyness, and social withdrawal. In contrast, externalizing behaviors are often the result of under-regulation of ego-control, as seen in hyperactivity, aggression, and antisocial behaviors (Al-Yagon, 2003).

In addition to studying generalized internalizing and externalizing problems, it is important to assess specific psychopathologies associated with these general domains of socioemotional development. This perspective allows for investigations of the causes and correlates of various psychopathologies and provides suggestions for the development of new prevention and intervention approaches. In the following sections, we provide an overview of disorders related to internalizing and externalizing problems, focusing on Depression, Anxiety, ADHD, ODD, and CD during childhood and adolescence.

Disorders Associated With Internalizing Behaviors: Depression and Anxiety

Depression and anxiety disorders are clinical manifestations of internalizing problems. Depressive symptomatology is a core feature of Major Depressive Disorder (MDD), Dysthymic Disorder, and Bipolar Disorder (American Psychiatric Association [APA], 1994). Likewise, anxiety is a defining feature of Generalized Anxiety Disorder (GAD), Posttraumatic Stress Disorder, and Obsessive Compulsive Disorder. For the purposes of this chapter, we use the terms *depression* and *anxiety* to refer to symptomatology associated with Major Depressive Disorder (MDD) and Generalized Anxiety Disorder (GAD).

In order to meet criteria for Major Depressive Disorder, an individual must have experienced a major depressive episode for at least 2 weeks (APA, 1994). Individuals experiencing a major depressive episode display a variety of characteristics, such as tearfulness, irritability, brooding, anxiety, and complaints of pain. Although the core symptoms of a major depressive episode are the same for children and adolescents, certain symptoms such as somatic complaints, irritability, and social withdrawal are particularly common in children; psychomotor retardation, hypersomnia, and delusions are more common in adolescence and adulthood than before the onset of puberty. MDD is associated with a high mortality rate; 15% of individuals suffering from this disorder will die by suicide. In typical populations, MDD is twice as common in adolescent and adult females as adolescent and adult males; there are no known sex differences among prepubescent children. In the general population, the prevalence rate for MDD appears to be unrelated to ethnicity, education, income or marital status.

Generalized Anxiety Disorder is marked by excessive anxiety and worry for more than 6 months, to such an extent that social and occupational life is hindered (APA, 1994). In children, anxiety and worry are typically accompanied by at least one of the following symptoms: restlessness, fatigue, difficulty concentrating, irritability, and muscle tension. Children with GAD tend to worry about their general competence and the quality of their performance in daily life activities, such as sports and school, even when not being evaluated; other fears range from punctuality to catastrophic events. Among adults, women are diagnosed with this disorder somewhat more frequently than men in clinical settings, with a sex ratio approximately 2:1, female versus male. The sex ratio has not been clearly established among children and adolescents.

Disorders Associated With Externalizing Behaviors: ADHD, ODD, and CD

The three most common and troubling externalizing disorders that develop during childhood and adolescence are ADHD, ODD, and CD. ADHD is associated with problematic behavior at home and school (APA, 1994). Diagnostic criteria stipulate that inattentive, hyperactive, or impulsive symptoms must occur prior to age 7; also, symptoms must be pervasive across settings (e.g., home and school). The onset of symptoms may occur at a young age–excessive motor activity during toddlerhood is often the first recognizable symptom–yet initial diagnosis usually does not happen until the child enters school. Clinical diagnoses of ADHD tend to be more frequent among boys than girls, although sex ratios have not been clearly established in community-based samples.

ODD is marked by a recurrent pattern of negativistic, defiant, disobedient, and hostile behaviors toward authority figures (APA, 1994). Frequently occurring behaviors in individuals with ODD include losing their temper; arguing; actively defying or refusing to comply with rules; and being angry, resentful, spiteful, or vindictive. Individuals with ODD tend not to perceive themselves as oppositional or defiant; rather, they justify their behaviors as a reaction to unreasonable demands placed upon them. Although ODD is thought to be more prevalent in males than females prior to puberty, the rates appear to become similar across sexes after puberty.

CD is a behavioral disturbance consisting of a persistent pattern in which the basic rights of others or age-appropriate norms and rules are violated (APA, 1994). Common CD symptomatology includes bullying, physical cruelty to people or animals, stealing, forcing another individual into sexual activity, deliberate destruction of others' property, use of weapons, and frequent lying or breaking promises. Children and adolescents with CD often display a host of associated adverse behaviors, including early onset of sexual behavior, drinking, smoking, use of illegal substances, and reckless behavior. CD is generally thought to be more common among males than females, but symptoms seem to vary by sex (APA, 1994; Loeber, Burke, Lahey, Winters, & Zera, 2000). Boys with CD tend to display behaviors such as fighting, stealing, vandalism, and school discipline problems, whereas girls with CD are more likely to display behaviors such as lying, truancy, running away from home, substance use, and prostitution (APA, 1994). Onset of CD symptomatology may occur as early as age 5, but more often occurs in late childhood or early adolescence. Onset by age 10 is associated with less favorable prognoses, including an increased likelihood of substance-related disorders and Antisocial Personality Disorder in adulthood.

SOCIOEMOTIONAL DEVELOPMENT IN CHILDREN OF ADOLESCENT MOTHERS

Due to the multiple risk factors present in their lives (Whitman, Borkowski, Keogh, & Weed, 2001), children of adolescent mothers are at high risk for socioemotional problems during childhood and adolescence. For example, the Baltimore Study followed a sample of children born to adolescent mothers for 20 years, into late adolescence and early adulthood. Although children showed normal emotional functioning during childhood (Furstenberg, 1976), major problems surfaced by late adolescence. At the 17-year assessment, 32% of the parents reported that they felt their children needed emotional, mental, or behavioral help (Furstenberg, Brooks-Gunn, & Morgan, 1987). These children were more likely to engage in risky delinquent behaviors such as running away from home, stealing, substance use, and sexual intercourse when compared to adolescents who were born to adult mothers. By the time the children were 17 years old, 60% had consumed alcohol, 46% had smoked marijuana, 5% had tried other drugs, and 78% had engaged in sexual activity.

In addition to emotional distress, delinquency, and substance abuse, children in the Baltimore sample also exhibited behavior problems in school. For example, 34% of children had skipped school, 28% were reported for fighting, and 4% had damaged school property (Furstenberg et al., 1987). Reports indicated that 52% of parents had received notification from school about behavior problems and 44% of the children had been expelled or suspended in the past 5 years. Furstenberg et al. (1987) projected that a significant portion of the sample was headed for a "life on the streets" and had already spent, or would spend, time in a juvenile home or prison. These statistics reflect the high-risk status of children born to teen mothers. In the following section we discuss specific risk factors associated with adolescent parenting, describing ways in which these risks may influence children's adjustment over time.

Risks for Socioemotional Delays and Psychopathologies

Although the relationships between adolescent parenting and clinical disorders in children have not been clearly established, there are many risk factors associated with adolescent parenting that can jeopardize children's socioemotional well-being. In the following sections we describe specific risk factors for socioemotional delays and psychopathologies. Given that maternal characteristics have been shown to account for a substantial proportion of variance in the development of children of adolescent mothers (Jaffee, Caspi, Moffitt, Belsky, & Silva, 2001), we begin by focusing our discussion on maternal factors that impact child well-being. Research is also reviewed identifying important child characteristics and environmental situations affecting developmental outcomes, particularly in children of adolescent mothers.

Maternal Well-Being and Children's Socioemotional Adjustment. Impairments in maternal psychological adjustment have been associated with children's socioemotional development. Specifically, maternal depression and anxiety are risk factors for socioemotional problems and psychopathologies during childhood and adolescence (Cummings, Davies, & Campbell, 2000; Leadbeater & Bishop, 1994; Sommer et al., 2000; Spieker, Larson, Lewis, Keller, & Gilchrist, 1999). These effects extend beyond children's psychological well-being and may impact other developmental domains. For example, children whose mothers are depressed and anxious are more likely to have disruptive behavior problems in classroom settings (Spieker et al., 1999), which diminishes their learning environment and may hinder cognitive development (cf. chap. 3).

Maternal Behavior Problems and Children's Socioemotional Development. Women who become pregnant as teenagers often have personal histories of conduct problems (Miller-Johnson et al., 1999; Wakschlag et al., 2000). In the National Longitudinal Survey of Youth, histories of maternal antisocial behaviors as teenagers predicted children's behavioral and emotional development at age 6 (Wolpin, 1983). Moreover, the association between maternal nondrug offenses and children's problem behavior was stronger for dyads where mothers had histories of severe delinquency problems (Martin & Burchinal, 1992). Although the intergenerational transmission of conduct related disorders seems plausible, it is unclear whether this transmission is due to genetic or environmental factors, or a combination of both factors.

Family Status, Social Support, and Socioemotional Development.
The place of residence, number of children in the family, and availability of social support are all related to the development of behavior problems. Children have been shown to display more
internalization or externalization if their mothers lived at the grandmother's residence or had another baby within 3 years of the first
child's birth (Leadbeater & Bishop, 1994). Children's behavior problems may also be influenced by the fact that teenage mothers are unlikely to have adequate social supports to help them counteract the
elevated stress levels associated with an off-timed pregnancy
(Borkowski et al., 2002; Whitman et al., 2001). Moreover, teen mothers often live in poverty at the time of childbirth (Whitman et al.,
2001), thereby placing their children in situations where the provision of adequate supports may be unlikely.

*Parenting Practices and Children's Socioemotional Develop-
ment.*   Harsh, insensitive, and/or neglectful parenting practices
also place children at risk for socioemotional maladjustment and
psychopathology. Teenage mothers are more likely than adult mothers to engage in abusive and neglectful parenting practices
(Borkowski et al., 2002; Klerman, 1993). Engagement in these practices may be associated with impairments in knowledge of child development and endorsement of harsh and insensitive parenting
practices, which are common among adolescent mothers (Whitman
et al., 2001). Abuse and neglect are, in turn, associated with
socioemotional delays or psychopathologies during childhood and
adolescence (Dukewich, Borkowski, & Whitman, 1999). Previous research with adolescent mothers has suggested that abuse and neglect negatively impact children's development by hindering the
emergence of mature forms of cognitive and emotional self-regulation (Borkowski et al., 2002). Difficulties with regulation can lead to
impairments in children's academic achievement (cf. chap. 3) and
associated developmental delays (Borkowski et al., 2002). Children
who lack social or emotional control are especially likely to develop
behavioral problems when faced with the stress and instability inherent in most families with an adolescent mother. Because many teenage mothers have not developed mature self-regulation skills prior

to having children it is often difficult for them to teach these skills to their children (Borkowski et al., 2002; Martinez-Pons, 1996).

Sex, Ethnicity, and Socioemotional Development. The risks associated with having an adolescent mother may be exacerbated as a result of a child's sex. Researchers and clinicians have typically accepted the notion that girls experience a higher prevalence of internalizing behaviors and boys a higher prevalence of externalizing behaviors (Else-Quest, Hyde, Goldsmith, & Van Hulle, 2006). Recent work, however, is challenging this view. For instance, boys of adolescent mothers often have higher rates of attention problems and aggressive behaviors than girls (Spieker, Larson, Lewis, White, & Gilchrist, 1997), but rates of internalizing problems do not always differ across sexes (Else-Quest et al., 2006). Future research is necessary to clarify sex differences in psychopathologies, especially in community-based samples. Because of its focus on both boys and girls, the NDAPP holds promise for assessment of sex differences in childhood and adolescent disorders.

Race/ethnicity has also been found to alter the relationship between maternal control and children's behavior problems (Spieker et al., 1999). Specifically, African American children have been shown to experience fewer behavior problems when mothers provided higher levels of negative control, possibly because African American mothers attend more closely and respond more vigilantly to aggressive behavior in their children. The interaction of sex and race/ethnicity can also be important in the prediction of developmental outcomes. For example, a study of children born to adolescent mothers indicated that African American boys showed the highest levels of behavior problems and Puerto Rican boys showed the lowest levels; aggressive behavior in girls fell between these two extremes, regardless of ethnicity (Leadbeater & Bishop, 1994). These findings are relevant to the NDAPP sample, as the majority of mothers were African American.

Summing Up: Multiple Risks for Socioemotional Problems. Although any particular maternal or child characteristic may place children at risk for socioemotional problems, it is important to recognize that vulnerability increases when the child is exposed to multiple risk factors (Sameroff & Seifer, 1995). In addition, multiple factors may interact to determine whether the child will be resilient in the face of risk (Werner & Smith, 1982, 1992). Because children of adolescent mothers are often exposed to multiple risk factors, it seems more likely that they will develop delays and socioemotional problems, which at the extreme could result in psychopathology. The following section discusses recent contributions of the NDAPP in furthering the understanding of at-risk children's socioemotional development during early adolescence.

SOCIOEMOTIONAL DELAYS
AND PSYCHOPATHOLOGIES IN THE NDAPP

Adolescent mothers and their first-born children have participated in the NDAPP since the third trimester of the mother's pregnancy. Children's socioemotional development and symptoms of psychopathologies were assessed at 3, 5, 8, 10, and 14 years of age. The Child Behavior Checklist for Ages 4–18 (CBCL; Achenbach, 1991) was administered to mothers when their children were 3, 5, 8, and 10 years of age. The Youth Self Report for Ages 11–18 (YSR; Achenbach & Rescorla, 2001) was completed by children at age 14. The CBCL and YSR include assessment of symptoms which relate to DSM–IV diagnostic categories (Achenbach & Rescorla, 2001). Studies have shown significant associations between DSM-oriented scale scores from these assessments and clinical diagnoses of psychopathology (e.g., Arend, Lavigne, Rosenbaum, Binns, & Christoffel, 1996; Edelbrock & Costello, 1988; Kasius, Ferdinand, van den Berg, & Verhulst, 1997). In the previous book reporting on the NDAPP, (Whitman et al., 2001), 36.9% of children at age 3 were in the borderline or clinical range for internalizing behaviors and 35.5% for externalizing behaviors (Whitman et al., 2001). At 5 years, 24.5% were in the borderline or clinical range for internalizing behaviors and 14.4% for externalizing behaviors. Externalizing behaviors in the borderline or clinical range decreased from 3 to 5 years by 21.2%, while internalizing problems decreased by only 6.6%. This discrepancy could be a result of a normative decrease in externalizing behaviors as a result of maturation for the sample as a whole, because social competence emerges during the early school years due to the development of the child's language competencies and emotional self-regulatory skills (Mendez, Fantuzzo, & Cicchetti, 2001).

Follow-up assessments since the publication of *Interwoven Lives* have allowed for the examination of internalizing and externalizing behaviors through adolescence. Standardized *T*–scores for internalizing and externalizing behaviors at 3, 5, 8, 10, and 14 years are presented in Table 4.1. CBCL and YSR scoring norms are standardized to account for sex differences, so results are presented for the sample as a whole rather than separately for boys and girls. Average externalizing scores ranged from 51.20 to 53.99, with a slight but nonsignificant decrease occurring over time. Average internalizing scores ranged from 50.47 to 56.13, with the greatest decrease seen from 3 to 5 years, though this change was not significant. Overall, average internalizing and externalizing scores at each time point were within the normal range (i.e., $T < 60$), indicating that, on average, our sample did not report socioemotional problems as a group. However, it is important to note that the distribution of scores was skewed. In a typical population, it is expected that 7% of children will attain scores in the borderline or clinical range (According to CBCL and YSR norms, borderline/clinical scores begin at the 93rd percentile; Achenbach & Rescorla, 2001). Our analyses suggested that, despite mean scores in the normal range, more children than expected

TABLE 4.1
Mean Scores for Internalizing and Externalizing Behaviors

Age	N	Internalizing T-Score	Externalizing T-Score
3	141	56.13	53.77
5	139	50.47	53.99
8	111	51.40	52.75
10	119	51.64	52.06
14	83	50.84	51.20

Note. Behavior measured with the Child Behavior Checklist

(CBCL) at 3, 5, 8, and 10 years and by Youth Self Report (YSR) at 14 years.

were in the borderline/clinical level for socioemotional problems (Nicholson, Farris, & Borkowski, 2006). Given these elevated rates, our next step was to assess the prevalence of symptoms of specific psychopathologies, rather than the general levels of internalizing and externalizing behaviors.

Internalizing and Externalizing Problems

Few studies have examined the relationships between adolescent parenting and specific psychopathologies. The NDAPP provides an ideal dataset for assessing the onset, prevalence, and course of youth psychopathologies for three reasons: (a) it consists of prospective, rather than retrospective, reports of clinical symptomatology; (b) the sample includes both boys and girls; and (3) the longitudinal design allows for investigations of symptomatology from early childhood through adolescence.

Farris, Villines, Borkowski, and Whitman (2005) examined the prevalence, sex differences, age of onset, intraindividual stability, and co-occurrence of clinical symptomatologies in the NDAPP at ages 5, 8, 10, and 14. This study provided a unique opportunity to investigate clinical symptomatologies in a longitudinal, community-based sample of at-risk boys and girls. In contrast, past research of youth psychopathology has focused only on clinic-referred samples of boys or girls or has merely examined socioemotional problems in the clinical range for children of adolescent mothers (Leadbeater & Bishop, 1994; Spieker et al., 1997).

Design.   Normative DSM–oriented guidelines were used to categorize participants' ADHD, ODD, CD, Affective, and Anxiety scores from the CBCL (Achenbach, 1991) at ages 5, 8, and 10 and the YSR (Achenbach & Rescorla, 2001) at age 14 into two groups: (a) average, and (b) borderline or clinical (Farris et al., 2005). Borderline and clinical scores were collapsed in order to provide a dichotomous categorization. As with internalizing and externalizing scores, borderline/clinical scores for DSM–oriented problems begin at the 93rd percentile; thus, 7% of children in the general population are expected to report scores in this range (Achenbach & Rescorla, 2001).

Results and Implications.   The percentages of children meeting borderline or clinical criteria for Depressive, Anxiety, ADHD, ODD, and CD problems at ages 5, 8, 10, and 14 are presented in Table 4.2. Results indicated that boys and girls in the NDAPP displayed significantly higher than expected rates of ADHD, ODD, and CD symptomatology during childhood and adolescence (see Table 4.2). Specifically, girls displayed substantially elevated rates of ADHD and ODD problems at ages 5 and 14, and notably elevated rates of CD problems at ages 5, 10, and 14. Boys displayed elevated rates of ODD problems at age 10 and elevated rates of CD problems at ages 10 and 14. It should be noted that the proportions of boys and girls with borderline/clinical Affective and Anxiety problems were not significantly greater than would be expected in a typical sample at any time point. Thus, on average, elevated rates of externalization were reported for both sexes, but internalization was not a problem for either sex.

Although the rates of problematic behavior in the NDAPP sample tended to be higher than in a normative population, the data suggested considerable interindividual instability in symptomatology over time (Farris et al., 2005). In other words, it was difficult to predict later diagnostic classifications based on prior identification of symptomatologies. For example, among children who ever received a borderline/clinical classification for ADHD, 88% of them displayed

TABLE 4.2

Percentages of Boys and Girls in the Borderline/Clinical Range of DSM-Oriented Symptomatology

Age	Sex	Depression	Anxiety	ADHD	ODD	CD
5	Boys	7.0	11.0	9.5	8.4	7.1
	Girls	9.4	12.1	13.6*	12.5+	17.2**
8	Boys	5.2	8.8	5.1	8.6	6.9
	Girls	8.0	6.0	6.1	4.0	10.2
10	Boys	7.9	7.9	11.1	15.8*	16.4*
	Girls	10.7	5.4	5.4	12.5	16.1*
14	Boys	10.8	6.8	7.3	14.6	17.5*
	Girls	6.5	7.7	25.0**	15.7+	17.2*

Note. Norms for these measures indicate that 7% of scores are expected to be in the borderline/clinical range. Results that differ significantly from the expected 7% are indicated.

$*p < .05. **p = .001. +p < .1.$

this symptomatology at only one time point. In other words, only 12% of the children with borderline/clinical ADHD scores on at least one occasion had ADHD problems more than once. Similar patterns were evidenced for ODD, CD, Affective, and Anxiety symptomatology. None of the children received a borderline/clinical rating for any specific disorder at all four time points. Thus, in contrast to the literature that suggests a higher degree of intraindividual stability in youth psychopathology (APA, 1994), children in the community-based NDAPP sample moved into and out of diagnostic classifications over time.

Farris et al. (2005) also investigated co-occurrence across psychopathologies at 5, 8, 10, and 14. Of children who received at least one borderline/clinical rating at any given age, the majority reported average levels of functioning in the other domains of psychopathology. Specifically, 52% of 5-year-olds, 72% of 8-year-olds, 53% of 10-year-olds, and 64% of 14-year-olds met borderline/clinical criteria for only one of five possible disorders. The co-occurrence of several disorders was unlikely: Only 15% of 5-year-olds, 4% of 8-year-olds, 17% of 10-year-olds, and 5% of 14-year-olds reported borderline/clinical criteria for more than three psychopathologies.

Findings from the NDAPP offered a unique perspective on clinically significant externalizing and internalizing psychopathologies in a community-based sample of boys and girls (Farris et al., 2005). Results provided support for the conclusion that children of adolescent mothers were at increased risk for symptomatology of clinical disorders and suggested unexpected sex differences in rates of psychopathologies. Our findings indicated that: (a) the age of onset of clinically significant internalizing and externalizing problems was younger among children of teen mothers as compared to the age of onset that occurs in the general population (cf. APA, 1994); (b) girls born to teen mothers tended to display more symptoms of externalizing pathologies than boys, especially at younger ages; (c) neither boys nor girls reported an elevated prevalence of internalizing psychopathologies; and (d) there was a greater degree of intra-individual instability and less co-occurrence of psychopathologies than in previous studies of clinic-referred children (Farris et al., 2005; cf. Lahey, Loeber, Burke, Rathouz, & McBurnett, 2002).

On average, girls displayed problematic levels of CD symptomatology beginning in early childhood and continued to show elevated rates into adolescence. Boys, on the other hand, demonstrated normal levels of CD symptomatology until later childhood, at which time their average rates of borderline/clinical CD symptomatology became equal to that of girls. Interestingly, neither boys nor girls, on average, displayed elevated rates of internalizing-related psychopathologies. Although the literature tends to suggest that girls are more at risk for internalizing psychopathologies and boys more at risk for externalizing psychopathologies (Spieker et al., 1999), children in the NDAPP were more likely to display externalizing problems regardless of sex. This finding reflects the potential intergenerational transmission of externalizing problems from adolescent mothers to their children, as well as negative implications of violence in the broader society (cf. chap. 6).

High intraindividual instability within disorders and low co-occurrence across disorders (Farris et al., 2005) suggested that there is substantial variability in symptoms of psychopathologies among children of adolescent mothers. These findings are in contrast to the broader literature, which indicates a more consistent course within any given disorder and a greater degree of predictability across disorders (Lahey et al., 1995). It should be noted that intraindividual stability was more likely among children whose scores fell in the average (i.e., nonproblematic) range for any one disorder at a specific age; these children were more likely to have average scores on the same outcome over time, as well as average scores for the other four disorders at the same time point. In sum, children with average scores tended to remain problem-free, whereas children with symptoms of psychopathology at any one time showed varied courses of problems at other times points.

It should be noted that the intraindividual instability of socioemotional problems among children of adolescent mothers may be associated with changes in their exposure to risks over time. For example, stress levels have been shown to increase as residential, school, and familial instability is experienced (Wood, Halfon, Scarlata, Newacheck, & Nessin, 1993). Such turmoil is not uncommon for children living with adolescent mothers (cf. chap. 7) and has been associated with poor academic achievement and behavior problems at school (Smith, 2004). It is possible that at-risk children will display symptoms of psychopathologies at times of greater stress, and that these symptoms will remit during less stressful times. Thus, intraindividual instability in symptoms of psychopathology may reflect the personal instability in the lives of at-risk children.

Childhood and Adolescent Psychopathology: Contributions From the NDAPP

Because data collection began prenatally and was conducted on a regular basis throughout childhood and early adolescence, the NDAPP dataset provided a unique opportunity to investigate children's socioemotional development and symptoms of psychopathology. Research that is less measurement intensive across time is likely to present an incomplete and limited picture of socioemotional functioning. For example, Brooks-Gunn, Guo, and Furstenberg (1993) followed trajectories of socioemotional development from childhood through early adulthood, but lacked data between the ages of 5 and 17. As a result, conclusions could not be drawn about the age of onset or developmental course of psychopathologies. Several other studies have concentrated on socioemotional changes only during early childhood (Leadbeater & Bishop, 1994; Spieker et al., 1999), whereas others focused on a single point during later childhood (Martin & Burchinal, 1992; Spieker et al., 1997). In contrast, as a result of the repeated, prospective measures in the NDAPP, our findings offer more complete information about the onset, prevalence, and course of socioemotional problems in at-risk community-based boys and girls. Several findings from the NDAPP contribute to our understanding of socioemotional development and psychopathologies during adolescence:

- On average, the onset of externalizing problems was earlier for girls than boys; specifically, girls were 1½ to 2½ times more likely than boys to be in the borderline/clinical range for ADHD, ODD, and CD problems at age 5.
- By adolescence, the prevalence of ODD and CD converged across sexes, with both boys and girls reporting more than twice the expected rates; girls, however, continued to report

borderline/clinical ADHD symptoms approximately three times more frequently than boys.

- During childhood and adolescence, rates of externalizing problems were, on average, approximately double those of internalizing problems; although the rates of externalizing disorders were often more than double the expected for boys and girls, the prevalence of internalizing disorders was not significantly elevated for either sex during this time period.

- There were high rates of intraindividual instability in diagnostic classifications and low rates of co-occurrence across a range of psychopathologies.

Many findings from NDAPP stand in contrast with those in the broader literature on the emergence and progression of youth psychopathologies. For example, children in our sample tended to develop problems at younger ages than typically expected; girls often displayed higher rates of problems than boys; a high degree of intraindividual instability was observed; and low rates of co-occurrence were commonplace. The essential difference between previous findings and the results from the NDAPP may well be due to the populations under study; previous findings were often based on clinic-referred samples of boys (Lahey et al., 1995), whereas the NDAPP dataset was a community-based sample of boys and girls. The severity of behavioral problems is likely to be worse in clinic-referred, as opposed to community-based, groups (Goodman et al., 1997). In the NDAPP, this trend was observed specifically; despite the high prevalence of DSM-oriented symptoms, the severity of these problems was not as high as in clinic referred samples.

Our findings on the onset and progression of psychopathologies may be relevant to a specific subgroup of at risk, but nonreferred, children and adolescents. Although participants often reported elevated levels of symptomatologies, their problems were not especially severe. Severity of symptoms may play an important role in influencing the consistency of diagnostic classifications over time. Moreover, severity may be associated with stability and co-occurrence, such that when symptoms of any one disorder are more severe they are more likely to persist over time as well as co-occur with symptoms associated with other disorders. Thus, the low levels of severity of psychopathology symptoms in the NDAPP may partially account for their unexpected instability and inconsistency.

SOCIOEMOTIONAL RESILIENCE AND FUTURE RESEARCH DIRECTIONS

Although the rates of psychopathologies in the NDAPP were higher than would be expected in a typical population, the majority of children and adolescents reported scores in the normal range of socioemotional development. In other words, many children in the NDAPP appeared to be resilient in terms of their socioemotional development.

Early intervention and provision of adequate health care services have been shown to increase the likelihood of resilience (Thomlison, 1997). Therefore, it is possible that high-risk individuals whose symptoms begin early in life were less likely to maintain a specific psychopathology into adolescence because they were more apt to be referred for treatment. Children with higher levels of psychopathology and family impairment are more likely to be referred for clinical treatment (Lavigne et al., 1998). It is possible that teachers, school counselors, priests or pastors, or other community members recognize high early levels of psychopathology in at-risk children and, in turn, refer the children and their families for early intervention. "Therefore, when adults who are involved in the child's life are aware that a child is at risk for psychopathology, they may be more likely to carefully attend to early symptoms. Thus, children who are exposed to risks may sometimes be more likely to receive formal assistance, such as school counseling, psychiatric treatment, or government assistance, thereby contributing to their socioemotional resilience and diagnostic instability.

In order to understand whether this may have been the case in our sample, we recently conducted analyses regarding the provision of psychopharmacology and therapy in the NDAPP. Retrospective data suggested that many children received at least one source of formal support services by the onset of adolescence. Specifically, 22% reported having seen a therapist, psychiatrist, or other mental health professional; a third of these children had been admitted at least once to a mental health facility, and 20% of the sample had received psychopharmacological treatment for an emotional or behavioral problem. In these cases, the treatment for mental health problems may have played a protective role, thereby contributing to resilience despite exposure to multiple risks.

Future research on socioemotional resilience would benefit from moving beyond the mere analysis of risk factors to include an assessment of protective factors that facilitate resilience among high-risk youth. The exploration of protective factors in the face of multiple risks should focus on multiple factors (Burke, Loeber, & Birmaher, 2002), such as children's intelligence, higher SES, and maternal aggression that impact the onset and progression of psychopathologies (Lahey, Loeber, Burke, & Rathouz, 2002).

In addition, this field of research would also benefit from incorporating observational measures of psychopathological symptoms or actual psychiatric diagnoses into the assessment scheme, in order to avoid the bias that may result from using self-report measures. Research should include boys and girls from various backgrounds, such as low-risk community-based, high-risk community-based, and clinic-referred samples. Increasing the frequency of assessments allows for an examination of higher-order trends, especially when embedded in sophisticated longitudinal designs, appropriate for Hierarchical Linear Modeling (HLM), Structural Equation Modeling (SEM), and Dynamical Systems analyses (see chap. 9 for a detailed description of these advanced analytic techniques). These designs and related statistical approaches can provide more accurate reflections of long-term trends in diagnostic classifications, trajectories of underlying symptomatology, and treatment effectiveness as well as information about how changes in risk and protective factors influence socioemotional development during adolescence.

REFERENCES

Achenbach, T. (1991). *Manual for the Child Behavior Checklist/4–18 and 1991 Profile*. Burlington, VT: University of Vermont Department of Psychiatry.

Achenbach, T. M., & Rescorla, L. A. (2001). *Manual for the ASEBA School-Age Forms & Profiles*. Burlington, VT: University of Vermont, Research Center for Children, Youth, & Families.

Al-Yagon, M. (2003). Children at risk for learning disorders: Multiple perspectives. *Journal of Learning Disabilities, 36*, 318–335.

American Psychiatric Association (1994). *Diagnostic and statistical manual of mental disorders* (4th ed.). Washington, DC: APA.

Arend, R., Lavigne, J. V., Rosenbaum, D., Binns, H. J., & Christoffel, K. K. (1996). Relation between taxonomic and quantitative diagnostic systems in preschool children: Emphasis on disruptive disorders. *Journal of Clinical Child Psychology, 25*, 388–397.

Borkowski, J. G., Bisconti, T., Willard, C. C., Keogh, D. A., Whitman, T. L., & Weed, K. (2002). The adolescent as parent: Influences on children's intellectual, academic, and socioemotional development. In J. G. Borkowski, S. L. Ramey, & M. Bristol–Power (Eds.), *Parenting and the child's world: Influences on academic, intellectual, and social-emotional development* (pp. 161–184). Mahwah, NJ: Lawrence Erlbaum Associates.

Brooks-Gunn, J., Guo, G., & Furstenberg, F. F., Jr. (1993). Who drops out of and who continues beyond high school? A 20-year follow-up of Black urban youth. *Journal of Research on Adolescence, 3*, 271–294.

Burke, J. D., Loeber, R., & Birmaher, B. (2002). Oppositional Defiant Disorder and Conduct Disorder: A review of the past 10 years, part II. *Journal of the American Academy of Child and Adolescent Psychiatry, 41*, 1275–1293.

Cicchetti, D., Rogosch, F. A., Lynch, M., & Holt, K. D. (1993). Resilience in maltreated children: Processes leading to adaptive outcome. *Development and Psychopathology, 5*, 629–647.

Cummings, E. M., Davies, P. T., & Campbell, S. B. (2000). *Developmental psychopathology and family process: Theory, research, and clinical implications.* New York: Guilford Press.

Dukewich, T. L., Borkowski, J. G., & Whitman, T. L. (1999). A longitudinal analysis of maternal abuse potential and developmental delays in children of adolescent mothers. *Child Abuse and Neglect, 23*, 405–420.

Edelbrock, C., & Costello, A. J. (1988). Convergence between statistically derived behavior problem syndromes and child psychiatric diagnoses. *Journal of Abnormal Child Psychology, 16*, 219–231.

Else-Quest, N. M., Hyde, J. S., Goldsmith, H. H., & Van Hulle, C. A. (2006). Gender differences in temperament: A meta-analysis. *Psychological Bulletin, 132*, 33–72.

Farris, J. R., Villines, D., Borkowski, J. G., & Whitman, T. L. (2005, April). *ADHD and disruptive behavior disorders in children with adolescent mothers: A prospective longitudinal analysis.* Poster session presented at the biennial meeting of the Society for Research in Child Development (SRCD), Atlanta, GA.

Furstenberg, F. F., Jr. (1976). *Unplanned parenthood: The social consequences of teenage childbearing.* New York: Free Press.

Furstenberg, F. F., Jr., Brooks-Gunn, J., & Morgan, S. P. (1987). *Adolescent mothers in later life.* New York: Cambridge University Press.

Goodman, S. H., Lahey, B. B., Fielding, B., Dulcan, M., Narrow, W., & Reiger, D. (1997). Representativeness of clinical samples of youths with mental disorders: A preliminary population-based study. *Journal of Abnormal Psychology, 106*, 3–14.

Jaffee, S., Caspi, A., Moffitt, T. E., Belsky, J., & Silva, P. (2001). Why are children born to teen mothers at risk for adverse outcomes in young adulthood? Results from a 20-year longitudinal study. *Development and Psychopathology, 13*, 377–397.

Kasius, M. C., Ferdinand, R. F., van den Berg, H., & Verhulst, F. C. (1997). Associations between different diagnostic approaches for child and adolescent psychopathology. *Journal of Child Psychology and Psychiatry, 38*, 625–632.

Klerman, L. V. (1993). The relationship between adolescent parenthood and inadequate parenting. *Children and Youth Services Review, 15*, 309–320.

Lahey, B. B., Loeber, R., Burke, J., & Rathouz, P. J. (2002). Adolescent outcomes of childhood conduct disorder among clinic-referred boys: Predictors of improvement. *Journal of Abnormal Psychology, 30*, 333–348.

Lahey, B. B., Loeber, R., Burke, J., Rathouz, P. J., & McBurnett, K. (2002). Waxing and waning in concert: Dynamic comorbidity of Conduct Disorder with other disruptive and emotional problems over 7 years among clinic-referred boys. *Journal of Abnormal Psychology, 111*, 556–567.

Lahey, B. B., Loeber, R., Hart, E. L., Frick, P., Applegate, B., Zhang, Q., et al. (1995). Four-year longitudinal study of conduct disorder in boys: Patterns and predictors of persistence. *Journal of Abnormal Psychology, 104*, 83–93.

Lavigne, J. V., Arend, R., Rosenbaum, D., Binns, H. J., Chrostoffel, K. K., Burns, A., et al. (1998). Mental health service use among young children receiving pediatric primary care. *Journal of the American Academy of Child and Adolescent Psychiatry, 37*, 1175–1183.

Leadbeater, B. J., & Bishop, S. J. (1994). Predictors of behavior problems in preschool children of inner-city Afro-American and Puerto Rican adolescent mothers. *Child Development, 65*, 638–648.

Loeber, R., Burke, J. D., Lahey, B. B., Winters, A., & Zera, M. (2000). Oppositional defiant and conduct disorder: A review of the past 10 years, part I. *Journal of the American Academy of Child and Adolescent Psychiatry, 39*, 1468–1484.

Martin, S. L., & Burchinal, M. R. (1992). Young women's antisocial behavior and the later emotional and behavioral health of their children. *American Journal of Public Health, 82*, 1007–1010.

Martinez-Pons, M. (1996). Test of a model of parental inducement of academic self-regulation. *Journal of Experimental Education, 64*, 213–227.

Mendez, J. L., Fantuzzo, J., & Cicchetti, D. (2001). Profiles of social competence among low-income African American preschool children. *Child Development, 73*, 1085–1100.

Miller-Johnson, S., Winn, D. M., Coie, J., Maumary-Gremaud, A., Hyman, C., Terry, R., et al. (1999). Motherhood during the teen years: A developmental perspective on risk factors for childbearing. *Development and Psychopathology, 11*, 85–100.

Nicholson, J. S., Farris, J. R., & Borkowski, J. G. (2006, May). *Data analysis approaches with atypical populations: Going beyond the mean.* Poster session presented at the 2006 Midwestern Psychological Association (MPA) Annual Meeting, Chicago, IL.

Office of Applied Studies. (2005, December 30). *The National Survey on Drug Use and Health [NSDUH] Report: Depression among adolescents.* Rockville, MD: Substance Abuse and Mental Health Services Administration.

Sameroff, A. J., & Seifer, R. (1995). Accumulation of environmental risk and child mental health. In H. E. Fitzgerald, B. M. Lester, & B. S. Zuckerman (Eds.), *Children of poverty: Research, health, and policy issues* (pp. 233–268). New York: Garland Publishing, Inc.

Smith, L. E. (2004, March). *Impact of environmental instability on children with developmental delays.* Poster session presented at the Gatlinburg Conference, San Diego, CA.

Sommer, K. S., Whitman, T. L., Borkowski, J. G., Gondoli, D. M., Burke, J., Maxwell, S. E., et al. (2000). Prenatal maternal predictors of cognitive and emotional delays in children of adolescent mothers. *Adolescence, 35*, 87–112.

Spieker, S. J., Larson, N. C., Lewis, S. M., Keller, T. E., & Gilchrist, L. (1999). Developmental trajectories of disruptive behavior problems in preschool children of adolescent mothers. *Child Development, 70*, 443–458.

Spieker, S. J., Larson, N. C., Lewis, S. M., White, R. D., & Gilchrist, L. (1997). Children of adolescent mothers: Cognitive and behavioral status at age six. *Child and Adolescent Social Work Journal, 14*, 355–364.

Thomlison, B. (1997). Risk and protective factors in child maltreatment. In M. W. Fraser (Ed.), *Risk and resilience in childhood: An ecological perspective* (pp. 50–72). Washington, DC: NASW Press.

Visser, S. N., & Lesesne, C. A. (2005, September 2). Mental health in the United States: Prevalence of diagnosis and medication treatment for Attention-Deficit/Hyperactivity Disorder–United States 2003. *Morbidity and Mortality Weekly Report, 54*, 842–847.

Wakschlag, L. S., Gordon, R. A., Lahey, B. B., Loeber, R., Green, S. M., & Leventhal, B. L. (2000). Maternal age at first birth and boys' risk for conduct disorder. *Journal of Research on Adolescence, 10*, 417–441.

Werner, E. E., & Smith, R. S. (Eds.). (1992). *Overcoming the odds: High risk children from birth to adulthood.* Ithaca, NY: Cornell University Press.

Werner, E., & Smith, R. (1982). *Vulnerable but invincible: A study of resilient children.* New York: McGraw-Hill.

Whitman, T. L., Borkowski, J. G., Keogh, D. A., & Weed, K. (2001). *Interwoven lives: Adolescent mothers and their children*. Mahwah, NJ: Lawrence Erlbaum Associates.

Wolpin, K. (1983). *The National Longitudinal Surveys handbook 1983–1984*. Columbus: Center for Human Resource Research, Ohio State University.

Wood, D., Halfon, N., Scarlata, D., Newacheck, P., & Nessim, S. (1993). Impact of family relocation on children's growth, development, school function, and behavior. *Journal of the American Medical Association, 270*, 1334–1338.

5

Child Maltreatment:
Precursors of Developmental Delays

Julie N. Schatz
Julie J. Lounds

*Child abuse has a domino effect that spreads to all who touch the family.
It takes its greatest toll on the child and spreads into the immediate
family to the spouse, who is often torn between the child and their mate.
From there it goes to other children in the family who do not understand
and also feel threatened. Also involved are neighbors who hear the
screams but do not react, teachers who see the bruises and must deal
with a child too distracted to learn, and relatives who want to intervene
but do not want to risk relationships.*

—David Pelzer (1995, pp. 164–165).

N early 1 million children were substantiated victims of child
maltreatment in 2002 (U.S. Department of Health and Human Services [DHHS], 2004). Sixty percent were victims of neglect; 20%
were physically abused; 10% experienced sexual abuse; and 7%

were victims of emotional maltreatment (DHHS, 2004). Victimized children are represented across all ages, from infancy through late adolescence. Evidence suggests that younger children are at heightened risk for the most serious consequences of maltreatment, life-threatening injuries and death; out of the 1,400 children who died as a result of maltreatment in 2002, 76% were younger than 4 years of age (DHHS, 2004). More than 80% of the perpetrators were the children's parents and more women were found to be perpetrators than men (DHHS, 2004).

Maltreated children are also represented across racial groups. American Indian or Alaska Native (21.7 per 1,000 children) and African American (20.2 per 1,000) children had the highest rates of substantiated maltreatment; however, in terms of the total number of cases, European American children made up more than 50% of all victims (DHHS, 2004).

MALTREATMENT AND ITS DEVELOPMENTAL CONSEQUENCES

Victims of childhood maltreatment generally experience developmental difficulties, with the most frequently observed problems occurring in behavioral and emotional domains. For example, Bousha and Twentyman (1984) studied the behaviors of preschool and school-aged children within the context of mother–child observations and found that abused and neglected children were more physically and verbally aggressive than their nonmaltreated peers. Internalizing symptomatologies and withdrawn behaviors have also been documented in victimized children (Todd–Manly, Kim, Rogosch, & Cicchetti, 2001). In a classroom context, Kendall–Tackett and Eckenrode (1996) examined behavioral problems in a sample of maltreated and nonmaltreated children: Maltreated children were found to have more discipline problems and referrals for suspensions.

It is not surprising to find that abused and neglected children experience academic difficulties in addition to problems in adaptive behaviors, especially as their classroom performance requires sustained attention. For instance, maltreated children have been found to have lower grades as well as more grade repetitions than nonmaltreated children (Kendall–Tackett & Eckenrode, 1996). They also score lower than nonmaltreated children on tests of reading and math (Wodarski, Kurtz, Gaudin, & Howing, 1990) and on measures of home, peer, and school adjustments (Wodarski, et al., 1990).

Problems in socialization, as evidenced by negative peer relationships and immature social skills, have been repeatedly documented (Carlson, Cicchetti, Barnett, & Braunwald, 1989; George & Main, 1979; Shields & Cicchetti, 2001). For instance, Carlson and colleagues (1989) studied disorganized/disoriented (Type D) attachments in 12-month-old maltreated and nonmaltreated infants; the overwhelming majority of maltreated children (80%) were classified as having Type D attachments in contrast to a demographically-matched comparison group of children (19%). Among preschool children, problems in peer relationships have been observed, with abused preschoolers responding more aggressively to the distress of others (George & Main, 1979). Bullying and becoming a victim of bullying were commonplace among older maltreated children (Kim & Cicchetti, 2003).

Because maltreatment, as a societal problem, has reached epidemic proportions (DHHS, 2004), researchers have begun to investigate the major factors that place mothers at risk for abusing or neglecting their children. Several maternal risk variables have been identified such as low intelligence, depression, aggression, and anxiety as well as variables related to parenting practices such as knowledge of infant and child development and the quality of mother–child interactions (Ethier, Lacharite, & Couture, 1995; Gauthier, Stollak, Messe, & Aronoff, 1996; Twentyman & Plotkin, 1982).

A number of studies have found that children born to younger mothers are more likely to be abused or neglected (Black, Heyman, & Slep, 2001; Bolton, 1990). In fact, it has been suggested that up to 50% of maltreated children reside with an adolescent mother (Bolton, 1990). Several reasons have been discussed for the heightened risk of child abuse and neglect found among adolescent mothers such as age and immaturity at first childbirth, poor education, depression, and inadequate social supports; it is clear, however, that maltreatment is almost always multiply determined, arising from the interaction of cumulative risk factors (Azar, 1991; Belsky, 1980,

1993). Furthermore, shared environmental, familial, and maternal characteristics of most adolescent mothers and adult mothers who maltreat likely account for the similar developmental difficulties observed in their children. Before describing the contributions of the NDAPP to understanding the problem of child maltreatment, we briefly review Belsky's (1980; 1993) theoretical model as well as the existing literature on the causes and consequences of abuse and neglect among teen mothers.

UNDERSTANDING THE RISK FOR MALTREATMENT: BELSKY'S ECOLOGICAL MODEL

Belsky (1980, 1993) has proposed an ecological model of child maltreatment in which abuse and neglect are determined by influences at the individual, family, community, and cultural levels. His ecologically-based model has four levels that have been associated with child maltreatment in low and high-risk samples: ontogenic development, the microsystem, exosystem, and macrosystem (Belsky, 1980). The model synthesizes previous research in child abuse and neglect through stressing the interplay among child characteristics, family interactional patterns, maternal stress, and cultural expectations and mores.

The first level of Belsky's (1980) model, ontogenic development, includes personal characteristics such as past histories of maltreatment and current psychopathologies. The second level, the microsystem, represents the immediate context (i.e., the family environment) in which maltreatment occurs. At this level, family dynamics and characteristics of each of the family members are included. The third level, the exosystem, represents the broader social structures surrounding the family; this level includes the family's neighborhood and the work environment. Factors in the exosystem often influence child maltreatment through their impact on the microsystem (i.e., the family system and immediate environment). The macrosystem is the fourth level in Belsky's ecological model and is represented by social attitudes, including attitudes toward violence and how children should be treated. The macrosystem is the broadest system and influences each of the other levels, but is generally the most difficult to measure.

ADOLESCENT MOTHERS AND CHILD
MALTREATMENT

A number of characteristics associated with the first level of Belsky's model, ontogenic development, have been linked to the risk for child maltreatment among adolescent mothers. First, adolescent mothers are more likely than adult mothers to have histories of abuse and neglect (Herrenkohl, Herrenkohl, Egolf, & Russo, 1998). The proportion of maltreated parents who go on to maltreat their own children ranges from 30% to 70% (Kaufman & Zigler, 1987). Maternal adjustment, including anxiety, depression, and low self-esteem, is also an important determinant of child maltreatment, (Ethier et al., 1995; Gauthier et al., 1996; Lahey, Conger, Atkeson, & Treiber, 1984), with teen mothers exhibiting elevated rates in comparison to adult mothers (Passino, et al., 1993; Whitman, et al., 2001). Additionally, maternal beliefs about parenting are part of Belsky's ontogenic level: Adolescent mothers have been found to have inaccurate knowledge about child development and unrealistic expectations for their children (Whitman, et al., 2001); these parenting characteristics have been frequently identified as correlates of abusive and neglectful behaviors, and of their severity (Chance & Scannapieco, 2002; Twentyman & Plotkin, 1982).

Broader microsystem factors related to maltreatment include poor quality of partner relationships and/or single parenthood (Brown, Cohen, Johnson, & Salzinger, 1998; Spearly and Lauderdale, 1983; Zuravin, 1987). Many teenage mothers are not married (Moore, Manlove, & Franzetta, 2005), thus lacking an important source of social support. Adolescent mothers, much like other girls of the same age, often show instability in their romantic relationships and have multiple relationships over the course of a few months or year (Gee & Rhodes, 1999; Schamess, 1993). Relational instability increases the risk for child maltreatment, distracting the mother from childcare duties and exposing the child to other possible perpetrators of maltreatment, their romantic partners (Margolin, 1992).

Another microsystem factor associated with child maltreatment is the quality of interactions between the parent and child. For instance, abusive mothers display more verbal and physical aggression in their interactions with their children than nonmaltreating mothers (Bousha & Twentyman, 1984; Lahey et al., 1984), these parenting behaviors are also observed in adolescent mothers (Whitman, et al., 2001). Although the direction of causality is difficult to discern, children's personal characteristics, such as having a difficult temperament, have been associated with maltreatment risk (Horton & Cruise, 2001; Nesbitt & Karagianis, 1982).

Low socioeconomic status (SES) is the main exosystem factor that has been associated with risk for child maltreatment. For example, Sedlak and Broadhurst (1996) found that families with yearly incomes below $15,000 were more likely to be identified as neglectful in comparison to families with yearly incomes above $30,000. Families with documented cases of child maltreatment were more likely to be recipients of governmental benefits, such as welfare, TANF, or Medicaid (Ovwigho, Leavitt, & Born, 2003). For teen mothers, many of whom fail to complete high school and lack functional reading and math skills (cf. Furstenberg, Brooks–Gunn, & Morgan, 1987; Horowitz, Klerman, Kuo, & Jekel, 1991), their earning potential and financial success is compromised throughout their life course. It is important to identify teen mothers most at risk for maltreatment in order to mount prevention programs before problems surface. To aid the early identification process, we turn to the measurement approaches we have used in the NDAPP to assess risks for abuse and neglect.

MEASURING THE RISK FOR MALTREATMENT

Despite significant progress in uncovering the predictors and consequences of child maltreatment, few advances have been made in the measurement of abuse and neglect. Although nearly 5 million children were brought to the attention of child protective agencies in 2002, more than half of these cases were found to be unsubstantiated. For some children, unsubstantiated conclusions may be valid, whereas for others evaluative procedures were likely affected by flaws in the substantiating processes, including overburdened caseworkers and insufficient evidence regarding perpetration.

Most alarming, however, is the discrepancy across the United States in handling reports about child maltreatment. Different states require varying levels of evidence, have considerable variability in time from the first report to the actual investigation (e.g., allowing physical wounds resulting from maltreatment to heal), and hold divergent views on the types of abuse and neglect that determine substantiated maltreatment (e.g., recognizing the validity of emotional neglect).

These issues draw attention to problems inherent in identifying cases of maltreatment for research purposes. The main problem here is that a sizable portion of victimized children are missing from documented case records, and only the most serious cases are represented. For these reasons, alternative measures are needed in order to determine the potential for child maltreatment. Most of the newly created measures of abuse and neglect have been based on a "parenting deficit model." According to this perspective, parents who maltreat their children are not considered qualitatively different than from those who do not. Rather, abusive or neglectful parenting is on one end of a continuum and optimal parenting at the other. Two examples of alternative assessments of maltreatment, based on the parenting deficit model, are the Child Abuse Potential Inventory (CAPI; Milner, 1989) and the Mother–Child Neglect Scale (MCNS; Lounds, Borkowski, Whitman, and the Centers for the Prevention of Child Neglect, 2004).

Child Abuse Potential Inventory.   The CAPI, a self-report scale (Milner, 1989), measures attitudes that place a mother at risk for becoming physically abusive and includes scales assessing psychological distress, rigidity, unhappiness, problems with child and self, problems with family, and problems with others. The CAPI is widely used in research and has been found to have reliability and validity in both low-risk and high-risk populations, including adolescent mothers (Blinn–Pike & Mingus, 2000; Burrell, Thompson, & Sexton, 1992; Milner, 1980; Milner, 1994). Using cutoff scores suggested by Milner (1989), the CAPI was able to correctly discriminate between abusing and nonabusing parents 93% of the time.

Mother–Child Neglect Scale.   The NDAPP addressed the issue of unreported neglectful behaviors and identified low levels of child neglect through a newly developed maternal report questionnaire, the Mother–Child Neglect Scale (MCNS; Lounds, Borkowski, Whitman, & the Centers for the Prevention of Child Neglect, 2004). The MCNS consists of 20 statements about specific parenting behaviors, to which participants respond using a 4-point Likert-type scale to indicate their agreement, ranging from strongly agree to strongly disagree.

Four different domains are evaluated in the MCNS; emotional, cognitive, supervision, and physical neglect. Examples of items from each subscale include: "I comforted my child when he/she was upset," "I helped my child with homework," "I wanted to know what my child was doing when he/she was not home," and "I kept my child clean." The overall neglect score exhibited high internal consistency ($\propto = .94$) as well as moderate test–retest reliability ($r = .60$) (Lounds, Borkowski, Whitman, & the Centers for the Prevention of Child Neglect, 2004). Due to its ease of administration, the MCNS is applicable to many research projects, allowing for the identification of low levels of neglect, which we label as neglect potential, that are likely to be missed when relying on reports to child protective service agencies. We have used self-report measures of maltreatment, such as the CAPI and MCNS, in the NDAPP to assess the antecedents of maltreatment and role that abuse and neglect play in children's development.

CHILD MALTREATMENT IN THE NDAPP

Findings from the NDAPP have provided several advancements to the extant literature on child maltreatment. First, its longitudinal nature makes possible a prospective examination of psychosocial processes through which mothers are likely to maltreat their children. Second, characteristics of the mothers in the NDAPP, such as low SES and teenage status at first birth, have been shown in the literature to place children at risk for maltreatment (Black et al., 2001; Brown et al., 1998; Zuravin, 1988). Because participants in the NDAPP had little variability in SES, age at first childbirth, and educational experiences, these characteristics were essentially held constant in our dataset, permitting an examination of more proximal social and psychological predictors of abuse and neglect and their consequences for children's development.

Set within a longitudinal framework, the research we report contributes to understanding both antecedents and consequences of child maltreatment over a 10-year time span. The chapter contains a set of studies that (a) examine the effects of abuse potential during early infancy and childhood and its relationship to early development; (b) explore relationships among early risk characteristics (e.g., depression, low intelligence) and maternal abuse potential during middle childhood and between abuse potential and children's development at age 10; and (c) investigate the role of neglect potential during childhood, including its predictors and developmental consequences.

Abuse Potential During Early Childhood

In an initial study, Dukewich, Borkowski, and Whitman (1996) examined abuse potential during infancy, focusing on relations among prenatal maternal characteristics—such as social support, psychological adjustment, and preparation for parenting—and abuse potential during infancy. A second study followed up the same mothers and children exploring how early abuse potential was related to two of the components of mild mental retardation, intelligence and behavioral adaptation, during early childhood (Dukewich, Borkowski, & Whitman, 1999).

Design. Data for both studies were collected prenatally, and again when the children were 1, 3, and 5 years. Maternal preparedness for parenting, social support, and psychological adjustment were measured prenatally. A short form of the CAPI was developed for use in both studies, this version consisted of 25 items drawn primarily from the unhappiness and rigidity subscales of the full CAPI (Milner, 1989); and demonstrated good reliability and internal consistency (Whitman, et al., 2001). The short form of the CAPI was then used to measure abuse potential at 1, 3, and 5 years. Children's intelligence and adaptive behaviors were measured at 3 and 5 years through standardized testing and maternal interviews.

Results and Implications. In the first study that examined early risks and their relationship to abuse potential, regression analyses revealed that prenatal parenting preparedness, but not social support or psychological adjustment, predicted abuse potential during infancy (Dukewich et al., 1996). In fact, parenting preparedness (consisting of knowledge and expectations about child development and behaviors and beliefs about the parenting role) accounted for 16% of the unique variance in abuse potential. More specifically, mothers who had less knowledge of and inappropriate attitudes and expectations about children's development had greater potential for physical abuse when they were 1 year of age. These findings highlight the influence that prenatal risks, especially being unprepared for assuming the parenting role, had on abuse potential 1 year later (Dukewich et al., 1996).

In a second study, abuse potential was strongly associated with children's development prior to school entry, predicting both current and future intellectual and adaptive functioning (Dukewich et al., 1999). More specifically, at both 3 and 5 years, abuse potential was significantly related to children's concurrent intelligence and adaptive behaviors. Additional analyses revealed that abuse potential at 1 and 3 years predicted children's intelligence and adaptive behaviors at 3 and 5 years. Similar relationships did not hold when examining the reverse direction of these effects: Children's developmental outcomes at 3 years did not predict abuse potential at 5. These results, using a cross-lag panel design, point to a possible causal relationship between abuse potential during early childhood and two major components of mild mental retardation, intelligence, and adaptive behaviors.

Antecedents and Consequences of Abuse Potential During Middle Childhood

The relationship of abuse potential to development during middle childhood was an important focus of research in the NDAPP (Lounds, Borkowski, & Whitman, 2004). This project sought to disentangle how maternal risks and abuse potential influenced children's development. More specifically, early risks such as depression have been shown to predict maltreatment and to be related to children's development (Ethier, Lacharite, & Couture, 1995; Gauthier et al., 1996; Lahey et al., 1984). However, these findings are difficult to interpret unambiguously. For instance, when a relationship between abuse and development is observed, is the causal mechanism abuse or the result of a preexisting maternal characteristic such as depression? The present study explored abuse potential as a possible causal mediator of the relationship between early risks and later development. The project had two goals: (1) explore maternal characteristics assessed prenatally as predictors of abuse potential scores when children were 10 years of age, and (2) examine abuse potential as the mediator of the association between maternal risks and children's socioemotional functioning.

Design.   Data collection for this project occurred at multiple timepoints and included both maternal and child assessments. Prenatal variables were collected during the last trimester of pregnancy, including maternal IQ, externalizing behaviors (aggression), cognitive readiness to parent, and internalizing problems (depression). Parenting was measured postnatally and defined by the quality of mother–child interactions. Child abuse potential and children's behavior problems, both aggression and depression, were assessed at age 10.

Results and Implications.   The mean full scale CAPI score at age 10 was 121.05 ($SD = 91.45$), with a median of 94. Participants were divided into two categories using established cutoff points: Those likely to abuse their children (CAPI scores > 166) and those at less risk for abuse (scores < 166; Milner, 1980). Interestingly, 27% of the participants scored above the cutoff point and were judged at risk for child abuse. This percentage is higher than the 16% reported by Milner (1980) in samples of middle class, primarily European American parents. Prenatal intelligence and depression were found to be important predictors of abuse potential at age 10. Regression analyses showed that lower levels of maternal intelligence and higher levels of depression were significantly related to abuse potential, accounting for 6% and 7% of the variance, respectively. It may be that depression—and not merely an off-timed pregnancy—was a major reason for the high levels of reported abuse potential. The significant relationship between prenatal risks (e.g., depression and IQ) and abuse potential also extends past research that has shown neonatal risks, including depression, to be related to reports of abuse at age 4 (Kotch, Browne, Dufort, Winsor, & Catellier, 1999).

The second part of the project explored the impact of early maternal risks and abuse potential on children's development during middle childhood. At age 10, the typical child in the NDAPP had difficulty in a number of developmental domains, as can be seen in their academic, cognitive, and socioemotional functioning, presented in Table 5.1. For instance, compared to normative samples, nearly twice as many children had externalizing scores at or above the cutoff indicating clinical problems with aggression. More importantly, mean scores for reading and math achievement and intelligence fell nearly 1 *SD* below the population means (cf. Lounds, Borkowski, & Whitman, 2004).

Two sets of regression analyses were employed to understand the mediational role of abuse potential between prenatal maternal characteristics and children's development. If the relationship between a maternal characteristic and a child outcome became nonsignificant after controlling for abuse potential, it was possible to infer that abuse potential was the mechanism through which prenatal variables affected children's development (Baron & Kenny, 1986).

Table 5.1

Descriptive Statistics for Children's 10-year Academic, Cognitive, and Socio-Emotional Development

	N	*M*	*SD*
Academic Achievement			
Math	117	89.10	16.87
Reading	117	88.50	19.13
Cognitive Development			
Intelligence	117	88.67	14.25
Socio-Emotional Development			
Internalizing – Teacher Report	117	51.95	10.12
Externalizing – Teacher Report	117	55.53	10.28
Internalizing – Parent Report	117	52.01	9.86
Externalizing – Parent Report	117	52.74	10.19

Analyses revealed that abuse potential mediated the relationship between prenatal maternal characteristics, including intelligence and depression, and children's depression and aggression at age 10. Figure 5.1 highlights the results of three different mediational mod-

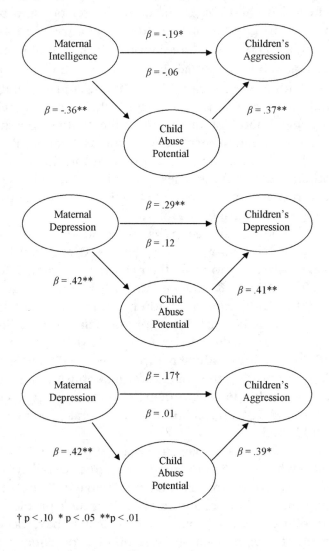

Figure 5.1.   Child abuse potential as a mediator of the relations between prenatal intelligence and depression, and children's 10-year depression and aggression.

els. In the top panel, relationships among prenatal maternal intelligence, child abuse potential, and children's aggression are shown. In the initial regression analysis, maternal intelligence was significantly related to children's aggression ($\beta= -.19$). In a second analysis that included child abuse potential, the relationship between maternal intelligence and children's aggression became nonsignificant ($\beta = -.06$). More importantly, maternal intelligence predicted child abuse potential ($\beta = -.36$), which was significantly related to children's aggression ($\beta = .37$): Lower maternal IQs were associated with higher abuse potential which, in turn, was related to children's aggression. The mediational role of abuse potential can also be seen between maternal depression and children's depression (middle panel) and maternal depression and children's aggression (bottom panel). In both cases, higher levels of depression were related to increased abuse potential which then influenced children's depression and aggression.

Each of the above relationships has been found in prior cross-sectional designs: Mothers who were depressed and had lower IQ scores were more likely to abuse their children (Mammen, Kolko, & Pikonis, 2002; Milner & Chilamkurti, 1991; Pianta, Egeland, & Erikson, 1989). Additionally, children who had been physically abused were at higher risk for poor socioemotional adjustment (Finzi et al., 2001; Kazdin, Moser, Colbus, & Bell, 1985; Scerbo & Kolko, 1995). The longitudinal nature of the NDAPP furthered past research by supporting the conclusion that abuse potential mediated the relationship between preexisting maternal characteristics (depression and IQ) and children's behavioral problems during middle childhood.

Children in the NDAPP may have reacted to potentially abusive mothers in two ways: (1) modeling the aggressive behavior of the mother as evidenced by externalizing behaviors, or (2) over-controlling their behaviors and internalizing their problems as reflected in depressive symptoms. That is, it may have been more adaptive not to express emotions around a potentially abusive mother and risk provoking her aggressive behaviors.

Neglect Potential During Middle Childhood

Although we found important relationships between early risk, abuse potential, and children's development, earlier research has shown that different forms of maltreatment have differential effects on children's developmental outcomes (Todd-Manly et al., 2001). For this reason, the NDAPP examined neglect potential, as measured by the Mother–Child Neglect Scale (MCNS), and the role that it played in the development of adolescent mother–child dyads, both in terms of risk factors that predicted neglect as well as its effects on development during middle childhood (Lounds, Borkowski, Whitman, & the Centers for Prevention of Child Neglect, 2006). The purpose of this study was threefold: (1) to determine whether variables related to prenatal maternal functioning (e.g., intelligence, depression), parenting, or children's characteristics (e.g., temperament, attachment) during early childhood predicted low levels of neglect during middle childhood; (2) to assess children's developmental outcomes at 8 and 10 years of age, including academic performance, intelligence, behavioral adaptation, and personal adjustment as a function of low levels of neglect; and (3) to examine the possibility that neglect mediated the relationship between important maternal risk factors and children's development.

Design.   Data collection occurred at seven time points: the third trimester of pregnancy and when each child reached 6 months, 12 months, 3 years of age, 5 years, 8 years, and 10 years of age. During the last trimester of pregnancy, maternal IQ and adjustment as indicated by internalizing, depression and anxiety, and aggression were assessed. Children's temperament was measured at 6 and 12 months, and attachment, using the Strange Situation paradigm, was measured at 12 months. The quality of mother–child interactions and child abuse potential was measured at 3 years of age and again at 5 years. Aggregates for both constructs were formed by averaging the measures across the two time points. At 8 and 10, children's school achievement, intelligence, adaptive behaviors, and problem behaviors were assessed. The 8- and 10-year scores for each outcomes variable were also averaged in order to obtain more stable representations of children's characteristics (Rushton, Brainerd, & Pressley, 1983).

Mothers were also contacted by telephone when their children were between 9 and 15 years of age. The Neglect Scale and MCNS were administered to assess each mother's recollection of neglect when she was a child as well as her reports of low levels of neglect toward her own child. Because of difficulties in defining specific behaviors that were indicative of neglect at different ages, mothers were asked to answer the questions on the MCNS at a common time point (age 8), regardless of the actual age of the child at the time of assessment (for further details, see Lounds, Borkowski, Whitman, & the Centers for the Prevention of Child Neglect, 2006).

Results and Implications.   The first goal of this study was to explore possible predictors of neglect potential and included four variables related to earlier maternal functioning—past experiences of neglect, intelligence, depression, and aggression—as well as the overall quality of mother–child interactions during childhood and two variables related to children's earlier functioning, temperament and attachment. Out of the six possible predictors, only past experiences of neglect during childhood and adolescence and the quality of mother–child interactions predicted neglect potential at 8, accounting for 8% and 7% of unique variance in the MCNS, respectively. Similar to the findings with abuse potential, none of the child variables were predictive of later neglect potential, highlighting the importance of maternal characteristics in determining the potential for maltreatment.

Previous studies have reported a strong relationship between the quality of mother–child interactions and substantiated reports of neglect to child protective agencies (Bousha & Twentyman, 1984); relatedly, we found that these same relationships held with lower, nonreportable levels. Moreover, we found evidence for the intergenerational transmission of neglect: After controlling for maternal intelligence and depression, past histories of neglect remained significantly associated with current propensities for child neglect.

The next step was to explore the effects of neglect potential on children's development during middle childhood. Children's adaptive behaviors and aggression at age 10 were predicted by neglect potential but not academic achievement or intelligence. These relations were important for two reasons: (1) neglect was an important predictor of development, even at levels not severe enough to warrant substantiated reports to child protective services; and (2) low levels of neglect increased the risk for aggression, acting out, and problems in social adaptation among children who were already at an increased risk for these problems due to being raised by an adolescent parent.

Teen mothers may be less focused than adult mothers on teaching socialization skills to their children because they are forced to deal with high levels of stress and often do not possess mature socioemotional regulation skills themselves, perhaps because of their own histories of maltreatment. In turn, neglected children experienced difficulties in school settings, because they failed to learn the necessary regulatory skills to function independently and adaptively.

Further analyses in this project explored how earlier parenting behaviors and later neglect potential worked in combination to influence children's aggression (Lounds, Borkowski, Whitman, & the Centers for the Prevention of Child Neglect, 2006). Figure 5.2 high-

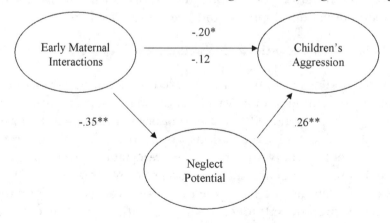

†$p < .10$ *$p < .05$ **$p < .01$

Figure 5.2.   Low levels of neglect as a mediator of the relations between early parenting quality and children's aggression during middle childhood.

lights the role of neglect potential as a potential mediator of the relationship between early maternal–child interactions and children's aggression at age 10. Following procedures outlined by Baron and Kenny (1986), the quality of maternal interactions significantly predicted children's aggression ($\beta = -.20$). In the next set of analyses that included neglect potential, the relationship between maternal interactions and children's aggression became nonsignificant ($\beta = -.12$). Finally, the quality of early maternal interactions predicted neglect potential ($\beta = -.35$) which was significantly related to children's aggression ($\beta = .26$): Insensitive and unresponsive maternal interactions were associated with neglect potential, which in turn was related to children's aggression. It appears that early parenting behaviors impacted children's aggression through the mechanism of emotional and physical neglect.

The NDAPP is one of the first projects on abuse and neglect to determine the processes through which maternal characteristics, parenting, and maltreatment exerted their interactive influence on children's development. Our findings, using two different measures of maltreatment (CAPI and MCNS), offer evidence for the unique effects of maltreatment, beyond the impact of earlier negative parenting practices and maternal depression on children's socioemotional development and behavioral problems.

Early Identification of the Risk for Abuse and Neglect

Previous findings from the NDAPP have revealed the importance of maternal parenting orientations in understanding parenting behaviors (Dukewich et al., 1996). Parenting orientations include maternal knowledge and expectations about the pace of children's development, rigidity toward these expectations, and attitudes about being a mother and the parenting role (Whitman et al., 2001). These orientations provide a "mental model" that guides parenting behavior, thereby influencing the potential for maltreatment (Borkowski, Ramey, & Stile, 2002).

The lack of knowledge about children's development can foster unintentional neglect. For instance, a baby's constant sleeping or failure to urinate may be alarming for those mothers who recognize these characteristics as signs of dehydration. For others—not prepared for the stress and demands of parenting—sleeping may be a welcomed reprieve from the daily hassles of motherhood. Because of the established link between negative parenting orientations and maltreatment, Schatz and Burke-Lefever (2003) explored the utility of a screening tool that assessed at-risk parenting orientations in order to identify teen mothers with potential for maltreatment.

The screening tool, referred to as the Child Abuse and Neglect Risk Evaluation–Short Form (CARE–S), was drawn from a more comprehensive 126-item index, consisting of four measures that assessed parenting orientations: knowledge about child development, parenting expectations, rigidity about children's behaviors, and attitudes about parenting (Schatz & Burke-Lefever, 2003).

TABLE 5.2
Child Abuse and Neglect Risk Evaluation–Short Form (CARE–S)

1. Having kids and taking care of them is one of the most important things a woman can do.

2. A good child will make both parents feel better after the parents have been fighting.

3. Parents will spoil their children by picking them up and comforting them when they cry.

4. Children should be taught to control their feelings at all times.

5. It's usually a good idea to physically punish a 6-year-old with a belt for acting out on the school bus because the child will learn how to behave next time.

6. Children should always pay the price for misbehaving.

7. A parent can expect a 3- or 4-year old child to know enough to behave in a supermarket so the parents won't look foolish in front of others.

8. It is at this age that a child will be most afraid when an adult stranger picks them up:

    (a) birth to 4-months; (b) 6- to 12-months; (c) 24- to 36-months; (d) 18- to 24-months.

9. I am really, really looking forward to being a mother.

10. A 1-year-old can usually feed himself/herself without spilling.

11. Little boys should never learn sissy games.

12. A home should be spotless.

The CARE–S was composed of 12 items listed in Table 1, including "Children should always 'pay the price' for misbehaving" and "Parents will spoil their children by picking them up and comforting them when they cry." Responses indicating risk were scored with 1 while nonrisk responses received a 0. The total score was derived from the summation of the 12 items, with higher scores pointing to risk for maltreatment. The measure can be administered in a short time and the total score quickly derived, making this an ideal screening tool for utilization with at-risk populations where length of assessment is an important consideration.

The CARE–S was utilized to analyze relationships between maltreatment risks during pregnancy and infancy and children's cognitive, adaptive, and behavioral development at age 8. The CARE–S explained significant portions of the variance in several domains of children's development (Schatz & Burke-Lefever, 2003). For instance, mothers with higher scores on the CARE–S had children who scored significantly lower on intelligence (12% of the variance explained), receptive language (16% of variance explained), and adaptive functioning (13% of variance explained). These results lend support for the CARE–S as a practical screening tool, with reasonable predictive validity. Prevention programs could employ this instrument to help evaluate the need for services and to select participants most at risk for maltreatment.

Contributions From the NDAPP to Understanding Maltreatment

Past research has shown that child maltreatment is determined by the interplay of multiple factors operating at different levels of the children's environments (Belsky, 1980) including age at childbirth, education, available economic resources, and single parenthood (Bolton, 1990; Sedlak & Broadhurst, 1996; Twentyman & Plotkin, 1982; Zuravin, 1987). Findings from the NDAPP supported the multifaceted nature of early maternal risks for abuse and neglect (cf. Belsky, 1980) and their impact on the potential for maltreatment later in life. Although previous research has shown prenatal risk factors to be related to reports of abuse 4 years later (Kotch et al., 1999), our research has extended these relationships to age 10.

Past research has also documented the developmental challenges that maltreated children face, including academic difficulties (Eckenrode, Laird, & Doris, 1993), adaptive behavior deficits (Wodarski et al., 1990), and socioecomotional problems (Kim & Cicchetti, 2003). Findings from the extant literature, coupled with those from the NDAPP, have shown that maltreatment is multiply determined and can have a long-term, adverse impact on children's cognitive, behavioral, and adaptive development. The NDAPP contributed to the research base with five important findings:

- 27% of mothers in the NDAPP scored in the elevated range on the 10-year CAPI, suggesting high potential for child abuse.
- Maternal histories of neglect, that occurred prior to age 18, predicted the potential for neglect when children were 8 years old.
- Prenatal maternal characteristics predicted abuse potential at age 10, with abuse potential surfacing as a possible mechanism through which maternal depression and intelligence influenced children's depression.
- Similarly, the potential for neglect appeared to be the mechanism through which early maternal interactions influenced children's aggression at 10.
- The CARE–S, consisting of 12 items presented to the mothers during pregnancy and early infancy, explained 12–16% of the variance in children's intelligence, receptive vocabulary, and adaptive behaviors at 8.

CONCLUSIONS, IMPLICATIONS, AND FUTURE DIRECTIONS

Maltreatment cuts across racial, ethnic, national, and economic boundaries, with elevated rates of abuse and neglect occurring in both low and high risk samples. For instance, Straus and Savage (2005) found high rates of neglect in nonrisk samples of university students across the world. In Europe, North America, Latin America, Asia, Australia, and New Zealand, college students were asked to report about their early childhood experiences of neglect. The percentage that experienced neglectful caregiving ranged from 3% to nearly 40%, with an average of 13.4% (Straus & Savage, 2005). In the United States, the overall rate of neglect was 11.2% (Straus & Savage, 2005).

In the NDAPP, the Childhood Trauma Questionnaire (Bernstein & Fink, 1998), a self-report measure of abuse and neglect during childhood and adolescence, was used to determine maltreatment rates for the mothers in the NDAPP prior to age 18. Five types of maltreatment were assessed: physical abuse, emotional abuse, sexual abuse, as well as physical and emotional neglect. According to maternal reports, almost 40% of NDAPP mothers had suffered physical abuse; nearly 50% reported emotional abuse; 39% experienced sexual abuse; 30% experienced physical neglect; and more than one half were subjected to emotional neglect. In addition, nearly 80% reported the presence of abuse or neglect on at least one subscale, and 59% experienced two or more types of maltreatment. Given their past histories of maltreatment, it is not surprising to find that 27% of mothers had elevated scores on the CAPI, suggesting they were at risk for abusing their own children (Lounds, Borkowski, & Whitman, 2004). The cycle of maltreatment appears to be repeating itself within families and across generations, with no known geographical boundaries.

Because of the transmission of maltreatment from one generation to the next, prevention programs hold the key to reducing its prevalence in the United States and around the world. The utilization of valid screening measures, such as the CARE–S, to select at-risk mothers will help to ensure the delivery of needed services as early as possible, often before the birth of a child at risk for later maltreatment. In addition, findings from the NDAPP showed that several prenatal maternal characteristics, especially depression, were consistent predictors of maltreatment potential during infancy and throughout middle childhood; programs that target these early risk factors may help to ameliorate the onset of abusive and neglectful behaviors. Relatedly, chapter 10 extends our research on child maltreatment by presenting a comprehensive model prevention program, beginning prenatally and lasting for 3 years, designed and implemented by the Centers for the Prevention of Child Neglect. Based on the active collaboration between researchers, community leaders, and service delivery professionals, similar prevention programs can be developed to help ensure that all children develop to their fullest potential in environments free of maltreatment.

REFERENCES

Azar, S. T. (1991). Models of child abuse: A metatheoretical analysis. *Criminal Justice and Behavior, 18*, 30–46.

Baron, R. M., & Kenny, D. A. (1986). The moderator–mediator variable distinction in social psychological research: Conceptual, strategic, and statistical considerations. *Journal of Personality and Social Psychology, 51*, 1173–1182.

Belsky, J. (1980). Child maltreatment: An ecological approach. *American Psychologist, 35*, 320–335.

Belsky, J. (1993). Etiology of child maltreatment: A developmental–ecological analysis. *Psychological Bulletin, 114*, 419–434.

Bernstein, D. P., & Fink, L. (1998). *Childhood Trauma Questionnaire: A retrospective self-report.* San Antonio, TX: Psychological Corporation Harcourt Brace and Company.

Black, D. A., Heyman, R. E., & Slep, A. M S. (2001). Risk factors for child physical abuse. *Aggression and Violent Behavior, 6*, 121–188.

Blinn-Pike, L., & Mingus, S. (2000). The internal consistency of the Child Abuse Potential Inventory with adolescent mothers. *Journal of Adolescence, 23*, 107–111.

Bolton, F. G. (1990). The risk of child maltreatment in adolescent parenting. *Advances in Adolescent Mental Health, 4*, 223–237.

Borkowski, J. G., Ramey, S. L., & Stile, C. (2002). Parenting research: Translations to parenting practices. In J. G. Borkowski, S. L. Ramey, & M. Bristol-Power (Eds.), *Parenting and the child's world: Influences on academic, intellectual, and social-emotional development* (pp. 365–386). Mahwah, NJ: Lawrence Erlbaum Associates.

Bousha, D. M., & Twentyman, C. T. (1984). Mother–child interactional style in abuse, neglect, and control groups: Naturalistic observations in the home. *Journal of Abnormal Psychology, 93*, 106–114.

Brown, J., Cohen, P., Johnson, J. G., & Salzinger, S. (1998). A longitudinal analysis of risk factors for child maltreatment: Findings of a 17-year prospective study of officially recorded and self-reported child abuse and neglect. *Child Abuse and Neglect, 22*, 1065–1078.

Burrell, B., Thompson, B., & Sexton, D. (1992). The measurement integrity of data collected using the Child Abuse Potential Inventory. *Educational and Psychological Measurement, 52*, 993–1001.

Carlson, V., Cicchetti, D., Barnett, D., & Braunwald, K. (1989). Disorganized/disoriented attachment relationships in maltreated infants. *Developmental Psychology, 25*, 525–531.

Chance, T., & Scannapieco, M. (2002). Ecological correlates of child maltreatment: Similarities and differences between child fatality and nonfatality cases. *Child and Adolescent Social Work Journal, 19,* 139–161.

Dukewich, T. L., Borkowski, J. G., & Whitman, T. L. (1996). Adolescent mothers and child abuse potential: An evaluation of risk factors. *Child Abuse and Neglect, 20,* 1031–1047.

Dukewich, T. L., Borkowski, J. G., & Whitman, T. L. (1999). A longitudinal analysis of maternal abuse potential and developmental delays in children of adolescent mothers. *Child Abuse and Neglect, 23,* 405–420.

Eckenrode, J., Laird, M., & Doris, J. (1993). School performance and disciplinary problems among abused and neglected children. *Developmental Psychology, 29,* 53–62.

Ethier, L. S., Lacharite, C., & Couture, G. (1995). Childhood adversity, parental stress, and depression of negligent mothers. *Child Abuse and Neglect, 19,* 619–632.

Finzi, R., Ram, A., Shnit, D., Har-Even, D., Tyano, S., & Weizman, A. (2001). Depressive symptoms and suicidality in physically abused children. *American Journal of Orthopsychiatry, 71,* 98–107.

Furstenberg, F. F., Brooks-Gunn, J., & Morgan, S. P. (1987). *Adolescent mothers in later life.* New York: Cambridge University Press.

Gauthier, L., Stollak, G., Messe, G., & Aronoff, J. (1996). Recall of childhood neglect and physical abuse as differential predictors of current psychological functioning. *Child Abuse and Neglect, 20,* 549–559.

George, C., & Main, M. (1979). Social interactions of young abused children: Approach, avoidance, and aggression. *Child Development, 50,* 306–318.

Gee, C. B., & Rhodes, J. E. (1999). Postpartum transitions in adolescent mothers' romantic and maternal relationships. *Merrill-Palmer Quaterly, 45,* 512–525.

Herrenkohl, E. C., Herrenkohl, R. C., Egolf, B. P., & Russo, M. J. (1998). The relationship between early maltreatment and teenage parenthood. *Journal of Adolescence, 21,* 291–303.

Horowitz, S. M., Klerman, L. V., Kuo, H. S., & Jekel, J. F. (1991). Intergenerational transmission of school-age parenthood. *Family Planning Perspectives, 23,* 166–172.

Horton, C. B., & Cruise, T. K. (2001). *Child Abuse and Neglect.* New York: Guilford Press.

Kaufman, J., & Zigler, E. (1987). Do abused children become abusive parents? *American Journal of Orthopsychiatry, 57,* 186–192.

Kazdin, A. E., Moser, J., Colbus, D., & Bell, R. (1985). Depressive symptoms among physically abused and psychiatrically disturbed children. *Journal of Abnormal Psychology, 94,* 298–307.

Kendall-Tackett, K. A., & Eckenrode, J. (1996). The effects of neglect on academic achievement and disciplinary problems: A developmental perspective. *Child Abuse and Neglect, 20,* 161–169.

Kim, J., & Cicchetti, D. (2003). Social self-efficacy and behavior problems in maltreated and nonmaltreated children. *Journal of Clinical Child and Adolescent Psychology, 32*, 106–117.

Kotch, J. G., Browne, D. C., Dufort, V., Winsor, J., & Catellier, D. (1999). Predicting child maltreatment in the first 4 years of life from characteristics assessed in the neonatal period. *Child Abuse and Neglect, 23*, 305–319.

Lahey, B. B., Conger, R. D., Atkeson, B. M., & Treiber, F. A. (1984). Parenting behavior and emotional status of physically abusive mothers. *Journal of Consulting and Clinical Psychology, 52*, 1062–1071.

Lounds, J. J., Borkowski, J. G., & Whitman, T. L. (2004, July). *Abuse potential and behavior problems in children of adolescent mothers.* Poster presented at the annual meeting of the American Psychological Association, Honolulu, HI.

Lounds, J. J., Borkowski J. G., Whitman. T. L., & The Centers for the Prevention of Child Neglect (2004). Reliability and validity of the Mother–Child Neglect Scale. *Child Maltreatment, 9*, 371–381.

Lounds, J.J., Borkowski J. G., Whitman. T. L., & The Centers for the Prevention of Child Neglect (2006). The potential for child neglect: The case of adolescent mothers and their children. *Child Maltreatment, 11*, 281–294.

Mammen, O. K., Kolko, D. J., & Pilkonis, P. A. (2002). Negative affect and parental aggression in child physical abuse. *Child Abuse and Neglect, 26*, 407–424.

Margolin, L. (1992). Child abuse by mothers' boyfriends: Why the overrepresentation? *Child Abuse and Neglect, 16*, 541–551.

Milner, J. S. (1980). *The Child Abuse Potential Inventory: Manual* (2nd Ed.). DeKalb, IL: Psytec Inc.

Milner, J. S. (1989). Additional cross-validation of the child abuse potential inventory. *Psychological Assessment, 1*, 219–223.

Milner, J. S. (1994). Assessing physical child abuse risk: The Child Abuse Potential Inventory. *Clinical Psychology Review, 14*, 547–583.

Milner, J. S., & Chilamkurti, C. (1991). Physical child abuse perpetrator characteristics. *Journal of Interpersonal Violence, 6*, 345–366.

Nesbitt, W., & Karagianis, L. (1982). Child abuse: Exceptionality as a risk factor. *Alberta Journal of Educational Research, 28*, 69–76.

Ovwigho, P. C., Leavitt, K. L., & Born, C. E. (2003). Risk factors for child abuse and neglect among former TANF families: Do later leavers experience greater risk? *Children and Youth Services Review, 25*(1/2), 139–163.

Passino, A., Whitman, T. L., Borkowski, J. G., Shellenbach, C. J., Maxwell, S. E., Keogh, D. A., et al. (1993). Personal adjustment during pregnancy and adolescent parenting. *Adolescence, 28*, 97–122.

Pelzer, D. (1995). *A child called 'it.'* Health Communications, Inc: Deerfield Beach, FL.

Pianta, R., Egeland, B., & Erikson, M. F. (1989). The antecedents of maltreatment: Results of the mother–child interaction project. In D. Cicchetti & V. Carlson (Eds.), *Child maltreatment: Theory and research on the causes and consequences of child abuse and neglect.* New York: Cambridge University Press.

Rushton, P. J., Brainerd, C. J., & Pressley, M. (1983). Behavioral development and construct validity: The principle of aggregation. *Psychological Bulletin, 94,* 18–38.

Scerbo, A. S., & Kolko, D. J. (1995). Child physical abuse and aggression: Preliminary findings on the role of internalizing problems. *Journal of the American Academy of Child and Adolescent Psychiatry, 34,* 1060–1066.

Schamness, S. (1993). The search for love: Unmarried adolescent mothers' views of, and relationships with, men. *Adolescence, 28,* 425–438.

Schatz, J. N., & Burke-Lefever, J. (2003, February). Understanding maltreatment: The interplay between mothers' parenting orientations and children's vulnerability. Paper presented at the Gatlinburg Conference on Research and Theory in Intellectual and developmental Disabilities, Annapolis, MD.

Sedlak, A., & Broadhurst, D. (1996). Third National Incidence Study of Child Abuse and Neglect (NIS–3): Executive Summary. Washington, DC: U.S. Department of Health and Human Services, Administration on Children, Youth and Families.

Shields, A., & Cicchetti, D. (2001). Parental maltreatment and emotion dysregulation as risk factors for bullying and victimization in middle childhood. *Journal of Clinical Child Psychology, 30,* 349–363.

Spearly, J. L., & Lauderdale, M. (1983). Community characteristics and ethnicity in the prediction of child maltreatment rates. *Child Abuse and Neglect, 7,* 91–105.

Straus, M. A., & Savage, S. A. (2005). Neglectful behavior by parents in the life history of university students in 17 countries and its relation to violence against dating partners. *Child Maltreatment, 10,* 125–135.

Todd-Manly, J., Kim, J. E., Rogosch, F. A., & Cicchetti, D. (2001). Dimensions of child maltreatment and children's adjustment: Contributions of developmental timing and subtype. *Development and Psychopathology, 13,* 759–782.

Twentyman, C. T., & Plotkin, R. C. (1982). Unrealistic expectations of parents who maltreat their children: An educational deficit that pertains to child development. *Journal of Clinical Psychology, 38,* 497–503.

U.S. Department of Health and Human Services, Children's Bureau. (2004). Child Maltreatment 2002. Retrieved December 15, 2004 from http://www.acf.hhs.gov/programs/cb/publications/cmreports.htm.

Whitman, T. L., Borkwoski, J. G., Keogh, D., & Weed, K. (2001). *Interwoven lives: Adolescent mothers and their children.* Mahwah, NJ: Lawrence Erlbaum Associates.

Wodarski, J. S., Kurtz, P. D., Gaudin, J. M., & Howing, P. T. (1990). Maltreatment and the school-aged child: Major academic, socioemotional, and adaptive outcomes. *Social Work, 35,* 506–513.

Zuravin, S. J. (1987). Unplanned pregnancies, family planning problems, and child maltreatment. *Family Relations, 36,* 135–139.

6

Understanding the Cycle: Violence in the Lives of At-Risk Children

Chelsea M. Weaver
Carol E. Akai

Peace is not the absence of conflict but the presence of creative alternatives for responding to conflict—alternatives to passive or aggressive responses, alternatives to violence.

—Dorothy Thompson

Violence not only threatens children's physical safety but also their psychological well-being (Osofsky, 1997). Exposure to violence, in the forms of witnessing violence and/or victimization, often results in emotional harm such as depression, anxiety, and substance abuse during the teenage years (Saunders, 2003). Often, exposure to violence leads to an increased likelihood of adolescent aggression (Blum, Ireland, & Blum, 2003; Durant, Cadenhead, Pendergrast, Slavens, & Linder, 1994; Flannery, Singer, & Wester, 2001).

The effects of exposure to violence may be magnified or diminished by contextual risk and protective factors, such as dangerous neighborhoods or family cohesion. For example, warm and supportive family environments may serve as buffers for children living in violent neighborhoods. In contrast, children with families entrenched in poverty may be more susceptible to the negative consequences associated with repeated exposure to violence. As discussed in previous chapters, adolescent mothers and their children are often influenced by problems in multiple domains, such as low socioeconomic status, unemployment, family dysfunction, cognitive deficits, and socioemotional maladjustment (Whitman, Borkowski, Keogh, & Weed, 2001). For these reasons, children of adolescent mothers are at increased risk for exposure to violence and its detrimental impact on their long-term development.

It is important to investigate the factors associated with youth violence, particularly among at-risk children. In addition to understanding the antecedents and consequences of exposure to violence, it is essential to identify the moderating roles of risk and protective factors on adolescent development. Only then can researchers and practitioners begin to address the multifaceted problem of youth violence in the United States in an effort to promote optimal development among children of adolescent mothers and other at-risk children who are surrounded by violence in their daily lives.

PREVALENCE AND CORRELATES OF EXPOSURE TO VIOLENCE

In 2001, the U.S. Surgeon General announced that violence among adolescents had become a public health epidemic, even though violent crime victimization has steadily declined over the past decade (Satcher, 2001), with younger teens (12 to 14) experiencing the steepest drop (Baum, 2005). A study of children in Washington, DC found that nearly 33% of children 6 to 8 years of age had witnessed a shooting and 11% were actually shot or shot at (Richters & Martinez, 1993). Similarly, elevated rates of violence exposure were found among adolescents living in urban, suburban, and rural areas of Cleveland, Ohio (Singer, Anglin, Song, & Lunghofer, 1995). In the previous year, 56% of teenagers had witnessed a shooting, 56% had witnessed a stabbing, 22% had been shot at or shot, and 13% had been attacked with a knife, with urban children experiencing the highest levels of violence (Singer et al., 1995). Furthermore, youth between the ages of 12 and 17 were more than twice as likely to be victims of violent crimes than adults (Baum, 2005). In light of these facts, it is important to examine and understand the ramifications that exposure to violence can have on child and adolescent development.

The consequences of exposure to youth violence depend upon the place of occurrence (e.g., home or community), the proximity of the event (e.g., direct or indirect exposure), and the duration (e.g., isolated or chronic) of exposure. In terms of the place of occurrence, the negative impact of community violence exposure has been well-documented (e.g., Henrich, Schwab-Stone, Fanti, Jones, & Ruchkin, 2004; Salzinger, Feldman, Stockhammer, & Hood, 2002) and is often directly related to poverty. For example, disadvantaged neighborhoods have high rates of violence and victimization (Leventhal & Brooks-Gunn, 2000). Community violence exposure is typically defined in the literature as witnessing of, or victimization from, violent events in the neighborhood, such as beatings, stabbings, or shootings (e.g., Cooley-Quille, Turner, & Beidel, 1995; Singer et al., 1995).

Recently, exposure to chronic community violence has been found to impact physical health. A study of urban African American children found that exposure to violence was associated with stress and somatic complaints, even after controlling for socioeconomic status, prenatal and postnatal alcohol exposure, history of maltreatment as well as maternal age and psychopathology (Bailey et al., 2005). Witnessing neighborhood violence was associated with sleeping problems and headaches, whereas victimization predicted decreased appetite, difficulties in sleeping, and stomachaches. Exposure to chronic community violence has also been linked with symptoms of upper respiratory illnesses among urban minority adolescents, with psychological distress mediating this relationship (Wilson, Rosenthal, & Austin, 2005).

Schools are another context for exposure to violence. A study of urban, suburban, and rural students in Grades 3 through 8 found that 87% of children reported witnessing someone being hit, and

44% reported being threatened with physical harm at school (Flannery, Wester, & Singer, 2004). Interestingly, older students reported witnessing higher levels of violence at school; however, elementary school students reported the highest rates of victimization. Similar rates of violence exposure have been found among children in urban and nonurban school environments (Flannery et al., 2004).

In addition to neighborhood and school violence, violence in the home is also detrimental to the social and emotional development of children (cf. Edleson & Graham-Bermann, 2001). For instance, children's exposure to marital violence has been associated with aggression toward peers and parents as well as later depression (McCloskey & Lichter, 2003). In terms of physiological functioning, children exposed to marital violence were found to have elevated heart rates and higher levels of cortisol (a stress hormone) than comparison children (Salzman, Holden, & Holahan, 2005). Child abuse is an aspect of home violence exposure, with children of adolescent mothers at increased risk for maltreatment by their caregivers (Lee & Goerge, 1999; Stouthamer-Loeber, Wei, Homish, & Loeber, 2002). Not surprisingly, high levels of maltreatment have been found among violent families (Appel & Holden, 1998; Lee, Kotch, & Cox, 2004), suggesting that some children may be "doubly" victimized through witnessing the abuse of a parent combined with being abused themselves.

The negative consequences of home violence may be due, in part, to the fact that family violence often translates into children's direct exposure rather than the indirect exposure sometimes associated with community violence. For example, exposure to community violence typically includes hearing gunshots at night, which may make a child feel scared or unsafe, although the actual exposure is indirect. In contrast, domestic conflict that turns violent often occurs in the child's presence, thereby compromising the typical "safe haven" of home. Relatedly, Jenkins and Bell (1994) demonstrated that family victimization was as strongly associated with distress as was personal victimization. Thus, even though a child may not be directly victimized, violence exposure through the victimization of a loved one may be just as detrimental. Another factor that increases a child's proximity to violence is age. As children approach middle childhood, exposure to community violence may increase as children gain greater autonomy (Ingoldsby & Shaw, 2002). For example, a 12-year-old child who is permitted to play outside unsupervised or walk to a neighborhood store alone has an increased likelihood of direct exposure to community violence. In turn, physical proximity to a traumatic event has been directly related to the severity of posttraumatic symptoms (Nader, Pynoos, Fairbanks, & Frederick, 1990).

In addition to context and proximity, the duration of violence exposure can also adversely impact children's development. In general, chronic exposure has been related to higher levels of pathology than exposure to isolated events (Osofsky, 1997). In a study of the relationship between violence exposure and trauma symptoms, exposure to chronic community violence was associated with higher levels of internalizing and externalizing problems, even after accounting for socioeconomic status and exposure to family violence (Lineras & Cloitre, 2004). Because exposure to community violence occurred in the presence of the mother, children's exposure to maternal trauma symptoms may have acted as the mediating mechanism by which maladjustment manifested (Lineras & Cloitre, 2004).

An alternative explanation of children's reactions to exposure to violence resides in their perceptions of themselves and their environments. For example, violence exposure predicted at-risk children's internalizing and externalizing problems, even after controlling for maternal psychological distress (Buckner, Beardslee, & Bassuk, 2004). Furthermore, self-esteem and perceived chronic danger partially mediated these relationships, suggesting mechanisms through which children's exposure to violence acted to negatively impact their socioemotional development. Collectively, these studies provide evidence that chronic exposure to violence is associated with serious negative consequences; however, the mechanisms to explain how this phenomenon typically occurs vary from maternal distress to children's distress. It is likely that there are transactional effects between mother and children as they react to witnessing violence and related victimization.

It is evident that the characteristics of violence exposure among youth are complex, intertwined, and often cumulative, making it difficult to establish the differential effect of any one facet in isolation.

For instance, children who are maltreated at home may have a higher risk for living in a violent community and for being chronically abused. Most likely, the combination of these factors is not additive, but instead the negative impact of violence exposure increases exponentially with each added risk. Whereas multiple risks jeopardize both psychological and physiological outcomes for children and adolescents, the presence of protective factors must also be considered in terms of their ability to ameliorate the impact of exposure to violence. For example, an analysis of violence prevention programs found that at-risk youth who had a supportive relationship with at least one adult had more favorable developmental outcomes (Nation et al., 2003). Religiosity and parent involvement also protect against the development of conduct problems among violence-exposed youth (Pearce, Jones, Schwab-Stone, & Ruchkin, 2003). The examination of youth violence in the context of risk and resilience provides a more complete understanding of the complex patterns surrounding this phenomenon.

THE CYCLICAL NATURE OF EXPOSURE TO VIOLENCE

Youth violence is commonly thought of as a cyclical process. Research indicates that conduct problems are not only a consequence of exposure to violence (Blum et al, 2003; Durant et al., 1994; Flannery et al., 2001; Lynch & Cicchetti, 1998; Stouthamer-Loeber et al., 2002), but also that conduct problems themselves predict higher levels of violence exposure (Esbensen & Huizinga, 1991; Lauritsen, Laub, & Sampson, 1992). For example, children's aggression is likely associated with environments that are conducive to violence (e.g., harsh and punitive parents and antisocial peers). In turn, violence exposure then contributes to the development of new aggressive behaviors, which likely lead to more exposure to violence. The pattern of these causal effects is often difficult to untangle, highlighting the need for prospective longitudinal designs that enable researchers to distinguish between the differential impact of multiple antecedents and consequences of violence exposure on children's development over time.

Antecedents of Youth Violence Exposure

Demographic Risks and Violence Exposure. In the United States, people from all walks of life are affected by violence; however, consistent differences in levels of violence exposure have revealed increased susceptibility for specific at-risk populations. For example, African American youth have been found to be at highest risk for exposure to violence, followed by Latinos and European Americans (Crouch, Hanson, Saunders, Kilpatrick, & Resnick, 2000). More recently, African American juveniles were found to be five times more likely than European American teens to be a victim of homicide (Baum, 2005). Furthermore, youth from lower income households witnessed violence more often than those from higher income households (Crouch et al, 2000). Generally, the percentage of minority youth compared to the percentage of European American youth living in low income households has been shown to be disproportionately high, suggesting that violence exposure for minority youth may be attributed, in part, to income-related factors such as high-crime neighborhoods and overcrowded schools.

The relationship between race, socioeconomic status, and exposure to violence is likely more complex than just described. For example, the National Family Violence Surveys revealed a significant negative relationship between familial income level and exposure to violence for European American youth but not for African American or Latino youth (Crouch et al., 2000). In other words, higher income levels protected against both witnessing of, and victimization from, violence only for European American children. Family income did not matter for exposure to violence among minority youth. In addition, males living in public housing were found to be more likely to engage in delinquent activities than peers living in more advantaged communities, even in the context of favorable indexes of both risk and protective factors (Wikström & Loeber, 2000). These findings suggest that a culturally-sensitive, sociological perspective should be taken when attempting to conceptualize and understand differential risks for exposure to violence among youth in the United States and, perhaps, internationally.

Family Functioning and Violence Exposure.   Much of the attention surrounding youth violence exposure has investigated the impact of children's social surroundings, particularly the adequacy of family functioning and the quality of relationships between family members. Parent–child relationships are typically the most important social interactions experienced by children and, in turn, may have a strong influence on their exposure to violence. For example, those from "struggling" families (defined in terms of poor parenting and low cohesion) are more likely to be exposed to community violence than those from more optimally functioning families (Gorman-Smith, Henry, & Tolan, 2004). Similarly, among youth exposed to high levels of community violence, favorable family functioning protected against later violence perpetration (Gorman-Smith et al., 2004). On the other hand, antisocial behaviors among adolescent mothers have been associated with elevated rates of children's conduct problems (Rhule, McMahon, & Speiker, 2004). The delinquent behaviors of teen mothers likely translated into an elevated risk for exposure to violence in their children's daily lives.

Interestingly, relationships between parenting behaviors and violence exposure sometimes vary depending upon children's sex. For instance, reports of maternal overprotective behaviors have been related to preadolescent boys' peer victimization, with heightened levels of fear during mother–child conflicts exacerbating this relationship for males (Finnegan, Hodges, & Perry, 1998). Peer victimization was related to maternal threat of rejection among girls (Finnegan et al., 1998). In contrast, more recent research examining preadolescent peer victimization demonstrated that parenting, including emotional warmth, overprotection, or rejection, did not affect victimization (Veenstra et al., 2005). Contemporary research investigating the impact of family relationships on children's violence exposure is inconclusive. It is likely, however, that specific facets of family functioning, such as cohesion and parenting practices, affect both the parent–child relationship as well as the development of children's social skills and their likelihood of exposure to violence.

In terms of parenting practices, monitoring strategies, such as supervising youth activities, regulating peer involvement, and imposing rules, may be important factors affecting the rates and consequences of children's exposure to violence. A qualitative study of families living in violent urban communities revealed that both mothers and fathers used a variety of monitoring strategies when children were preschool-aged in an attempt to protect their children from violence (Letiecq & Koblinsky, 2003). These strategies included keeping a close watch on children in the neighborhood, teaching children survival skills and emergency responses, and promoting avoidance of delinquent peers. Higher rates of parental monitoring have been associated with lower rates of witnessing of, and victimization from, community violence (Ceballo, Ramirez, Hearn, & Maltese, 2003). Moreover, monitoring was shown to protect against the negative effects of children's exposure to violence, but only when rates of community violence exposure were low. When children were exposed to higher rates of neighborhood violence, monitoring did not protect against children's psychological distress, suggesting that the cumulative effect of chronically dangerous environments undercut the positive effects of high-quality parenting (Ceballo et al., 2003).

It should be noted that mother–child agreement regarding the rates of children's exposure to violence has been associated with more positive child adjustment (i.e., lower trauma symptoms and internalizing problems) among inner-city families, suggesting that parental monitoring and awareness may increase children's support systems and improve their abilities to cope with stress (Ceballo, Dahl, Aretakis, & Ramirez, 2001). Also, children may be more likely to confide in their parents within the context of healthy parent–child relationships, which may serve as a vehicle for both soliciting and providing support.

Children's Characteristics and Exposure to Violence.   Along with demographic and family risk factors, children's adjustment contributes to the likelihood of being exposed to violence. A prospective study of male and female children found that parent and teacher reports of aggression in first grade were positively associated with violence exposure during middle school, both victimization and witnessing violence (Boyd, Cooley, Lambert, & Ialongo, 2003); for boys, this relationship was attenuated by higher anxiety. The connection between children's aggression and youth violence exposure was consistent with earlier findings on aggressive children and subsequent victimization (e.g., Schwartz, McFadyen-Ketchum, Dodge, Pettit, & Bates, 1999).

In addition to early aggression, children's perceptions of stressful situations have been associated with their exposure to violence, with greater distress being related to higher levels of violence exposure (Raviv et al., 2001). For instance, self-reported life stress among inner-city, clinically-referred adolescents was a unique predictor of violence exposure, both in term of witnessing violence and being victimized, even after accounting for other demographic and risk variables (Weist, Acosta, & Youngstrom, 2001). Rather than stress actually leading to violence exposure, it may be that high-risk adolescents have elevated stress levels because of their histories of chronic exposure to violence. More specifically, violence exposure during childhood contributes to the development of stress responses, which likely persist in the face of chronic exposure that continued into adolescence.

An alternative explanation is that urban youth, with high levels of stress, may be hypersensitive to exposure to violence, and may overestimate their rates of exposure, whereas youth with lower stress levels may have more realistic perceptions about exposure, even underestimating their exposure due to desensitization. For instance, youth from dangerous communities may develop dysfunctional coping mechanisms, such as numbness and low empathy, when confronted with chronic violence (Garbarino, Dubrow, Kostelny, & Pardo, 1992). More research is needed to determine the impact of stress on violence exposure among at-risk children and adolescents as well as among youth who are not from inner-city neighborhoods, such as those living in rural and suburban communities.

The impact of children's demographic, family, and individual risk on exposure to violence has been well-documented; however, the precise contributions of these factors in isolation are less clear for a variety of reasons. For example, studies of children's violence exposure have typically been conducted with inner-city or minority children, making an evaluation of the impact of poverty or ethnicity impossible. Furthermore, research conducted with high-risk groups presents challenges in terms of maintaining participation over time in the face of potentially high levels of personal stress and adversity. It is difficult to conceptualize a priori definitions of what should be considered risk and resilience because of the dynamic interplay between environmental context, familial functioning, and individual characteristics. There is a need for well-designed, longitudinal studies investigating the antecedents of exposure to violence. Until then, conclusions about the effects of risk and protective factors on exposure to violence must be drawn with care.

Consequences of Exposure to Violence

Youth violence has been considered a public health epidemic due mainly to its pervasive impact on children, particularly in terms of their socioemotional adjustment (Satcher, 2001). Children's exposure to violence has been linked to later maladjustment in multiple developmental domains, including cognitive, social, and emotional functioning (e.g., Ingoldsby & Shaw, 2002; Salzinger et al., 2002). Our discussion here will focus on two particularly salient and well-documented consequences of children's exposure that best illustrate the cycle of violence: conduct problems and posttraumatic stress.

Conduct Problems.   Violence exposure has been linked to adolescent conduct problems and juvenile delinquency. For example, rates of violence perpetration among adolescents with high levels of home violence were found to be three times higher for girls and two times higher for boys than for those from low violence homes (Flannery, Singer, Williams, & Castro, 1998). Flannery et al. (2001) demonstrated that dangerously violent adolescents (e.g., those who engaged in interpersonal violence perpetration) reported higher levels of exposure to violence and victimization than did matched controls. Furthermore, maternal age was related to conduct problems among a clinical sample of adolescent males (Wakschlag et al., 2000). In turn, female adolescents with conduct disorders have an increased risk of teen motherhood (Bardone, Moffitt, Caspi, Dickson, & Silva, 1996). Relatedly, seriously delinquent adolescent males were found to be more likely than less serious delinquents to have fathered a child by age 19 (Wei, Loeber, & Stouthamer-Loeber, 2002). This cycle of violence and teen parenthood intensifies the problems within families, homes, schools, and communities, extending to involvement with the juvenile justice system. If incarceration occurs, it often serves to exacerbate the personal difficulties experienced by troubled youth (Lamberg, 2002; Steinberg, 2003).

Posttraumatic Stress.   Traumatic symptomatology is another potential consequence of violence exposure that may contribute to the quality and severity of negative adolescent outcomes and juvenile offending. Symptoms of Posttraumatic Stress Disorder fall into three categories: (a) recurring and intrusive recollections of the event (e.g., flashbacks, nightmares), (b) avoidance of activities and a numbing of responsiveness to stimuli, and (c) increased arousal such as hypervigilance and irritability (American Psychiatric Association, 1994). Children must experience symptoms in all three categories in order to warrant the diagnosis. Reactions to traumatic experiences may include emotional, behavioral, and cognitive components such as extreme terror, feelings of helplessness, incessant worry, avoidance, and sudden changes in vigilance and attention (Pynoos, Steinberg, & Aronson, 1997),

Traumatic responses have been associated with violence exposure among children and adolescents. For example, higher rates of adolescent violence exposure were found to predict not only higher levels of overall trauma, depression, anxiety, anger, dissociation, and posttraumatic stress, but also conduct problems (Singer et al., 1995). Children's relationships to victims of violence also affect traumatic sequelae, with closer personal bonds leading to higher levels of distress (Richters & Martinez, 1993). Other factors that may influence the nature of a child's response to a violent incident include whether he or she witnessed the event or was personally victimized and whether the violence was acute or chronic (Osofsky, 1997). These variables can contribute to the severity of posttraumatic symptoms that are experienced by children.

Posttraumatic stress symptoms have also been related to youth violence perpetration. For example, exposure to violence at school was related to both clinical levels of trauma symptoms and violence perpetration among children in Grades 3 through 12 (Flannery et al., 2004). Additionally, the most violent adolescents, (that is, the top 10%) in six public high schools reported higher levels of violence exposure and psychological trauma symptoms as compared to less violent and nonviolent peers (Flannery, Singer, & Wester, 2003).

In sum, both conduct problems and posttraumatic stress exemplify the cyclical nature of violence exposure and violent behaviors. It appears that in both cases, initial exposure to violence through witnessing or victimization can become the catalyst for perpetuating a pattern of violence in the lives of children and adolescents. Evidence also has suggested that problems, such as delinquent and antisocial behaviors, may precede exposure to violence among children.

The NDAPP has explored both the antecedents and consequences of youth violence exposure. Because at-risk youth, including children of adolescent mothers, are likely to have higher levels of exposure to violence (Baum, 2005; Crouch et al., 2000; Gorman-Smith et al., 2004; Lee & Goerge, 1999; Stouthamer-Loeber et al., 2002), maternal factors that may have contributed to violent events in the lives of children of teen mothers, as well as their consequences, are systematically examined in the next section. In addition, the role of risk and protective factors were explored in an attempt to tease apart some of the interrelated components of the cycle of violence.

YOUTH VIOLENCE IN THE NDAPP

Maternal Antecedents of Youth Violence

The NDAPP provided a unique opportunity to test the effects of early maternal factors such as parenting styles and histories of victimization on children's violence exposure and violent behaviors during adolescence (Weaver, Borkowski, & Whitman, under review). The purpose of this study was threefold: (a) to examine the incidence of witnessing of, and victimization from, violence as well as violent behaviors in an at-risk sample; (b) to determine if adolescent violence exposure and violent behaviors can be predicted from early maternal parenting style expectations and maternal histories of victimization; and (c) to investigate whether relationships between early maternal factors and adolescent violence exposure and violent behaviors differed depending on early childhood socioemotional adjustment.

Design.   Violence exposure during adolescence was defined as the witnessing of, and/or victimization from, violent acts such as physical threats, beatings, and shootings that occurred in the home, school, or neighborhood. Violent behaviors were assessed through adolescent reports about engaging in these acts of violence. Maternal attitudes toward how they intended to parent their children were defined by two scales: responsive and abusive parenting styles. Responsive parenting attitudes were measured using the Empathetic Awareness subscale of the Adult–Adolescent Parenting Inventory (Bavolek, 1984), and consisted of items such as "Children will quit crying faster if ignored" and "Children who are given too much love by their parents will grow up to be stubborn and spoiled." Abusive parenting styles were defined by harsh, punitive parenting attitudes such as "It's good for parents to sit a 4-year-old on the toilet for an hour after the child messed up his/her pants" and "There is nothing wrong in punishing a 9-month-old child for crying too much" (Whitman et al., 2001). Finally, maternal histories of abuse were assessed using the physical abuse and emotional abuse subscales of the Childhood Trauma Questionnaire (Bernstein & Fink, 1998). A sample physical abuse item was, "People in my family hit me so hard that it left me with bruises or marks;" an emotional abuse item was, "People in my family called me things like 'stupid', 'lazy,' or 'ugly'."

Data were collected at three time points: Maternal parenting style expectations (e.g., abusive and empathy/responsive orientations) were measured when children were 6-months old; children's socioemotional adjustment (internalizing and externalizing behaviors) was assessed at 3 years; and maternal histories of victimization from abuse during childhood and adolescence (e.g., physical and emotional), children's violence exposure, and violent behaviors during adolescence were measured during a follow-up assessment when the adolescents were between 12 and 17 years of age.

Results and Interpretations.   At the time of the follow-up assessment, 21% of the adolescents reported witnessing a knife attack or stabbing, 21% witnessed a shooting, more than 4% were attacked with a knife or stabbed, and more than 4% were shot at or shot. Violent beatings were most frequently witnessed at school (74.5%); however, lower rates of victimization from beatings occurred in neighborhoods and at school (8.9% and 10%, respectively).

Multiple regression analyses were conducted to test the effects of abusive parental expectations, responsive parental expectations, and maternal histories of physical and emotional abuse on three adolescent outcomes: (a) witnessing violence, (b) victimization from violence, and (c) violent behaviors during adolescence. All four predictor variables were simultaneously entered into each of three regression models. In the first model, maternal characteristics were not significantly related to witnessing violence during adolescence.

In the second model, the independent variables accounted for 19.8% of the variance in adolescent victimization. Higher levels of responsive parental expectations and maternal histories of physical abuse predicted higher rates of adolescent victimization. In contrast, higher levels of maternal emotional abuse during childhood predicted lower rates of adolescent victimization. In terms of violence perpetration, both responsive and abusive parental expectations predicted adolescent violent behaviors, with the total model accounting for nearly 10% of the variance.

The fact that maternal expectations about the importance of being a responsive parent were related to both higher rates of victimization and violent behaviors for their adolescents may be reflective of the at-risk nature of the NDAPP sample. For example, adolescent mothers in this sample often live in poverty and have fewer than expected social supports during the first few years of parenting (Whitman et al., 2001). In addition, their children often displayed problem behaviors during early childhood. Because their parental beliefs and expectations were measured when their children were only 6 months old, mothers may have actually delivered less warm and responsive parenting after facing the daily struggles associated with raising children than they had hoped for during the early months of parenting.

In addition, findings suggested that experiencing emotional abuse during childhood served as a catalyst for mothers to protect their children from being victimized whereas their past physical abuse seemed to create a pattern of responding to domestic conflicts with violence and childhood victimization. Furthermore, there may be differences in personal adjustment and parenting among mothers who experienced co-occurring physical and emotional abuse versus those who experienced one type of maltreatment or the other. Further research is needed to investigate the individual and combined impact of histories of physical and emotional child abuse on adult adjustment and the intergenerational transmission of victimization and violent behavior.

In order to understand the role of children's characteristics in the previously descried relationships, externalizing behaviors at age 3 were tested as a potential moderator of the significant relationships between maternal characteristics and children's victimization and violent behaviors. Figure 6.1 shows that externalizing behaviors interacted with maternal histories of physical abuse to influence adolescent victimization. Specifically, among children with lower and average levels of externalizing behaviors at age 3, higher levels of maternal physical abuse during childhood were associated with higher rates of victimization during adolescence. This relationship was not found for children with higher levels of externalizing behaviors; in contrast, among those with higher externalizing problems at age 3, rates of victimization remained elevated regardless of maternal histories of abuse. This interaction suggested that maternal histories of physical abuse were important contributors to adolescent victimization only for children at low risk during early childhood, in terms of externalizing problems such as aggression. Children with

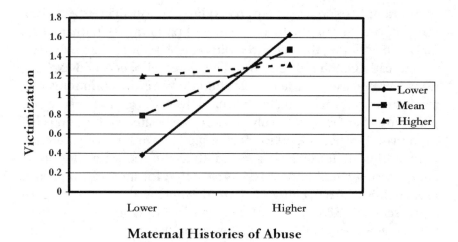

Figure 6.1. Children's externalizing behaviors at age 3 as a moderator of the relationship between maternal histories of physical abuse and adolescent victimization.

high rates of externalizing problems were already at risk for later victimization, regardless of their mothers' histories of abuse.

These findings illustrate the role of early maternal characteristics in predicting the incidence of violence exposure during childhood as well as their development of violent behaviors. For instance, maternal victimization during childhood predicted children's victimization, illustrating the intergenerational cycle of violence. Of particular importance is the fact that maternal parenting styles were measured during the third trimester of pregnancy and predict violence during adolescence, suggesting that prevention efforts should begin during infancy, based on harsh, punitive parenting styles and histories of abuse and neglect.

Violence Exposure and Later Conduct Problems

The impact of children's violence exposure prior to age 10 on the development of conduct problems during adolescence was investigated in a second, related study. To better isolate the effects of childhood violence exposure on later behavior problems, prenatal maternal and early childhood aggression were entered as covariates (Weaver, Borkowski, & Whitman, in press). The purpose of this study was threefold: (a) describe the incidences of violence exposure during childhood and delinquency during adolescence in an at-risk sample of children born to teen mothers; (b) determine if adolescent delinquency and violent behaviors can be predicted from violence exposure in childhood while controlling for prenatal maternal aggression and children's externalizing problems at age 3; and (c) investigate children's sex as well as social/emotional factors during middle childhood as potential moderators of adolescent conduct problems.

Design. Data were collected at six time points: maternal aggression was measured prenatally; children's externalizing problems at 3 years; children's social competency and depression at 10 years; and delinquency at 14 years. Children's exposure to violence prior to age 10 and violent behaviors during adolescence were measured during the follow-up assessment when the adolescents were between the ages of 14 and 17.

Results and Interpretations.   Prior to age 10, 60.2% of the adolescents reported witnessing a beating, 13.7% a stabbing, and 9.6% a shooting (Weaver et al., in press). Boys were more likely than girls to witness beatings. Based on self-reports of violence victimization, 8.2% were beaten; 3.8% were stabbed and nearly 2% were shot or shot at, with only boys reporting stabbings and shootings. There were no significant sex differences in rates of victimization.

During adolescence, about 46% of the sample participated in a serious fight and more than 30% engaged in a group fight. Males reported being significantly more likely than females to beat someone (53.8% versus 29.4%) and to hurt someone badly enough to require medical care (34.1% versus 15%). There were no reports of stabbings or shootings (Weaver et al., in press). In addition to sex differences, minority youth were more likely than white children to witness a stabbing during childhood as well as beat someone during adolescence. No other differences in ethnicity were found and poverty did not predict rates of violence exposure or violent behaviors.

It should be noted that the NDAPP sample is comprised exclusively of adolescent mothers and their children, and their socioeconomic statuses are somewhat lower than what would be expected in a national sample. Because of the higher rates of poverty across the entire sample, the nonsignificant relationships between socioeconomic status and violence exposure or perpetration must be interpreted with caution.

Regression analyses revealed that exposure to violence prior to age 10 predicted both adolescent delinquency and violent behaviors, even after controlling for prenatal maternal aggression and early children's aggression (Weaver et al., in press). In other words, adolescents who had higher levels of witnessing of, and victimization from, violence during childhood had higher rates of conduct problems in adolescence above and beyond the effects of early markers of behavioral problems and risk for maladjustment. More specifically, higher rates of witnessing violence predicted delinquency, explaining 12% of the variance. Victimization did not significantly predict delinquency, accounting for only 2% of the variance above the effect of witnessing. In contrast, both witnessing of, and victimization from, violence predicted higher levels of violent behaviors during adolescence, accounting for 16% and 4% of the variance, respectively.

Social competency at age 10 impacted the relationship between childhood exposure to violence and delinquency at age 14 differently for boys than for girls. This interaction is presented in Figure 6.2 (Weaver et al., in press). Among girls with lower social competency, rates of delinquency increased as levels of childhood violence victimization increased. In other words, low social competency seemed to function as a risk factor for delinquency among girls victimized by violence. There was no evidence of high social competency acting as a protective factor, and competency among boys did not impact the relationship between victimization and later delinquency.

Additionally, depression during middle childhood and children's sex moderated the relationship between victimization prior to age 10 and adolescent delinquency. Specifically for girls with lower levels of depressive symptomatology at age 10, rates of delinquent behaviors increased as victimization increased. In other words, lower levels of depression served as a risk factor for delinquency among girls victimized by violence; there was no evidence of higher depression magnifying this relationship. Similar to the findings with social competency, depression did not seem to impact this relationship for boys (Weaver et al., in press).

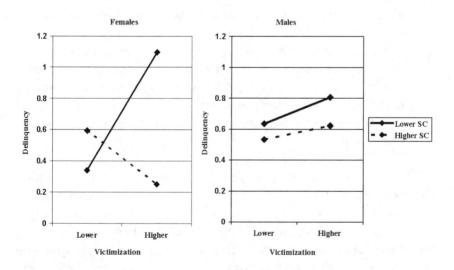

Figure 6.2.   Delinquency as a function of violence exposure, social competency (SC), and sex (Weaver et al., in press).

Summing Up: Contributions From the NDAPP

As shown in our review of the literature on the causes and consequences of youth violence as well as recent findings from the NDAPP,
evidence is emerging showing a cyclical pattern of violence that per-
petuates itself throughout families and communities, particularly
among those most entrenched in poverty and at-risk for delinquency. The important contributions to our understanding of youth
violence exposure that emerged from research on the NDAPP dataset
include the following findings:

- More than 60% of the children in the NDAPP witnessed a beating, 13% a stabbing, and 9% a shooting prior to age 10; during
  adolescence, more than 45% reported engaging in a serious
  fight, and more than 30% participated in a group fight.
- Early maternal expectations about parenting had a substantial
  influence on children's violence exposure and violent behaviors during adolescence.
- Maternal histories of physical abuse during childhood predicted higher levels of victimization among their children during adolescence; however, maternal experiences of emotional
  abuse during childhood were associated with lower rates of adolescent victimization.
- Children's early externalizing problems, such as aggression, were
  associated with increased risk for victimization during adolescence.
- Violence exposure during childhood had a significant impact
  on adolescent conduct problems, even after controlling for the
  effects of early signs of maternal and child aggression (Weaver
  et al., in press).

These findings provide unique contributions to the existing literature on youth violence. For example, several studies have shown that
parenting practices were associated with youth violence (e.g.,
Ceballo et al., 2003; Gorman-Smith et al., 2004). In our research, maternal expectations about parenting during infancy (e.g., espousing
responsive and abusive parenting styles) were associated with children's violence exposure and violence perpetration more than a decade later, suggesting that mothers at risk for engaging in poor

parenting practices can be identified and intervened with much earlier than previously thought.

Research has shown that early aggression was related to later exposure to violence (e.g., Boyd et al., 2003). By controlling for children's externalizing problems at age 3, Weaver et al. (in press) demonstrated that exposure to violence during childhood predicted adolescent conduct problems above and beyond the effect of early antisocial behaviors. Thus, violence exposure can have a detrimental effect on at-risk children's socioemotional development, regardless of the extent of early childhood behavioral problems.

Finally, research from the NDAPP has demonstrated that variables typically considered a risk, or a source of protection, should be interpreted within the context of children's lives. For example, depression, under certain conditions and for specific individuals, may serve to buffer rather than magnify children's risk for maladjustment (e.g., Weaver et al., in press). Because a positive relationship between depression and delinquency has been consistently demonstrated in the extant literature (e.g., Beyers & Loeber, 2003; Flannery et al., 2001; Ruffolo, Sarri, & Goodkind, 2004), it might be surprising that lower levels of depression were a risk factor for delinquency among girls victimized by violence, whereas depression was not a risk factor in exacerbating the relationship between childhood victimization and adolescent delinquency. This finding may be due to the fact that this sample included both boys and girls who demonstrated varying levels of risk in terms of their rates of victimization and antisocial behaviors. Nevertheless, this finding supports the notion that risk factors may not always result in negative outcomes and, in fact, may serve to protect vulnerable adolescents under specific circumstances.

FINAL THOUGHTS: DIRECTIONS FOR RESEARCH ON YOUTH VIOLENCE

In addition to evaluating its antecedents and consequences, research on youth violence should focus more on explaining how genetic and neurobiological risk factors interact with adverse environmental contexts to impede children's development. By gaining a more complete understanding of the interaction of vulnerabilities in multiple domains, we may be able to anticipate children who are at greatest risk for violence victimization as well as those likely to become violent. Research on the genetic markers of conduct problems and their interactions with environmental experiences provides a new window for understanding the causes and consequences of youth violence.

An interesting example of this approach to gene–environment interactions is the longitudinal investigation of the impact of a monoamine oxidase A (MAOA) polymorphism in the context of child maltreatment and antisocial behaviors among males (Caspi et al., 2002). The MAOA gene encodes the MAOA enzyme, which metabolizes neurotransmitters such as serotonin and dopamine. Genotypes that allowed higher activity levels of the MAOA gene protected against the development of antisocial behaviors among children who were severely abused (Caspi et al., 2002). On the other hand, low levels of expression exacerbated the effect of severe maltreatment and were associated with an increased likelihood of later conduct disorders. This study is a good example of how genetic–environment interactions help to explain why some children exhibit resilience in the face of adversity while others do not, setting the stage for more individualized and targeted intervention programs.

In addition to the biological bases of maladaptive patterns of behavior among violence-exposed youth, process variables, such as competence in peer interactions, may also be adversely affected by the early exposure to violence. For instance, in a sample of maltreated children, the relationship between maltreatment and behavioral problems was mediated by social competencies and ego resiliency (Shonk & Cicchetti, 2001). Socially competent adolescents have the ability to adapt according to contextual demands and to respond appropriately to interpersonal conflicts (Bierman & Welsh, 2000). Based on the compromising effects of exposure to violence, it is not surprising that children of adolescent mothers in the NDAPP often displayed deficits in social competency during middle childhood, which in turn exacerbated risks associated with violence exposure (Weaver et al., in press).

In summary, the cycle of violence, often seen in the lives of adolescents living in poverty, is characterized by complex patterns of interactions between exposure, risk, and protective factors. Findings from the NDAPP, in conjunction with the extant literature, have demonstrated that exposure to violence predicts violence perpetration. In turn, violent offending leads to additional violence exposure. It is important to note the important roles of risk and protective factors in ameliorating or exacerbating these relationships among at-risk children and adolescents.

Future research should bridge the gaps between the social and medical sciences, helping to integrate psychological, sociological, psychiatric, and physiological theories and methodological approaches to violence and human development. Through a careful, multidisciplinary examination of the cycle of violence, a multifaceted, holistic conception of the causes and consequences of violence may emerge. In turn, effective, precisely-targeted violence prevention programs designed to decrease risks and promote resilience among children at risk for violence exposure can be developed based on comprehensive models and implemented by skilled professionals.

REFERENCES

American Psychiatric Association. (1994). *Diagnostic and statistical manual of mental disorders* (4th ed.). Washington, DC: AUTHOR.

Appel, A. E., & Holden, G. W. (1998). The co-occurrence of spouse and physical child abuse: A review and appraisal. *Journal of Family Psychology, 12*, 578–599.

Bailey, B. N., Delaney-Black, V., Hannigan, J. H., Ager, J., Sokol, R. J., & Covington, C. Y. (2005). Somatic complaints in children and community violence exposure. *Journal of Developmental & Behavioral Pediatrics, 26*, 341–352.

Bardone, A. M., Moffitt, T. E., Caspi, A., Dickson, N., & Silva, P. A. (1996). Adult mental health and social outcomes of adolescent girls with depression and conduct disorder. *Development and Psychopathology, 8*, 811–829.

Bavolek, S. J. (1984). *Adult–Adolescent Parenting Inventory (AAPI)*. Park City, UT: Family Development Resources, Inc.

Bernstein, D. P., & Fink, L. (1998). Childhood Trauma Questionnaire: A retrospective self-report manual. San Antonio, TX: The Psychological Corporation.

Beyers, J. M., & Loeber, R. (2003). Untangling developmental relations between depressed mood and delinquency in male adolescents. *Journal of Abnormal Child Psychology, 31*, 247–266.

Bierman, K. L., & Welsh, J. A. (2000). Assessing social dysfunction: The contributions of laboratory and performance-based measures. *Journal of Clinical Child Psychology, 29*, 526–539.

Blum, J., Ireland, M., & Blum, R. W. (2003). Gender differences in juvenile violence: A report from Add Health. *Journal of Adolescent Health, 32*, 234–240.

Boyd, R. C., Cooley, M. R., Lambert, S. F., & Ialongo, N. S. (2003). First-grade child risk behaviors for community violence exposure in middle school. *Journal of Community Psychology, 31*, 297–314.

Buckner, J. C., Beardslee, W. R., & Bassuk, E. L. (2004). Exposure to violence and low-income children's mental health: Direct, moderated, and mediated relations. *American Journal of Orthopsychiatry, 74*, 413–423.

Caspi, A., McClay, J., Moffitt, T., Mill, J., Martin, J., Craig, I. W., et al. (2002). Role of genotype in the cycle of violence in maltreated children. *Science, 297*, 851–854.

Ceballo, R., Dahl, T. A., Aretakis, M. T., & Ramirez, C. (2001). Inner-city children's exposure to community violence: How much do parents really know?. *Journal of Marriage and Family, 63*, 927–940.

Ceballo, R., Ramirez, C., Hearn, K. D., & Maltese, K. L. (2003). Community violence and children's psychological well-being: Does parental monitoring matter? *Journal of Clinical Child and Adolescent Psychology, 32*, 586–592.

Cooley-Quille, M. R., Turner, S. M., & Beidel, D. C. (1995). Assessing community violence: The Children's Report of Exposure to Violence (CREV). *Journal of the American Academy of Child and Adolescent Psychiatry, 34*, 1362–1368.

Crouch, J. L., Hanson, R. F., Saunders, B. E., Kilpatrick, D. G., & Resnick, H. S. (2000). Income, race/ethnicity, and exposure to violence in youth: Results from the national survey of adolescents. *Journal of Community Psychology, 28*, 625–641.

Durant, R. H., Cadenhead, C., Pendergrast, R. A., Slavens, G., & Linder, C. W. (1994). Factors associated with the use of violence among urban black adolescents. *American Journal of Public Health, 84*, 612–617.

Edleson, J. L., & Graham-Bermann, S. A. (Eds.). (2001). *Domestic violence in the lives of children: The future of research, intervention, and social policy*. Washington, DC: American Psychological Association.

Esbensen, F., & Huizinga, D. (1991). Juvenile victimization and delinquency. *Youth and Society, 23*, 202–228.

Finnegan, R. A., Hodges, E. V., & Perry, D. G. (1998). Victimization by peers: Associations with children's reports of mother–child interaction. *Journal of Personality and Social Psychology, 75*, 1076–1086.

Flannery, D. J., Singer, M., & Wester, K. (2001). Violence exposure, psychological trauma, and suicide risk in a community sample of dangerously violent adolescents. *Journal of the American Academy of Child and Adolescent Psychiatry, 40*, 435–442.

Flannery, D. J., Singer, M., & Wester, K. (2003). Violence, coping, and mental health in a community sample of adolescents. *Violence and Victims, 18*, 403–418.

Flannery, D. J., Singer, M., Williams, L., & Castro, P. (1998). Adolescent violence exposure and victimization at home: Coping and psychological trauma symptoms. *International Review of Victimology, 6,* 63–82.

Flannery, D. J., Wester, K., & Singer, M. (2004). Impact of exposure to violence in school on child and adolescent mental health and behavior. *Journal of Community Psychology, 32,* 559–573.

Garbarino, J., Dubrow, N., Kostelny, K., & Pardo, C. (1992). *Children in danger: Coping with the consequences of community violence.* San Francisco, CA: Jossey-Bass.

Gorman-Smith, D., Henry, D. B., & Tolan, P. H. (2004). Exposure to community violence and violence perpetration: The protective effects of family functioning. *Journal of Clinical Child and Adolescent Psychology, 33,* 439–449.

Henrich, C. C., Schwab-Stone, M., Fanti, K., Jones, S. M., & Ruchkin, V. (2002). The association of community violence exposure with middle school achievement: A prospective study. *Applied Developmental Psychology, 25,* 327–348.

Ingoldsby, E. M., & Shaw, D. S. (2002). Neighborhood contextual factors and early-starting antisocial pathways. *Clinical Child and Family Psychology Review, 5,* 21–54.

Jenkins, E. J., & Bell, C. C. (1994). Adolescent violence: Can it be curbed? *Adolescent Medicine: State of the Art Reviews, 1,* 71–86.

Lamberg, L. (2002). Younger children, more girls commit acts of violence: Some get help, others receive only punishment. *Journal of the American Medical Association, 288,* 566–568.

Lauritsen, J. L., Laub, J. H., & Sampson, R. J. (1992). Conventional and delinquent activities: Implications of the prevention of violent victimization among adolescents. *Violence and Victims, 7,* 91–108.

Lee, B. J., & Goerge, R. M. (1999). Poverty, early childbearing and child maltreatment: A multinomial analysis. *Children and Youth Services Review, 21,* 755–780.

Lee, L. C., Kotch, J. B., & Cox, C. E. (2004). Child maltreatment in families experiencing domestic violence. *Violence and Victims, 19,* 573–591.

Letiecq, B. L., & Koblinsky, S. A. (2004). Parenting in violent neighborhoods: African American fathers share strategies for keeping children safe. *Journal of Family Issues, 25,* 715–734.

Leventhal, T., & Brooks-Gunn, J. (2003). Moving on up: Neighborhood effects on children and families. In R. H. Bradley & M. H. Bornstein (Eds.) *Socioeconomic status, parenting, and child development* (pp. 209–230). Mahwah, N.J.: Lawrence Erlbaum Associates.

Linares, L. O., & Cloitre, M. (2004). Intergenerational links between mothers and children with PTSD spectrum illness. In R. R. Silva (Ed.), Posttraumatic stress disorders in children and adolescents: Handbook. (pp. 177–201). New York, NY: W. W. Norton & Co.

Lynch, M., & Cicchetti, D. (1998). An ecological–transactional analysis of children and contexts: The longitudinal interplay among child maltreatment, community violence, and children's symptomatology. *Development and Psychopathology, 10*, 235–257.

McCloskey, L. A., & Lichter, E. L. (2003). The contribution of marital violence to adolescent aggression across different relationships. *Journal of Interpersonal Violence, 18*, 390–412.

Nader, K., Pynoos, R. S., Fairbanks, L., & Frederick, C. (1990). Childhood PTSD reactions one year after a sniper attack. *Journal of the American Psychiatric Association, 147*, 1526–1530.

Nation, M., Crusto, C., Wandersman, A., Kumpfer, K., Seybolt, D., Morrissey-Kane, E., et al. (2003). What works in prevention: Principles of effective prevention programs. *American Psychologist, 58*, 449–456.

Osofsky, J. D. (1997). Children and youth violence: An overview of the issues. In J. D. Osofsky (Ed.), *Children in a Violent Society.* (pp. 1–8). New York, NY: The Guilford Press.

Pearce, M. J., Jones, S. M., Schwab-Stone, M. E., & Ruchkin, V. (2003). The protective effects of religiousness and parent involvement on the development of conduct problems among youth exposed to violence. *Child Development, 74*, 1682–1696.

Pynoos, R. S., Steinberg, A. M., & Aronson, L. (1997). Traumatic experiences: The early organization of memory in school-age children and adolescents. In P. S. Appelbaum (Ed.). *Trauma and memory: Clinical and legal controversies.* (pp. 272–289). New York, NY: Oxford University Press.

Raviv, A., Erel, O., Fox, N. A., Leavitt, L. A., Raviv, A., Dar, I., et al. (2001). Individual measurement of exposure to everyday violence among elementary schoolchildren across various settings. *Journal of Community Psychology, 29*, 117–140.

Rhule, D. M., McMahon, R. J., & Speiker, S. J. (2004). Relation of adolescent mothers' history of antisocial behavior to child conduct problems and social competence. *Journal of Clinical Child and Adolescent Psychology, 33*, 524–535.

Richters, J., & Martinez, P. (1993). The NIMH Community Violence Project: I. Children as victims of and witnesses to violence. *Psychiatry, 56*, 7–12.

Ruffolo, M. C., Sarri, R., & Goodkind, S. (2004). Study of delinquent, diverted, and high-risk adolescent girls: Implications for mental health intervention. *Social Work Research, 28*, 237–245.

Salzinger, S., Feldman, R. S., Stockhammer, T, & Hood, J. (2002). An ecological framework for understanding risk for exposure to community violence and the effects of exposure on children and adolescents. *Aggression and Violent Behavior, 7*, 423–451.

Saltzman, K. M., Holden, G. W., & Holahan, C. J. (2005). The psychobiology of children exposed to marital violence. *Journal of Clinical Child and Adolescent Psychology, 34,* 129–139.

Satcher, D. (2001). *Youth violence: A report of the Surgeon General executive summary.* Washington, DC: U.S. Department of Health and Human Services.

Saunders, B. (2003). Understanding children exposed to violence: Toward an integration of overlapping fields. *Journal of Interpersonal Violence, 18,* 356–376.

Schwartz, D., McFadyen-Ketchum, S., Dodge, K. A., Pettit, G. S., & Bates, J. E. (1999). Early behavior problems as a predictor of later peer group victimization: Moderators and mediators in the pathways of social risk. *Journal of Abnormal Child Psychology, 27,* 191–201.

Shonk, S. M., & Cicchetti, D. (2001). Maltreatment, competency deficits, and risk for academic and behavioral maladjustment. *Developmental Psychology, 37,* 3–17.

Singer, M. I., Anglin, T. M., Song, L. Y., & Lunghofer, L. (1995). Adolescents' exposure to violence and associated symptoms of psychological trauma. *Journal of the American Medical Association, 273,* 477–482.

Steinberg, L. (2003). Less guilt by reason of adolescence: A developmental perspective on youth and the law. Invited Master Lecture at the Society for Research in Child Development Biennial Meeting, Tampa, FL.

Stouthamer-Loeber, M., Wei, E. H., Homish, D. L., & Loeber, R. (2002). Which family and demographic factors are related to both maltreatment and persistent serious juvenile delinquency? *Children's Services: Social Policy, Research, and Practice, 5,* 261–272.

Veenstra, R., Lindenberg, S., Oldehinkel, A. J., De Winter, A. F., Verhulst, F. C., & Ormel, J. (2005). Bullying and victimization in elementary schools: A comparison of bullies, victims, bully/victims, and uninvolved preadolescents. *Developmental Psychology, 41,* 672–682.

Wakschlag, L. S., Gordon, R. A., Lahey, B. B., Loeber, R., Green, S. M., & Leventhal, B. L. (2000). Maternal age at first birth and boys' risk for conduct disorder. *Journal of Research on Adolescence, 10,* 417–441.

Weaver, C. M., Borkowski, J. G., & Whitman, T. L. (in press). Violence breeds violence: Childhood exposure and adolescent conduct problems. *Journal of Community Psychology.*

Weaver, C. M., Borkowski, J. G., & Whitman, T. L. (under review). The effects of maternal histories of abuse and early parenting styles on adolescent violence exposure and perpetration.

Wei, E. H., Loeber, R., & Stouthamer-Loeber, M. (2002). How many of the offspring born to teenage fathers are produced by repeat serious delinquents? *Criminal Behaviour and Mental Health, 12,* 83–98.

Weist, M. D., Acosta, O. M., & Youngstrom, E. A. (2001). Predictors of violence exposure among inner-city youth. *Journal of Clinical Child Psychology, 30,* 187–198.

Whitman, T. L., Borkowski, J. G., Keogh, D. A., & Weed, K. (2001). *Interwoven lives: Adolescent mothers and their children*. Mahwah, NJ: Lawrence Erlbaum Associates.

Wikström, P. O., & Loeber, R. (2000). Do disadvantaged neighborhoods cause well-adjusted children to become adolescent delinquents? A study of male juvenile serious offending, risk and protective factors, and neighborhood context. *Criminology, 38*, 1109–1141.

Wilson, W. C., Rosenthal, B. S., & Austin, S. (2005). Exposure to community violence and upper respiratory illness in older adolescents. *Journal of Adolescent Health, 36*, 313–319.

7

Resilience and Vulnerability in the Context of Multiple Risks

Jaelyn R. Farris
Leann E. Smith
Keri Weed

The harder the conflict, the more glorious the triumph.

—Thomas Paine

Previous chapters have described specific risk factors for a range of developmental problems, such as child maltreatment and exposure to violence. Any single risk can increase a child's likelihood of maladjustment in one or more domains. However, as the number of risks to which an individual is exposed increases, or as risks accumulate over time, the odds of maladaptation increase substantially (Masten, Best, & Garmezy, 1990; Sameroff, Seifer, Baldwin, & Baldwin, 1993).

Because adolescent mothers and their children are exposed to a multitude of risks, it is essential to consider their impact on development. In this chapter, we discuss the influence of exposure to multiple risks on children's development and describe ways in which multiple risks pose a qualitatively different impact than exposure to any single risk. Next, we present three models of multiple risks—additive, multiplicative, and cumulative—and discuss the benefits and drawbacks of each model. Finally, we provide findings from five empirical studies that have investigated multiple risks and resilience using data from the Notre Dame Adolescent Parenting Project (NDAPP).

THE IMPACT OF MULTIPLE RISKS

Exposure to multiple risks almost always has a detrimental influence on development (Luthar, Cicchetti, & Becker, 2000; Masten et al., 1990; Sameroff et al., 1993; Werner, 1994). Multiple risks may be present across a variety of domains, including maternal psychopathology, authoritarian parenting, harsh or insensitive mother–child interactions, poverty, poor education, minority status, single motherhood, stressful life events, and large family size (Sameroff et al., 1993).

It has been suggested that the specific types of risk are less important in predicting children's outcomes than the number or chronicity of risks, even in high-risk samples (Sameroff & Seifer, 1995). This conclusion has been supported by research in a variety of developmental domains, such as intelligence, socioemotional adjustment, and academic achievement (Gutman, Sameroff, & Cole, 2003; Sameroff & Seifer, 1995; Sameroff et al., 1993). For example, children who were exposed to eight or nine risk factors scored more than 30 points (i.e., 2 SDs) lower in intelligence than children who were not exposed to environmental risks, with multiple risk scores accounting for one third to one half of the variance in children's intelligence (Sameroff & Seifer, 1995; Sameroff et al.,1993). These effects remained even after controlling for race, socioeconomic status, and prior measures of children's functioning. Another study utilizing the same risk index indicated that as the number of risks increased, the number of absences from school also increased and grades decreased (Gutman et al., 2003). Moreover, ratings of *clinically disturbed* were 30% more prevalent in high-risk children than in no-risk children (Sameroff & Seifer, 1995; Sameroff et al., 1993).

In general, children's short- and long-term socioemotional, cognitive, and academic development is increasingly put in jeopardy as exposure to social and environmental risks increases (Gutman et al., 2003; Sameroff et al., 1993; Sameroff, Seifer, Zax, & Barocas, 1987).

MODELS OF MULTIPLE RISKS: METHODOLOGICAL AND ANALYTICAL ISSUES

Based on the consensus that multiple risks are more influential than any single risk factor, the ensuing challenge for researchers has been to utilize appropriate models for conceptualizing and studying risks. To date, there has been substantial inconsistency in defining and assessing multiple risk models (Luthar et al., 2000). One of the primary goals of this chapter is to summarize and clarify the constructs that are utilized in the study of multiple risks. Although there are a variety of ways to define and analyze multiple risks, we focus on three approaches that have been used most frequently for research in this area: additive, multiplicative, and cumulative risk models. We provide a definition of each model, describe relevant methodological issues, explain the pros and cons of each approach, and outline questions that can be addressed with each model. Before describing differences between models, it is essential to acknowledge that all are based on the same underlying concept that multiple risks are more detrimental than any single risk factor. Distinctions between the models are primarily related to differences in methodology and type of analyses utilized.

Additive Models of Multiple Risks

Additive models, originally developed by Rutter (1979), are the most commonly used approach in studying multiple risks. This technique rests on the assumption that risks do not impact children's outcomes in isolation, but rather in combination. In other words, the number of risks present in a child's life, rather than the type of risks, is assumed to have the most important influence on development. Additive models postulate that each risk factor adds to the prediction of resilience or vulnerability, such that the predictive power of the overall model is increased when all of the individual factors are added together (Hooper, Burchinal, Roberts, Zeisel, & Neebe, 1998). These models are based on the assumptions that: (a) exposure to several risks at any given time is more detrimental than exposure to a lesser number of risks, and (b) the number of risk factors to which an individual is exposed is more influential than the types of risk.

An additive index is created by first dichotomizing or categorizing each predictor variable on the basis of whether the risk was present or absent. Dichotomization can be accomplished by conceptual classification (e.g., one-parent versus two-parent household), by normative or standardized assignment (e.g., scores of *average* versus *clinical* on measures of psychological well-being), or by utilizing a statistical cutoff (e.g., lowest 25% of the sample). Categorization can be accomplished using a similar approach, by dividing each factor into more than two classifications (e.g., scores of *absent*, *moderate*, and *severe* on measures of psychopathology). In either case, an additive risk index is created by summing the categorized variables. Higher scores typically indicate exposure to a greater number or severity of risk factors.

Additive risk indexes have three important limitations: (a) If the measures do not have standardized cutoff values, it becomes difficult to say with certainty whether a given risk factor was present or absent; (b) there is a loss of variability associated with dichotomizing or categorizing variables, which in turn may result in fewer significant findings than may have been evident if continuous variables had been used; and (c) these models do not provide process-related information as to how or why multiple risks influence development or which risks were more influential than others (MacCallum, Zhang, Preacher, & Rucker, 2002). Despite these drawbacks, additive models can be useful in studies with sample sizes that are not large enough to permit more sophisticated analytic approaches (cf. chap. 9).

The studies cited earlier in this chapter conducted by Sameroff and his colleagues (Sameroff et al., 1993; Sameroff et al., 1987) provide good examples of the use of additive risk models. In these projects, an additive index was created from 10 social and family risk factors that were dichotomized as present or absent in the children's lives. Children's intellectual, socioemotional, and academic outcomes were found to be compromised as the number of risk factors increased (Sameroff et al., 1993; Sameroff et al., 1987).

A more recent longitudinal study provides an alternative example of the use of an additive risk model over time (Appleyard, Egeland, van Dulmen, & Sroufe, 2005). In this study, risk status was assessed from birth until the sixth grade. Risk factors included child maltreatment, inter-parental violence, and low socioeconomic status among other variables. Results indicated that externalizing problems during adolescence (i.e., aggression) were associated with exposure to a higher number of childhood risks. The study also examined the connections between risks and developmental timing: Risks during early childhood were more predictive of adolescent behavior problems than risks during middle childhood (Appleyard et al., 2005).

Multiplicative Models of Multiple Risks

Multiplicative models assume that combinations of risk factors contribute to development in nonadditive, or disproportionate, ways (Hooper et al., 1998). Much like additive models, multiplicative models assume that each additional risk factor adds to the prediction of outcomes. In these models, the product of two or more risks is used to predict development. A benefit of multiplicative models is that they allow for the use of continuous rather than dichotomized or categorized variables, resulting in greater variability and, in turn, a greater likelihood of detecting significant results. In addition, interactions revealed by these models can be used to address process-related questions, such as identifying which individuals are most affected by multiple risks or determining when these effects are most likely to occur. The primary drawback of multiplicative models is that the interpretation of results becomes complicated as more variables are added to the models, especially when the interactions include three or more variables.

The Gutman et al. (2003) study described earlier—which examined interactions between maternal and child risk factors as predictors of children's grade point averages—provides a good example of the use of a multiplicative risk model. Interactive analyses revealed that child factors, such as preschool IQ and mental health, had significant effects only for low-risk individuals (Gutman et al., 2003). Higher IQs and better mental health were associated with higher grade point trajectories for low-risk, but not high-risk, children. This multiplicative, or interactive, risk model addressed process-related questions regarding which individuals were most, and which were least, likely to be affected by exposure to multiple risks.

Cumulative Models of Multiple Risks

Cumulative risk models represent an alternative to additive and multiplicative models in predicting developmental outcomes. These models can be conceptualized in two ways: (a) as *simultaneous* risk models that allow for the consideration of several different risk factors in a nonadditive and nonmultiplicative fashion, or (b) as *chronic* risk models that consider the accumulation of a single risk factor over time. Either way, cumulative risk models allow for the inclusion of continuous variables that would not fit neatly into an additive model, with the potential to include a greater number of factors than would be clearly interpretable in a multiplicative model.

Simultaneous Cumulative Risk Models.   Simultaneous cumulative risk models incorporate multiple risk factors in a nonadditive and nonmultiplicative manner. These models provide suggestions about which risk factors carry the most weight in the prediction of important outcomes. From an analytic perspective, this type of cumulative risk analysis can be accomplished in several ways. For example, multiple continuous variables can be entered into the predictive portion of a regression equation or used to form a latent risk construct within a structural equation model (cf. chap. 9).

There are several advantages associated with this conceptualization of simultaneous cumulative risk. The primary advantage is that a large number of risks can be included in a single model without the statistical demands of more complex multiple regression models (Evans, 2003). Moreover, these types of cumulative risk models do not forfeit degrees of freedom when adding factors to the model (Ackerman, Schoff, Levinson, Youngstrom, & Izard, 1999).

A study of the influence of multiple risk factors on children's functioning in a sample of low-income Latino families provides a good illustration of the use of a simultaneous cumulative risk model (Dumka, Roosa, & Jackson, 1997). Results from analyses using structural equation modeling suggested that inconsistent parenting mediated the relationship between the latent multiple risk construct and children's conduct disorders; in this model, all risks were included simultaneously as a latent risk construct. It was the number of risk variables, not the type of variable, that was important in predicting the developmental outcome. When approached in this way, simultaneous cumulative risk models address the same sorts of questions addressed by additive models. However, cumulative models do not suffer the drawbacks of the additive models that result from dichotomizing predictor variables.

Chronic Cumulative Risk Models.   Chronic cumulative risk models approach the study of multiple risks from a longitudinal perspective. Unlike the models discussed previously, this dynamic model considers the accumulation of one or more risk factors over time, instead of the static impact of multiple risk factors at a single point in time. Variables in this model may be continuous or discrete; the important point is to consider whether the risks are experienced in an acute or chronic manner.

There are several unique advantages to chronic cumulative risk models. First, the degree of risk can be evaluated over time and, in turn, the trajectories of risks can be related to other constructs, such as children's academic achievement or socioemotional functioning. Second, these models allow for the investigation of how acute versus chronic exposure to one or more risks may be related to changes in resilience or vulnerability over time. These analytic opportunities are not possible with the other multiple risk models described previously. Although the chronic cumulative risk model requires a longitudinal design, findings from this model often provide answers to questions that cannot be addressed with other models.

A recent study of the stability of family interactions from ages 6 to 18 provides an example of the use of a cumulative risk model (Loeber, Drinkwater, Yin, Anderson, Schmidt, & Crawford, 2000). In this study, various indicators of risk were used to predict longitudinal changes in multiple family-interaction attributes, such as physical punishment, communication, supervision, positive parenting, and the quality of parent–child relationships. Growth curve modeling analyses provided information about dynamic changes in risks and outcomes over time (see chap. 9 for a detailed description of this technique). Findings demonstrated the relative stability of most family-interaction measures, suggested that some of these measures change as children age, and indicated that family-interaction patterns differed among various parental risk groups (the overall risk construct was defined in terms of physical punishment, poor supervision, poor communication between child and primary caregiver, low positive parenting, and bad relationship between the child and the primary caregiver).

Longitudinal models of cumulative risk are particularly useful in that they evaluate dynamic changes in risk status over time, as well as examine the impact of early versus later risk and chronic versus acute risk. Although longitudinal designs may be taxing in terms of the time and resources required, investigating cumulative risk from a longitudinal framework is advantageous for researchers interested in testing complex hypotheses about changes in risks and children's development over a long time frame.

Choosing a Multiple Risks Model

Each model described above has benefits and limitations when used to address questions related to multiple risks. The final decision about which model to employ in any given study should be guided by the researcher's hypotheses and theoretical conceptualization. For example, researchers need to consider whether their study will be longitudinal or cross-sectional, the number of risk factors that are of interest, the sample size and its implications for the statistical power of different analytic approaches, and whether the focus is on the effects of static exposure to a variety of factors or the dynamic effects of chronic exposure to one or more risks. In addition, it is important to note that certain models provide not only different, but also more, information than other models. Ultimately, there is no "right" or "wrong" approach to studying multiple risks, but researchers should be careful to provide clear definitions and a theoretically-driven rationale for the technique that they utilize.

Given the multitude of risk factors that are typically associated with adolescent parenting, the NDAPP provides ideal opportunities for prospective longitudinal analyses of resilience and vulnerability. In the next section, we present findings from five studies of multiple risks in the NDAPP, followed by a description of how the major findings contribute to the literature on resilience and vulnerability in the face of multiple risks.

MULTIPLE RISKS IN THE NDAPP

Although adolescent parents are a heterogeneous group, they and their children are more likely to encounter adversities than adult parents and their children (Whitman, Borkowski, Keogh, & Weed, 2001), including daily stresses and challenges that arise from multiple sources, such as poor maternal resources, family instability, unemployment, and neighborhood violence. Teenage mothers tend to have lower levels of intelligence and educational attainment and higher levels of depression than adult mothers (Coll, Hoffman, & Oh, 1987; Passino et al., 1993; Sommer et al., 1993); equally important, they usually are less cognitively prepared to parent (Sommer et al., 1993; Whitman et al., 2001). The limited skills and abilities of many adolescent mothers pose serious risks for children's development, given that maternal resources have been shown to account for a substantial proportion of variance in the development of children of adolescent mothers (Jaffee, Caspi, Moffitt, Belsky, & Silva, 2001).

In addition to prenatal risks, children born to adolescent mothers are often exposed to turbulence and instability during childhood and adolescence. Frequent moves and school changes are typical of the instability in these familes (Wood, Halfon, Scarlata, Newacheck, & Nessim, 1993). Moreover, aspects of their social environment, particularly conditions associated with poverty such as crime and violence, play important roles as specific risk factors associated with adolescent parenting (Jaffee et al., 2001). For instance, children raised in poverty are at increased risk for adverse health outcomes, community violence, socioemotional problems, and cognitive and educational impairments (Duncan & Brooks-Gunn, 2000). It has been well-documented that adolescent mothers and their children often accumulate an array of risks across their lifespans; therefore, assessments of multiple risks are especially relevant for understanding development.

In the following sections, the predictive potential capabilities of five risk models from the NDAPP are described. First, we present findings from two studies that examined the impact of prenatal maternal risks on children's academic achievement and classroom behaviors at age 10. These studies both utilized additive risk indexes; the first used an index comprised of 3 risk factors, whereas the second index was based on a composite of 10 risk factors. Results are compared in terms of the predictive power of smaller versus larger additive risk indexes, especially when employed with the high risk NDAPP sample. Next, findings from studies that have utilized additive and cumulative models of environmental instability are provided as examples of the influence of multiple postnatal risks on children's development. Both models demonstrated that pervasive instability had a detrimental impact on children's academic and behavioral functioning. Finally, we present the results of a study that investigated the stability of children's resilience over time, in the face of multiple risks. This study demonstrated the value of an additive risk index in understanding resilience as a developmental outcome.

Multiple Prenatal Risks: A Contrast of Two Additive Models

Two studies assessed the impact of prenatal risks on children's academic achievement and behaviors at school at age 10. The first used an additive index comprised of three prenatal risk factors that represented the overall construct of cognitive readiness to parent. The second index tested a composite of 10 prenatal risk factors, including cognitive readiness to parent as well as prenatal measures of maternal intelligence, socioemotional adjustment, age, and socioeconomic status (SES). Results are discussed in terms of the utility of smaller versus larger additive risk indexes in high risk samples of children.

Design.   Data for both projects (Farris, Borkowski, & Weed, 2003; Farris, Borkowski, Whitman, & Lefever, 2006) were drawn from the prenatal and 10-year assessments in the NDAPP. Cognitive readiness to parent was assessed prenatally, based on three maternal self-report measures: the Knowledge of Child Development scale, the Parenting Style Expectations scale, and the Parenting Attitudes Questionnaire (Whitman et al., 2001). Maternal intelligence was assessed prenatally using the Vocabulary and Block Design subtests of the Wechsler Intelligence Scale for Children–Revised or the Wechsler Adult Intelligence Scale–Revised (Wechsler, 1974; Wechsler, 1981). Internalizing, externalizing, and social competence were evaluated with the Youth Self Report (Achenbach, 1991). Socioeconomic status was determined during the prenatal interview based on reports of the educational and occupational status of the adults with whom the mothers resided, since most the teens were not self-supporting during pregnancy (Whitman et al., 2001).

Four outcome measures were administered to assess children's school-related achievement and socioemotional adjustment at age 10. Reading and math achievement were assessed using the Peabody Individual Achievement Tests–Revised (Markwardt, 1989). Socioemotional adjustment at school was assessed through teachers' reports of children's internalizing and externalizing behaviors using the Teacher's Report Form (Achenbach, 1991).

Results and Implications: 3-Item Additive Index. Farris et al. (2006) assessed the impact of an additive risk index on children's academic achievement and behavioral adjustment in the classroom at 10 years of age. The additive index, comprised of the three prenatal cognitive readiness measures described above, was created by transforming raw scores from each of the three variables to standardized z scores, then averaging the three z scores to provide a single risk index score for each participant. This procedure falls under the broad conceptualization of an additive risk index because individual scores were added together to create a single risk index. It was hypothesized that children with mothers who had low prenatal levels of cognitive readiness would be more likely to display academic and behavioral impairments at school at age 10.

The 3-item additive index predicted children's reading achievement ($\beta = -.38, p < .001, R^2 = .14$), math achievement ($\beta = -.27, p < .01, R^2 = .07$), and externalizing problems at school ($\beta = .21, p < .05, R^2 = .05$) at age 10 (Farris et al., 2006). All results were in the hypothesized direction, such that children whose mothers had lower levels of prenatal cognitive readiness to parent had lower levels of reading and math achievement and higher levels of externalizing problems. The 3-item index accounted for 5% to 14% of variance in math and reading achievement and externalizing problems at school.

Results and Implications: 10-Item Additive Index. Given that maternal characteristics were shown to be important predictors of children's outcomes in families headed by adolescent mothers (Jaffee et al., 2001), Farris et al. (2003) created an additive index from 10 prenatal maternal characteristics to assess whether additional risks would add to the prediction of developmental outcomes. The 10-item index was comprised of the three measures of cognitive readiness to parent described above as well as two measures of intelligence (vocabulary and block IQ), three measures of socioemotional functioning (internalizing and externalizing problems, together with social competence), and two demographic characteristics (SES and age at time of childbirth).

Predictor variables were categorized such that each participant was assigned a score of 0, 1, or 2 for each of the 10 risk factors, with higher scores representing greater degrees of risk. Risk scores were set in comparison to standardized population norms or clinical cutoffs whenever available; for the remaining items, risk scores were set in comparison with scores obtained from a pregnant adult comparison sample in the NDAPP (Whitman et al., 2001). The 10 risk scores were summed to create an overall additive risk index for each participant. Scores on the risk index ranged from 1 through 15, with a mean of 8.97 ($SD = 3.16$).

The 10-item risk index significantly predicted children's math achievement ($\beta = -.24, p < .05, R^2 = .06$), internalization ($\beta = .16, p < .05, R^2 = .03$), and externalization ($\beta = .27, p < .05, R^2 = .07$). All significant predictions were in the hypothesized direction, such that children exposed to more severe degrees of prenatal risk performed significantly lower than other children on math achievement and higher on teachers' reports of aggression and depression. Although the predictions were statistically significant and similar to the outcomes predicted by the 3-item index, it should be noted that the 10-item risk index explained only 3% to 7% of the variance in the same outcome variables, whereas the 3-item index accounted for up to 14% of the variance.

Comparison of Prenatal Additive Risk Indexes. These two studies make a contribution to our understanding of additive risk; namely, that larger indexes are not necessarily better at predicting outcomes than indexes comprised of only a few variables. This point was illustrated by the facts that both indexes showed similar predictive power, with the smaller index accounting for a greater proportion of variance in major outcomes than the larger index.

It is possible that introducing additional variables into the additive risk index may have inadvertently created "noise" and, in turn, distorted the predictive power of the index. This effect may be particularly true in high-risk samples, such as the NDAPP, where nearly all participants were exposed to multiple risks. For instance, families with economic disadvantages are also likely to experience psychosocial problems and lower levels of intelligence and educational attainment (National Institute of Child Health and Human Development [NICHD] Early Child Care Research Network, 2005). In high-risk samples it may be irrelevant—both theoretically and analytically—to include risks that are encountered by nearly all participants. Many teen mothers score low on intelligence tests, have socioemotional problems, and live in poverty at the time of childbirth. The restricted variance in these domains may explain, in part, why additional risks in the 10-item index did not substantially increase predictive ability as compared to the 3-item index (Farris et al., 2003; Farris et al., 2006). In contrast to the broader literature on additive risk indexes (Gutman et al., 2003; Sameroff et al., 1993; Sameroff, Seifer, Zax, & Barocas, 1987), our findings suggest that it is important to consider the nature of the multiple risks rather than just the number of risks to which individuals have been exposed.

Although our use of additive models of multiple risks considered the impact of multiple prenatal risk factors, some of the risks may actually have endured long past childbirth. In order to understand the impact of the exposure to multiple risks after birth, the next section reviews findings from studies of additive and cumulative risk indexes composed of multiple postnatal risk factors in the NDAPP dataset.

Postnatal Risks: The Use of Additive and Cumulative Models

In addition to the early risks to which the children of teen mothers are often exposed, their lives frequently continue to be marked by turbulence and instability throughout childhood and adolescence. Instability in the lives of families with adolescent mothers may be manifested in several forms: frequent residential moves, multiple school changes, and/or numerous maternal romantic partners. Given the association between mobility and less-than-optimal developmental outcomes (Humke & Schaefer, 1995), and the fact that low-income adolescent mothers are relatively mobile (Wood et al., 1993), children in "unstable" families are particularly at risk for behavior problems. Using data from the NDAPP, two risk indexes were formed in order to assess the influence of postnatal environmental instabilities on the development of children of adolescent mothers (Smith, 2004).

Design: Additive Model.   Information on environmental instability was collected using the Life History Interview. Mothers reported the number of residential moves, the number of school changes, and the number of residential romantic partners between the time the child was born and his or her 10th birthday (Smith, 2004). Each variable (residential, school, and relationships) was rated with an instability score ranging from 0 to 2, indicating low, medium, and high instability. An additive index was then created by summing the instability ratings for each factor; the mean was 2.5, with a standard deviation of 1.5. Children's outcome measures at 10 years of age included reading achievement, assessed with the Peabody Individual Achievement Test–Revised, and classroom behaviors, assessed with the Conner's Teacher Rating Scales.

Results and Implications: Additive Model.   The environmental instability index predicted reading scores and teacher-reported conduct problems, with greater instability associated with more problematic outcomes. These findings point to the predictive utility of an additive index comprised of postnatal characteristics associated with family instability. Similar to the prenatal risk index used by Farris et al. (2006), the index of environmental instability was comprised of only three risk factors and yet predicted a significant proportion of the variance in both reading scores and problematic classroom behaviors, lending further support to the notion that in a high risk sample such as the NDAPP, an index based on a few, carefully selected factors may have the same explanatory power as a model with numerous variables.

Design: Cumulative Model.   Data from the NDAPP were also used to assess the impact of multiple risks using a cumulative risk index (Smith, 2004). In this study, the influence of chronic risks on children's development was investigated by comparing reading scores and teacher-reported classroom behaviors with different levels of cumulative instability. As in the study utilizing an additive risk model (Smith, 2004), three domains of environmental instability were assessed separately: residential, school, and romantic partner instability. The level of cumulative instability (low, medium, or high) within each domain was based on the number of residential (range 1 to 8), school (range 1 to 6), and maternal romantic partner changes (range 0 to 3) each child experienced from birth to 10 years of age. Cutoff points for the low, medium, and high categories were determined based on the distribution of scores within each factor. For instance, residential changes had a range of 1 to 8, a mean of 2.3 and a standard deviation of 1.7. Children with 1 to 3 moves were placed in the low instability category, children with 4 to 5 moves in the medium category, and children with 6 or more moves in the high category. Similar classifications were made for variables reflecting school and romantic partner instability.

Results and Implications: Cumulative Model.   Analyses of variance were conducted for each domain to examine how repeated exposure to environmental instability over time might impact children's developmental outcomes. The effect of instability (low, medium, and high) on reading scores and classroom behaviors at 10 was examined for each domain (residential, school, and maternal relationship). Children whose mothers had high relationship instability had significantly lower reading scores than children with medium or low relationship instability. Similarly, high levels of relationship and residential instability were both associated with teacher-reported conduct problems and children's hyperactive behaviors. Thus, children with an accumulation of risks over time (i.e., multiple maternal partner changes) displayed more behavior problems and poorer reading skills than children with fewer environmental changes.

These findings demonstrated how adolescent mothers and their children continued to experience numerous risks over the first 10 years of life. In the NDAPP, many children were exposed to postnatal environmental instability in multiple domains, in addition to chronic instability in just one domain; both forms of multiple risks were associated with poorer child outcomes at age 10. These data further underscore the importance of examining risks across domains and over time, particularly for groups with multiple, chronic risks, such as families with adolescent mothers.

Resilience Among Children Exposed to Multiple Risks

The studies described to this point have illustrated the detrimental impact of multiple prenatal and postnatal risks on the development of children born to adolescent mothers. Given that the probability of adverse developmental outcomes increases substantially as the duration and degree of risk accumulates (Dubow & Luster, 1990; Masten et al., 1990; Sameroff, 1994; Werner, 1994), the multiple risks to which children born to teen mothers were exposed would seem to imply an increased likelihood of adverse developmental outcomes. However, many children of adolescent mothers display resilience despite exposure to multiple risks (Furstenberg, Brooks-Gunn, & Morgan, 1987; Whitman et al., 2001).

Design. Although most children of adolescent mothers face greater adversity than children born to adult mothers, their actual caregiving environments vary considerably. Data from the NDAPP were used to create an index of the quality of maternal functioning to quantify the degree of adversity within caregiving environments (Whitman et al., 2001). The index was based on an additive model, with the dichotomization of seven variables based on both psychological functioning (self-esteem, depression, and anxiety) and achievement of socially valued outcomes (high school graduation, stable work history, current educational status, and current job status).

Scores on the additive index were categorized in order to provide criterion-referenced classifications of three levels of adversity. A highly adverse environment had multiple maternal risk factors present, including evidence of both psychological maladjustment and educational or occupational problems. In contrast, a low adversity environment was characterized by at least some evidence of psychological well-being combined with either educational or occupational success. Marginal environments were characterized by an approximately equivalent number of strengths and weaknesses in adjustment and social outcomes. After categorizing the adversity present in children's caregiving environments as high, marginal, or low, children's resilience in the face of risk was examined. Classifications of resilience were based on children's success in meeting age-appropriate standards for adaptive behavior, behavior problems, and intelligence (Whitman et al., 2001).

Results and Implications.   At 5 years of age, 31% of children from the NDAPP were considered resilient. Results indicated that only 22% from high adversity caregiving environments were resilient, whereas 54% from environments with low caregiving adversity were classified as resilient. A variety of constitutional and caregiving factors influenced the initial classification of children as resilient or vulnerable. In particular, partner support and caregiving support by grandmothers appeared to promote resilience by compensating for maternal adversity.

Next, the stability of resilience of children born in the NDAPP was examined by using the same additive risk index described above (Weed, Keogh, & Borkowski, 2006). Approximately 68% of the children retained their status as resilient or vulnerable when reassessed at age 8. Greater stability was observed for children in contexts characterized by either high or low levels of maternal adversity, in contrast to moderate adversity. Competence at age 8 was dependent on children's intelligence scores at age 5 as well as changes in maternal self-esteem and anxiety between the children's ages of 5 and 8.

Recent analyses of NDAPP data suggested that approximately 29% of the total sample continued to be considered resilient at age 14, based on competencies in intellectual, academic, behavioral, and social domains. Since resilience at 8 was difficult to achieve within caregiving environments characterized by high adversity, it was expected that long-term exposure to maternal adversity would further disrupt the process of resilience as children progressed into adolescence. Of 19 adolescents who were raised in highly adverse environments at ages 5 and 8, only 16% were considered resilient at age 14. Resilient teens were of particular interest as they were meeting age-appropriate standards in several important domains of life, despite extensive exposure to multiple environmental risks. In contrast, 28% of the adolescents raised in environments with low adversity at both time periods were found to be resilient at age 14. Follow-up analyses indicated that children's intelligence and improvements in maternal self-esteem were important predictors of children's stable resilience.

Summing Up: Contributions From the NDAPP Studies

The literature on multiple risks has established the utility of risk indexes comprised of variables that occur close in time to the predicted outcomes (cf. Sameroff et al., 1987). Research from the NDAPP has extended these findings by providing evidence that the accumulation of multiple risk factors impacted children's development over the course of a decade (Farris et al., 2003; Farris et al., 2006; Smith, 2004; Weed et al., 2006). The specific contributions of the NDAPP to our understanding of multiple risks include the following:

- At ages 5 and 14, respectively, 31% and 29% of the children were classified as resilient, with the majority of resilient children residing in caregiving environments marked by low levels of adversity. Resilient teens at 14 had higher levels of intelligence at age 5 and mothers who showed increases in self-esteem during children's early elementary school years.
- The impact of early exposure to risks does not fade with time. For instance, prenatal cognitive readiness to parent accounted for up to 14% of the variance in children's academic achievement and classroom behaviors at school at age 10.

- The lasting impact of early risks may be especially pronounced in high-risk samples, where early risks continue to accumulate and new risks are encountered throughout childhood and adolescence. For example, mothers in the NDAPP continued to endorse harsh parenting strategies, maintained unrealistic expectations of their children, and experienced residential and romantic instability during the first 10 years of their children's lives, illustrating the cumulative nature of risk over time.
- It may be difficult, at times, to detect statistically significant effects in high-risk samples, due to the restricted range of variance when nearly all participants are exposed to multiple risks. Use of sophisticated analytic techniques can provide solutions to this problem (cf. chap. 9).

Although findings from the NDAPP have demonstrated that prenatal risks impact children's development through late childhood and early adolescence, it is important to realize that risks for children of adolescent mothers are not limited to the prenatal period, but rather continue to be encountered throughout adolescence and adulthood. Specifically, many children in the NDAPP experienced environmental instability in multiple domains such as school mobility, residential changes, and multiple father figures. These kinds of instability across domains and over time were associated with negative child outcomes (Smith, 2004). In general, developmental delays were most likely for children born into a risky situation and then exposed to additional risks during late childhood and adolescence (Smith, 2004; Weed et al., 2006).

Findings from the NDAPP have shown that risk indexes do not always need to contain a large number of factors in order to reliably assess the impact of multiple risks (Farris et al., 2003; Farris et al., 2006). This conclusion contrasts with results from Sameroff et al. (1987) in which no single item was able to predict as much variability as an overall risk index. These differences are likely due to the types of samples that were used in the two projects. More specifically, Sameroff et al. (1987) utilized a more heterogeneous sample than the NDAPP, consisting of mothers and children from diverse age, SES, education, and family size groups. In short, sample variability is likely a major source of differences in the predictive power of single risk factors versus a risk index. The appropriate number of variables to include in a risk index appears to be somewhat dependent on the overall level of risk within the particular sample under study.

Findings from the NDAPP also illustrated that various types of multiple risk models can be used in combination to provide a more in-depth understanding of resilience and vulnerability (Weed et al., 2006). It is possible to begin a study with one model of multiple risks and then to conduct follow-up analyses using alternative models. This approach can provide in-depth, process-oriented answers to questions regarding the impact of multiple risks on children's development. Regardless of whether an additive, multiplicative, or cumulative model is used, multiple risk indexes can be useful in predicting short- and long-term developmental outcomes, in gauging the sample's overall level of risk, and in predicting changes in resilience or vulnerability over time.

FINAL THOUGHTS: FUTURE DIRECTIONS FOR RESEARCH ON MULTIPLE RISKS

The NDAPP findings presented in this chapter confirm the notion that children born to adolescent mothers are exposed to a multitude of risk factors, both prior to and following their births (Farris et al., 2003; Farris et al., 2006; Smith, 2004; Weed et al., 2006). Many children were unable to overcome these risks, resulting in impairments in school achievement, socioemotional adjustment, and/or behavior during childhood and early adolescence. It remains unclear, however, exactly why some children became more vulnerable to risks than others. Chapter 8 addresses the role of protective factors—including father presence, religiosity, and community support groups—in the lives of at-risk children.

Although there is general consensus that positive adaptation becomes less likely as the number of risks increases (Luthar et al., 2000; Masten et al., 1990; Werner, 1994), the processes underlying this relationship remain unclear. It has been suggested that the timing and/or duration of risks play important roles in determining children's outcomes. From this perspective, different risk factors may be more salient at certain points in children's development. For instance, exposure to inter-parental violence, family disruption, and life stress during early childhood predicted adolescent's internalizing and externalizing problems, but the same factors in middle childhood were not predictive of later development (Appleyard et al., 2005). On the other hand, peer relationships, neighborhood ecology, and academic achievement were salient risk factors during middle, but not early, childhood (Greenberg, Speltz, DeKlyen, & Jones, 2001).

Long-term impairments in development are more likely when risks persist over time. For example, children raised in chronic poverty generally have lower levels of language and preschool readiness skills and higher levels of internalizing and externalizing problems than children raised in homes marked by either no poverty or transient periods of poverty (NICHD Early Child Care Research Network, 2005). Future research should address process-related questions aimed at understanding issues such as the timing and duration of risks to which children are exposed.

Studies of risk and resilience need to make greater use of longitudinal designs in order to appropriately address questions regarding the timing and duration of risks. In addition, it is important to measure multiple risk factors on repeated occasions. This approach allows for investigations of chronic risks in a cumulative fashion. It is important to note that although most studies of multiple risks have used the term *cumulative risk*, the majority of risk indexes in the literature were created with an additive approach. However, it is not possible to understand fully the processes underlying multiple risks if risk factors are assessed only in an additive or multiplicative manner. Increases, decreases, or chronicity of risks over time can have important implications for children's development (Appleyard et al., 2005). Likewise, the developmental timing of exposure to the risks (e.g., exposure in childhood versus adolescence) may lead to variations in the prediction of developmental outcomes (Schulenberg, Sameroff, & Cicchetti, 2004). The use of more sophisticated designs enable the formulation and use of more complex cumulative risk models that address process-related questions regarding exposure to multiple risks over time. Analytic techniques appropriate for these models are described in chapter 9.

Evidence of resilience in the face of multiple risks suggests that it is possible for some children and adolescents to overcome severe degrees of risk exposure. In order to gain a more comprehensive understanding of which children are resilient and why, future research should focus not only on risks themselves, but also on the protective factors that mediate or moderate the potential negative impact of risks on children's development. The next chapter provides a detailed description of ways in which protective factors play important roles in facilitating children's successful adaptation despite risk-filled early environments. We contend that a greater understanding of multiple risk and protective factors will provide new and exciting opportunities for prevention research with high-risk children and their families.

REFERENCES

Achenbach, T. M. (1991). Integrative guide for the 1991 CBCL/4–18,YSR, and TRF profiles. Burlington, VT: University of Vermont, Department of Psychiatry.

Ackerman, B. P., Schloff, K., Levinson, K., Youngstrom, E., & Izard, C. E. (1999). The relations between cluster indices of risk and promotion and the problem behaviors of 6- and 7-year-old children from economically disadvantaged families. *Developmental Psychology, 35,* 1355–1366.

Appleyard, K., Egeland, B., van Dulmen, M. H. M., & Sroufe, L. A. (2005). When more is not better: The role of cumulative risk in child behavior outcomes. *Journal of Child Psychology and Psychiatry, 46,* 235–245.

Coll, C. G., Hoffman, J., & Oh, W. (1987). The social ecology and early parenting of Caucasian adolescent mothers. *Child Development, 58,* 955–963.

Dubow, E. F., & Luster, T. (1990). Adjustment of children born to teenage mothers: The contribution of risk and protective factors. *Journal of Marriage and the Family, 52,* 393–404.

Dumka, L. E., Roosa, M. W., & Jackson, K. M. (1997). Risk, conflict, mothers' parenting, and children's adjustment in low-income Mexican immigrant and Mexican American families. *Journal of Marriage and Family, 59,* 309–323.

Duncan, G. J., & Brooks-Gunn, J. (2000). Family poverty, welfare reform, and child development. *Child Development, 71,* 188–196.

Evans, G. W. (2003). A multimethodological analysis of cumulative risk and allostatic load among rural children. *Developmental Psychology, 39,* 924–933.

Farris, J. R., Borkowski, J. G., & Weed, K. (2003, April). *Risk, protection, and resilience in children of adolescent mothers.* Poster session presented at the biennial meeting of the Society for Research in Child Development, Tampa, FL.

Farris, J. R., Borkowski, J. G., Whitman, T. L., & Lefever, J. E. B. (2006). *Academic achievement and school behaviors of at-risk youth: Influences of cognitive readiness and self esteem.* Manuscript in preparation.

Furstenberg, F. F., Jr., Brooks-Gunn, J., & Morgan, S. P. (1987). *Adolescent mothers in later life.* New York: Cambridge University Press.

Greenberg, M. T., Speltz, M. L., DeKlyen, M., & Jones, K. (2001). Correlates of clinic referral for early conduct problems: Variable- and person-oriented approaches. *Development and Psychopathology, 13,* 255–276.

Gutman, L. M., Sameroff, A. J., & Cole, R. (2003). Academic growth curve trajectories from 1st grade to 12th grade: Effects of multiple social risk factors and preschool child factors. *Developmental Psychology, 39,* 777–790.

Hooper, S. R., Burchinal, M. R., Roberts, J. E., Zeisel, S., & Neebe, E. (1998). Social and family risk factors for infant development at one year: An application of the cumulative risk model. *Journal of Applied Developmental Psychology, 19,* 85–96.

Humke, C., & Schaefer, C. (1995). Relocation: A review of the effects of residential mobility on children and adolescents. *Psychology, A Journal of Human Behavior, 32,* 16–24.

Jaffee, S., Caspi, A., Moffitt, T. E., Belsky, J., & Silva, P. (2001). Why are children born to teen mothers at risk for adverse outcomes in young adulthood? Results from a 20-year longitudinal study. *Development and Psychopathology, 13,* 377–397.

Loeber, R., Drinkwater, M., Yin, Y., Anderson, S. J., Schmidt, L. C., & Crawford, A. (2000). Stability of family interaction from ages 6 to 18. *Journal of Abnormal Child Psychology, 28,* 353–369.

Luthar, S. S., Cicchetti, D., & Becker, B. (2000). The construct of resilience: A critical evaluation and guidelines for future work. *Child Development, 71,* 543–562.

MacCallum, R. C., Zhang, S., Preacher, K. J., & Rucker, D. D. (2002). On the practice of dichotomization of quantitative variables. *Psychological Methods, 7,* 19–40.

Markwardt, F. L. (1989). *Peabody Individual Achievement Test–Revised.* Circle Pines, MN: American Guidance Service.

Masten, A. S., Best, K. M., & Garmezy, N. (1990). Resilience and development: Contributions from the study of children who overcame adversity. *Development and Psychopathology, 2,* 425–444.

National Institute of Child Health and Human Development Early Child Care Research Network (2005). Duration and developmental timing of poverty and children's cognitive and social development from birth through third grade. *Child Development, 76,* 795–810.

Paine, T. (1894). The crisis (no. 1). In M. D. Conway (Ed.), *The writings of Thomas Paine: Vol. 1* (p. 170).

Passino, A. W., Whitman, T. L., Borkowski, J. G., Schellenbach, C. J., Maxwell, S. E., & Keogh, D., et al. (1993). Personal adjustment during pregnancy and adolescent parenting. *Adolescence, 28*, 97–122.

Rutter, M. (1979). Protective factors in children's responses to stress and disadvantage. In M. W. Kent & J. E. Rolf (Eds.), *Primary prevention of psychopathology: Vol. 3. Social competence in children* (pp. 49–74). Hanover, NH: University Press of New England.

Sameroff, A. J. (1994). Developmental systems and family functioning. In R. D. Parke & S. G. Kellam (Eds.), *Exploring family relationships with other social contexts* (pp. 199–214). Hillsdale, NJ: Lawrence Erlbaum Associates.

Sameroff, A. J., & Seifer, R. (1995). Accumulation of environmental risk and child mental health. In H. E. Fitzgerald, B. M. Lester, & B. S. Zuckerman (Eds.), *Children of poverty: Research, health, and policy issues* (pp. 233–268). New York: Garland Publishing, Inc.

Sameroff, A. J., Seifer, R., Baldwin, A., & Baldwin, C. (1993). Stability of intelligence from preschool to adolescence: The influence of social and family risk factors. *Child Development, 64*, 80–97.

Sameroff, A. J., Seifer, R., Zax, M., & Barocas, R. (1987). Early indicators of developmental risk: The Rochester Longitudinal Study. *Schizophrenia Bulletin, 13*, 383–394.

Schulenberg, J. E., Sameroff, A. J., & Cicchetti, D. (2004). The transition to adulthood as a critical juncture in the course of psychopathology and mental health. *Development and Psychopathology, 16*, 799–806.

Smith, L. E. (2004, March). *Impact of Environmental Instability on Children with Developmental Delays.* Poster session presented at the Gatlinburg Conference, San Diego, CA.

Sommer, K., Whitman, T. L., Borkowski, J. G., Schellenbach, C., Maxwell, S., & Keogh, D. (1993). Cognitive readiness and adolescent parenting. *Developmental Psychology, 29*, 389–398.

Wechsler, D. (1974). *Manual for the Wechsler Intelligence Scale for Children–Revised.* San Antonio, TX: The Psychological Corporation.

Wechsler, D. (1981). *Manual for the Wechsler Adult Intelligence Scale–Revised.* San Antonio, TX: The Psychological Corporation.

Weed, K., Keogh, D., & Borkowski, J. (2006). Stability of resilience in children of adolescent mothers. *Journal of Applied Developmental Psychology, 27*, 60–77.

Werner, E. E. (1994). Overcoming the odds. *Journal of Developmental and Behavioral Pediatrics, 15*, 131–136.

Whitman, T. L., Borkowski, J. G., Keogh, D. A., & Weed, K. (2001). *Interwoven lives: Adolescent mothers and their children.* Mahwah, NJ: Lawrence Erlbaum Associates.

Wood, D., Halfon, N., Scarlata, D., Newacheck, P., & Nessim, S. (1993). Impact of family relocation on children's growth, development, school function, and behavior. *Journal of the American Medical Association, 270*, 1334–1338.

8

Overcoming the Odds: Protective Factors in the Lives of Children

Kimberly S. Howard
Shannon S. Carothers
Leann E. Smith
Carol E. Akai

At a time of financial retrenchment, when many children are being placed at greater risk as a result of parental unemployment, other income losses, and reduction of health and family services, it is essential to determine which policies and programs can do most to enable families to perform the magic feat of which they alone are capable: making and keeping human beings human.

—Urie Bronfenbrenner (1986)

Although children born to adolescent mothers are generally more likely than children with adult mothers to demonstrate problems in social, emotional, behavioral, and academic domains, they often display successful adaptation despite heightened risks and adversities. Increased research on the concept of resilience has revealed that some at-risk children are able to adapt to, and persevere in, the face of challenging situations. In particular, highlighting the "twin themes" of risk and resilience has led many researchers to examine what have been referred to as protective factors or protective processes. Investigating sources of protection sheds some light on why children exposed to multiple stressful circumstances, such as poverty, neighborhood violence, or poor parenting practices, may experience positive developmental outcomes.

This chapter aims to enrich our current understanding of protection in terms of diminishing risk and promoting resilience for children of adolescent mothers. After defining protective mechanisms, we describe a number of sources of protection in the lives of at-risk children, guided by the systems approach proposed by Masten and Garmezy (1985). We then describe how three types of personal supports served protective functions for children in the Notre Dame Adolescent Parenting Project (NDAPP). Specifically, we summarize our research showing how father involvement, religious affiliation, and close ties to individuals in children's communities acted protectively when children were in high-risk environments. Finally, we conclude the chapter with a special emphasis on future directions for research in the areas of risk, protection, and resilience.

PROTECTION IN THE FACE OF ADVERSITY

Current approaches to the study of resilience identify stable characteristics in children and their surrounding environments that either buffer the negative effects associated with stressful conditions or foster recovery and successful adaptation following disruptions (Masten, 2001). Protective factors have been defined as individual or environmental safeguards that enhance a person's ability to resist stressful life events and hazards and, in turn, promote adaptation and competence (Rutter, 1987). Protective factors are specific characteristics that are conceptualized in terms of their ability to moderate or buffer the potentially negative impact of exposure to risks. Protective processes, on the other hand, refer to the mechanisms that allow children to develop in positive ways despite exposure to stressful experiences (Luthar, Cicchetti, & Becker, 2000). Protective processes are conceptualized in terms of their ability to mediate the potentially negative effects of risks; these characteristics explain how and why certain children are resilient despite exposure to multiple risks. Protective factors and processes are similar in the sense that both facilitate resilience among at-risk children; however important differences exist between protective factors and protective processes (Luthar et al., 2000). Whereas protective factors simply *describe* relationships between risk and resilience, an examination of protective processes *elucidate* the underlying mechanisms that account for positive adaptation in the face of risk.

Prevention and intervention programs achieve success by first identifying the protective factors functioning within the major systems associated with children's development, and subsequently strengthening the protective processes through which these variables operate to influence resilience (Luthar et al., 2000). Accordingly, this chapter will discuss some of the protective factors that have been identified for children of adolescent mothers and then expand on the ways that protective processes can be used to improve these children's functioning.

SOURCES OF PROTECTION IN THE LIVES OF ADOLESCENT MOTHERS AND THEIR CHILDREN

Protective factors in three domains have been shown to promote resilience: (a) dispositional attributes of the individual, (b) characteristics of the family, and (c) characteristics of the social environment. This conceptual approach, first proposed by Masten and Garmezy (1985), continues to be utilized in research on resilience (Luthar et al., 2000). The triarchic framework maintains that both internal and external factors serve important protective functions for children and adolescents characterized as resilient. Sometimes, positive internal characteristics shield children from risks, while external family and community support may also absorb some of the impact from risks on other occasions (Masten & Garmezy, 1985). In both cases, protective factors provide a barrier to risks, ultimately advancing the likelihood of resilience in at-risk children.

Masten and Garmezy's (1985) triarchic approach to protection is particularly useful for explaining resilience among children of adolescent mothers. As described in Whitman, Borkowski, Keogh, and

Weed (2001) and chapter 7, children of adolescent mothers in the NDAPP were exposed to multiple risks, often resulting in poor academic achievement and behavioral problems throughout childhood and early adolescence. Identifying sources of protection in individuals, families and communities helps researchers to better understand why some children who are exposed to significant risks do not exhibit the severity of developmental problems that other at-risk children may experience. Masten and Garmezy's approach suggests exploring a wide variety of characteristics that may play protective roles in the lives of high-risk children. We used the triarchic method in the next sections to organize a review of the literature, identifying protective factors in children, their immediate families, and communities, with an emphasis on describing how each source of protection facilitates resilience.

Protection Within the Individual

Dispositional attributes of the individual child have been investigated as potential sources of protection for children facing multiple risks. Children's intrinsic factors (such as gender, self-esteem, intelligence, attachment, temperament, or locus of control) serve important protective functions. For instance, self-esteem was identified as one protective factor that discriminated between groups of children, with resilient adolescents indicating higher levels of self-esteem than vulnerable adolescents (Dumont & Provost, 1999; Luthar, 2005). Additionally, higher levels of self-esteem and higher motivation toward school achievement have been considered protective factors against depression, decreased life satisfaction, and poor general well-being during adolescence (Dekovic, 1999). Resilient adolescents were also likely to use problem-solving coping strategies (Dumont & Provost, 1999) and have outgoing temperaments (Kim-Cohen, Moffitt, Caspi, & Taylor, 2004), suggesting that multiple internal qualities may buffer the influence of risks.

Cognitive protective factors, such as intelligence and possessing an internal locus of control, have also been identified as important for children's successful adjustment following exposure to stressful circumstances. For example, internal locus of control has been shown to operate as a protective mechanism through which personal experiences influence children's life satisfaction (Ash & Huebner, 2001). An internal locus of control also serves a protective function in classroom settings: Children with an internal locus of control have higher levels of assertiveness and lower levels of depression and anxiety than children with an external locus of control (Luthar, 1991). Specifically, an internal locus of control and high educational aspirations in the eighth grade were associated with resilience in 12th grade, even in the face of demographic risks such as low SES, minority status, or living in a single parent household (Cappella & Weinstein, 2001).

Protection Within the Family

For adolescent mothers and their children, family support is a critical source of protection because of the benefits provided by family members. Support from mothers, fathers, and grandmothers have all been shown to positively impact children. For example, lower psychological distress in children has been found in social networks marked by more satisfying contacts with family members (McLoyd & Wilson, 1990). Immediate family members can act as highly influential support agents for children of teenaged mothers (Hess, Papas, & Black, 2002).

Within the child's immediate family, mothers often shelter their children from harm associated with environmental risks. Despite the fact that adolescent mothers often place children at risk for developmental problems (see chap. 5), maternal characteristics (such as IQ, reading ability, school certification, or low conviction history) have been shown to attenuate some of the negative consequences associated with adolescent childbearing (Jaffee, Caspi, Moffitt, Belsky, & Silva, 2001). Similarly, Whitman et al. (2001) point out how maternal cognitive readiness to parent, intelligence, or socioemotional adjustment may act as protective factors, diminishing some of the problems that children of adolescent mothers encounter due to an association with a variety of difficult life circumstances such as neighborhood violence or father absence. Moreover, maternal characteristics together with family circumstances (such as SES, caretaker or residence changes, or parent–child relationship quality) have been shown to serve an important protective function for children of young mothers (Jaffee et al., 2001).

Although the majority of studies examining the protective aspects of parenting have focused on maternal contributions to children's well-being, the protective role of fathers in children's development is just beginning to be understood. The last two decades have, however, brought an increased awareness about the ways that fathers impact their families (Tamis-LeMonda & Cabrera, 2002). A growing body of literature suggests that fathers provide unique and important contributions to their children's development (Lamb, 2000; Paquette, 2004; Parke, 2000). Most research on fatherhood has examined resident fathers in two-parent families. In general, research suggests that fathers in these traditional families are in a better position than nonresident fathers to have a positive impact on children's lives (Brown, Michelsen, Halle, & Moore, 2001).

In contrast, there has been little exploration about the ways in which nonresident fathers influence their children's development (Amato & Gilbreth, 1999). The prevailing assumption of researchers and policymakers has been that if a father is absent from the home, he is also absent from his child's life. This perspective, however, is changing. Although paternal involvement with children tends to decline over time if the father is not married to the child's mother (Sobolewski & King, 2005), many nonresident fathers remain involved in their children's lives (Salem, Zimmerman & Notaro, 1998). Several researchers have found that the overall contact of many nonresident fathers with their children is fairly high and stable over time, particularly among fathers with steady jobs who live near their children (e.g., Halle & Menestrel, 1999).

Involved nonresident fathers often positively influence the lives of their children (Hawkins & Dollahite, 1997; Pleck, 1997). For instance, father involvement in childcare was strongly related to children's empathic concern for others, even when children became adults (Koestner, Franz, & Weinberger, 1990). Father availability and involvement have also been associated with cognitive gains and academic success in school-age children, including higher grades and achievement in math and reading (Jones, 2004). In addition, contact with nonresident fathers has been linked to improved psychological well-being for children (Menestrel, 1999). Not only did nonresident fathers protect children from psychological maladjustment during adolescence, but continued positive involvement during adolescence was also shown to defend against psychological distress as teens transitioned into adulthood (Flouri & Buchanan, 2001). Fathers maintain an important protective function, even when they do not reside with children. These findings are especially important for children of adolescent mothers, many of whom do not live with their fathers.

Grandmothers may become the primary sources of protection for children when fathers' involvement is inconsistent and teen mothers are constrained by school or work. Among families with adolescent mothers, grandmothers are instrumental figures in the early phase of adolescent parenting, as they often take on the primary responsibilities for childcare, especially during the first few years of life (Whitman et al., 2001). In these families, grandmothers have been shown to provide nurturance and advice to their daughters, guidance and care for their grandchildren, financial assistance for the entire household, and stability for their extended family members. Frequently, these types of protective supports have enabled teenage mothers to continue their education or to obtain job training (Black et al., 2002; Hess et al., 2002). In addition, shared caregiving with grandmothers has been shown to be a major source of support for African American adolescent mothers (George & Dickerson, 1995). As a result, grandmother support may promote children's resilience through direct protection for children or indirectly by influencing mothers.

Protection Within the Social Environment

The social environment surrounding children, consisting of peer networks, neighborhood environments, and community based organizations, can also provide protection for children of adolescent mothers. For instance, social competence—working, playing, loving, thinking, and serving others—increased when children were involved in either community or school service activities (Perry-Burney & Takyi, 2002). Communities can decrease the prevalence of problematic behaviors, such as crime or delinquency, by developing programs that increase positive relationships between children (Villarruel, Keith, Perkins, & Borden, 2003). In many cases, community programs have offered individuals the ability to interact and form social networks with peer groups and older adults (Villarruel et al., 2003). At-risk children have also benefitted from the character- and skill-building nature of community programs, such as 4–H, Scouts, YMCA, and YWCA. These types of programs, designed to prevent child and family problems, served as important resources for children and their families (Ganong, 1993). The availability of resources necessary for healthy human development, such as medical care, childcare, housing, education, job training, employment, and recreation, have connected families, schools, agencies, and organizations in order to address the needs of children and promote children's resilience (Benard, 1991).

Religious Involvement.   Religious affiliation is one specific source of protection for children that is found in the social environment. For example, church affiliation and attendance have been shown to promote resilience in children by providing positive role models and mentors in supportive and stable communities, assisting in developing self-regulatory abilities, aiding in identity development, and offering social relationships marked by unconditional love and support (Cook, 2000). In addition, church attendance also can function as a means of social control by inhibiting problematic antisocial behaviors and encouraging prosocial behaviors in both at-risk mothers and their children (Pearce, Jones, Schwab-Stone, & Ruchkin, 2003). Religious institutions have been shown to reinforce social norms by initiating positive belief systems that relate to children's personal competence (Brody, Stoneman, & Flor, 1996). Frequency of church attendance has been related to overall well-being and inversely related to distress and anxiety (Ellison, Boardman, Williams, & Jackson, 2001). Moreover, African American children whose parents had regular church attendance had fewer behavior problems than children whose parents attended less frequently (Christian & Barabrin, 2001).

Religious individuals have reported a greater sense of intrinsic self-worth and feelings of mastery than those who did not consider themselves religious (Ellison et al., 2001). Similarly, at-risk mothers who report high levels of religiosity tend to have higher self-esteem and self-worth (Commerford & Reznikoff, 1996; Hammermeister, Flint, Havens & Peterson, 2001) and fewer depressive symptoms (Cummings, Neff, & Husaini, 2003; Pearce, Little, & Perez, 2003; Smith, McCullough, & Poll, 2003) than mothers with lower levels of religiosity. At-risk children have also profited from parental religiosity. For instance, children's academic and socioemotional competence has been linked to the development of self-regulation and to parental religiosity (Cook, 2000). For mothers, religious involvement appears to work by minimizing everyday adversities and by increasing social support in a way that offers personal meaning, broader perspectives on conflict, and a greater capacity for inner resources in the face of stressful events (King & Schafer, 1992). Thus, children's resilience may be fostered directly through religious involvement or indirectly through the religious involvement of their mothers.

An explanation for the "religiosity effect" has been provided by Ellison (1993), who maintained that religious groups, especially in minority communities, fostered positive self-appraisals through positive feedback and fellowship, thus increasing the emotional well-being of their members. Theories about the protective nature of religiosity have maintained that the benefits of religiosity may be most evident among those confronted with a high degree of stress in their lives. They emphasize that factors associated with religious involvement have the potential to reduce the effects of high stress levels and improve general well-being (Ellison et al., 2001).

Culture and race appear to play significant roles in determining whether or not an individual is likely to become involved in, and benefit from, religious involvement. Some minority groups report that religious participation has provided both direction and meaning in their lives. For instance, Taylor and Chatters (1991) suggested that church attendance, where moral guidance, political leadership, and community life thrived, contributed to the solidarity of the African American community. Through participation in church activities that promote values, encourage positive interactions, and establish strong social bonds, personal competence appears to be increased (Brody et al., 1996).

Multiple Sources of Protection.   Following Rutter's (1987) view of protection as adaptation in the face of risk, it is plausible that even within the context of high-risk neighborhoods there may be a variety of protective mechanisms serving to promote children's resilience, such as positive influences within both the family and the community. Interpersonal relationships, and parental relationships in particular, are examples of protective factors that can impact children's development in the contexts of poor neighborhood quality (Leventhal & Brooks-Gunn, 2000). Parental involvement in school affairs is an example of protection in the milieu of neighborhood risk. Parents in low-income communities monitored their children's homework and other school activities less frequently than parents in middle or high income communities. Low-income parents also participated in fewer school activities and knew less about their children's school performance (Evans, 2004). These findings point to parental involvement as a potential source of protection for children living in high-risk neighborhoods. The assistance of supportive individuals discussed earlier in relation to religious involvement can also provide protective aid to children confronting environmental risk.

In summary, protective resources within the child, the child's family, and his or her social environment are critical in developing resilience for children of adolescent mothers in domains of academic, social, behavioral, and psychological functioning. The NDAPP explored the nature of protective factors for buffering the risks to which children of teenaged mothers are exposed in different contexts. The next section describes specific examples of how father involvement, religious affiliation, and supportive individuals in the community acted protectively for children by encouraging resilient outcomes as the children entered adolescence.

UNDERSTANDING PROTECTION: CONTRIBUTIONS FROM THE NDAPP

Findings from the NDAPP have examined the protective roles of child, family and community variables in facilitating positive outcomes among at-risk children. In the following sections we describe selective findings from our research that highlight the (a) protective role of fathers in high-risk families, many of whom were unmarried and did not reside with their children; (b) protective nature of religious involvement for both adolescent mothers and their children; and (c) the protective impact of multiple sources of community support in the face of negative life events.

The Impact of Father Involvement on Children's Development

Though existing literature provides solid evidence of the positive impact that resident fathers have on their children, few studies have explored the protective effects of fathers in high-risk families, where their involvement may be minimal. Howard, Lefever, Borkowski, & Whitman (in press) used data from the NDAPP to examine patterns of father presence in the lives of children of teen mothers and the subsequent impact of father involvement on children's development. In addition, maternal characteristics associated with variation in levels of father involvement were identified. Findings from this study provide insights into the protective nature of father involvement in the lives of at-risk children.

Design.   Using data from the NDAPP, Howard et al. (in press) gathered information about the amount and type of contact that the biological father had with his child over the course of 10 years. At each assessment (6 months, 12 months, 3, 5, 8 and 10 years), mothers were asked a series of questions about father involvement, such as whether the father had contact with the child and whether he helped with the child in any way. Prenatally, mothers were asked whether the biological father of the child was her current partner. At 6 months, mothers were asked if the biological father was still in contact with the baby. At 12 months, mothers reported whether the child's biological father lived with the mother and child, visited them, helped financially, and/or helped with childcare. Additionally, at 12 months, mothers reported whether the child's father helped with the child and also if he helped her with other things not related to the child. These questions were also asked at the 3- and 5-year assessments. Finally, at both 8 and 10 years, mothers indicated whether the biological fathers provided emotional support, financial support, childcare, or any other type of support for them and their child.

An important variable—father contact—was formed from the preceding questions in order to estimate consistency of father contact across the child's lifespan. When mothers answered positively to any of the questions related to father involvement at a particular time point, they were given a score of 1, indicating that the father was in contact at that time. These scores were then summed across all time points yielding a possible 0–6 range and a median split was used to obtain two groups: a contact with father group and a no-father-contact group. Fathers in the no-contact group were either not present at all or only very early in the child's life, whereas those in the contact group showed more consistent involvement over time, both early on as well as when the child was 8 years old (Howard et al., 2006).

Fathers were approximately 2 years older than mothers at the time the child was born ($M = 19.1$ years, $SD = 2.55$), and were predominately the same race (68% African American, 25% European American, 5% Latino, and 2% Native American). When children were 6 years old, mothers reported that 59% of the fathers had graduated from high school, 11% had obtained further education, and 66% were currently employed. For mothers who reported having a second child by the time the target child was 6 years old, 34% of these siblings had the same father.

Results and Implications.   Classifications of father contact revealed that at 1 year of age, 81% of children were in contact with their biological fathers, whereas by age 8 only 59% were in contact. This latter group of children also experienced relatively consistent father contact through age 10. The remaining 41% had either no contact or very limited contact with their biological fathers.

When children were 12 months old, 21.5% of fathers lived with them, and 60.5% visited. By the time the children were 8 years old, the number of fathers living with their children had decreased to 11% and the number who visited was only 24.5%. There was little change in father involvement between 8 and 10 years, as 9.8% of children lived with their fathers when they were 10 years old, and 27.2% had visits with them. There were no relationships between father involvement and mothers' or fathers' ethnicity (Howard et al., 2006).

Additional analyses revealed that one half of the 14-year-old teens received financial support from their fathers (50.7%), and 69% of the teens had some sort of contact with their fathers. Although only 8.5% of children were living with their fathers at this time, 37.2% identified their biological father as the most significant male role model in their lives. Among the 31% of fathers who did not have contact with their children, 13% were deceased, 13% were in prison, and the remaining 5% were alive and not incarcerated but still did not have any contact with their children.

Children who had more consistent contact with their biological fathers throughout their lives had fewer behavioral problems at school, as evidenced by lower rates of aggression and negative classroom behavior. They also had higher academic achievement, especially in reading. Interestingly, father contact interacted with children's sex on both reading and math achievement at age 10. Figure 8.1 shows that father contact was associated with higher math achievement for sons only. The pattern of results was the same for reading achievement.

The protective influence of fathers on their children was also highlighted by examining the effects of father contact in the face of maternal risk. Children who had high-risk mothers (defined by elevated

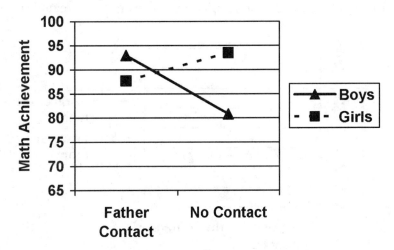

Figure 8.1.   Interaction of father contact and children's sex on Peabody Individual Achievement Test (PIAT) math achievement scores at age 10.

behavioral problems, low intelligence, and low cognitive readiness
to parent) and no father contact were evaluated as functioning in the
clinical range of externalizing problems such as aggression; whereas
children with high-risk mothers and father contact were functioning
within the normal range. Figure 8.2 illustrates the main effect of father contact on children's externalizing behaviors at age 8. It should
be noted that for children with no father contact, 54% had
externalizing scores in the borderline and clinical range (about 7%
would be expected in the population). Furthermore, 69% of children with high-risk mothers and no father contact had externalizing
scores in the borderline and clinical range (Howard et al., in press).

Consistent with the existing literature studying typically developing children, these results indicated the importance of father contact
for children's development (Jackson, 1999; Nord, Brimhall & West,
1998). In contrast, most fathers in the NDAPP resided only for a short
time with their children or had never lived with them. Fathers in our
sample who maintained contact with their children, either through
financial support, periodic visits, or childcare, positively influenced
children's behavioral and academic outcomes as well as higher levels
of academic achievement.

Although this study was limited to maternal reports about the extent of father contact, the results demonstrated that maternal per-

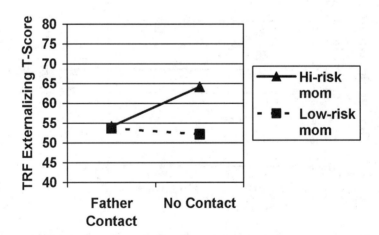

Figure 8.2.   Main effect of father contact on children's externalizing scores
at age 8.

ceptions of father involvement provided reliable information that predicted whether children were at risk for developmental problems. Fathers played an important role in their children's development, regardless of whether or not they resided with their children. Even in a society in which large percentages of children are raised in single-parent homes, fathers remain integral in providing optimal environments in which at-risk children can grow and develop to their full potential. The section that follows highlights the ways in which another form of social support, religiosity, serves as protection for at-risk children.

Religiosity's Impact on Adolescent Mothers and Their Children

Although adolescent mothers and their children are at risk for a variety of adverse developmental outcomes, they often demonstrate resilience even when confronted with significant personal and environmental risks. Using NDAPP data, Carothers, Borkowski, Lefever, and Whitman (2005) examined the role of another potential protective factor, religiosity. The purposes of the study were to investigate how adolescent mothers described their religious experience, and to determine if their self-described religiosity was related to the socioemotional and behavioral outcomes of both mothers and children over 10 years.

Design. Religiosity was defined in terms of the amount of contact with, and dependency on, the church community. Mothers were asked questions during a prenatal life history interview about their church attendance, closeness to the church community and physical and emotional support received from the church community. When children were 3, 5, and 8 years old, they were also asked to rate the frequency of contact and dependence on both church members and church leaders. Each response was dichotomized; a score of 0 represented no contact or dependence and a score of 1 represented some contact or dependence on the church community. These scores were then summed over each time of measurement, resulting in a total religiosity score ranging from 0 to 4 points, with 0 representing low religiosity and 4 representing high levels of religiosity. A religiosity index was created for each individual, resulting in 46 and 45 mothers being classified respectively as low and high in their religiosity (Carothers et al., 2005).

Results and Implications.   Mothers characterized as high on religious involvement had significantly higher self-esteem, were less likely to abuse their children, and had higher ratings of occupational and educational attainment than mothers rated low in their religious involvement at both 10 and 14 years (Carothers et al., 2005). These relationships were robust enough to persist even after controlling for intelligence, cognitive readiness to parent, socioeconomic status, stress, and grandmother support.

Maternal religious involvement was also associated with children's 10- and 14-year internalizing and externalizing behaviors. Children whose mothers were high on religious involvement were judged to have fewer problems in these socioemotional domains than children whose mothers were minimally involved with the church (Carothers et al., 2005). Most religions set standards for acceptable behavior and offer reinforcement when a child makes a wise or socially appropriate personal decision (Cook, 2000). In this case, church attendance appeared to assist teen mothers in developing socioemotional self-regulation by helping them refrain from negative behaviors and increasing their engagement in positive social activities. Thus, religiosity was a protective factor that influenced both mothers and children by acting as a buffer against potential risks associated with teenage parenting.

In the case of adolescent mothers in this study, church attendance may have initiated a protective process by providing job opportunities, daycare services, or other supports for mothers that allowed them to maintain steady employment or continue their education. Studies have suggested that mothers with high levels of religiosity who were involved with their local churches received social support as well as a framework for viewing stressful events in ways that provided meaning to their lives and empowered them in the face of stressful events (King & Schafer, 1992). It is possible that this explanation held true for the mothers in the NDAPP. In addition to the role of religious institutions in buffering children of adolescent mothers from adverse developmental outcomes, other supportive individuals in the community can also provide protection for children. The next section examines multiple sources of community support that are available to children of adolescent mothers.

Multiple Sources of Protection for Children of Adolescent Mothers

Utilizing data from the NDAPP, Carothers, Borkowksi, and Whitman (in press) analyzed the role of multiple protective factors in moderating the effects of exposure to negative life events on children's socioemotional and behavioral adjustment at age 10. The study's primary aim was to explore whether social support—as defined by relationship with parents, religiosity/spirituality, support networks, mentors, and social groups/sports activities—promoted resilience. The questions of major interest were the following: (a) What is the incidence of exposure to negative life events in a sample of children born to adolescent mothers in the late 1980s and early 1990s?; (b) Is exposure to negative life events—as defined by the Negative Events subscales of the Life Events Checklist—related to socioemotional and behavioral adjustment at age 10?; and (c) Is the impact of stressful life events on children's socioemotional adjustment moderated by a variety of supports such as relationship with their mothers, religiosity/spirituality, support networks/mentors, and social groups/sports activities?

Design.   At age 10, children's intelligence and socioemotional and behavioral adjustment were assessed. Next, children were given a memory task utilizing a timeline that asked them to remember back to when they were ages 3, 5, and 10 and to answer specific questions related to where they lived, who their teachers and friends were, and whether anything important happened to them at each time point. At the time of this retrospective assessment, they were between 11 and 17 years of age. Utilizing a measure specifically created for this study, children were then asked to report on exposure to negative life events, and the possible factors that helped them cope with stressful situations prior to age 10.

Results and Implications.   Fifty-six percent ($n = 54$) of the sample reported exposure to negative life events and 100% reported specific protective factors that help them cope with exposure to stressful circumstances. The relationship children had with their parents was the most commonly reported protective factor (64%), followed by self-esteem (11%). These data suggest that mothers were important coping resources in the face of children's exposure to stressful or negative life circumstances.

Hierarchical regression analyses, controlling for maternal stress, SES, children's age, and IQ, indicated that negative life events were associated with less favorable developmental outcomes, with social support serving as a buffer between exposure to these events and children's anxiety, internalization, externalization, and maladaptive behaviors. Summing over regression models, negative life events and social supports accounted for 40% of the variance in children's depression, 26% in anxiety, 42% in internalization, 37% in externalization, and 31% in maladaptive behavior. Thus, the combination of children's relationship with parents, religiosity/spirituality, support networks, and social groups/sports activities served as a buffer between negative life events and children's socioemotional and behavioral outcomes. Each of the four sources of support contributed to the predictive validity of the social support construct, with religiosity/spirituality and social/sports activities contributing the most.

Figure 8.3(a) shows the relationship between children's internalizing problems as a function of negative life events and social support. Social support was defined as a combination of the four contributing protective factors. Only children who had higher social support and few negative life events were protected from develop-

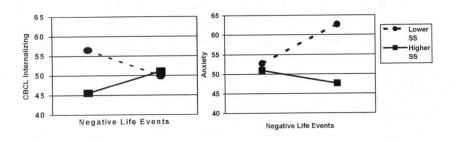

Figure 8.3. The effects of negative life events and social support on (a) internalization and (b) anxiety.

ing depression and withdrawal problems. As exposure to negative life events increased, social support was no longer protective; this same pattern was found for externalizing and maladaptive behaviors. Figure 8.3(b) presents the relationship between negative life events and social support on children's anxiety: Social support significantly differentiated scores on anxiety at higher levels of exposure to negative life events as opposed to lower levels; children with stressful life events and lower levels of social support were more likely to report high degrees of anxiety.

These findings support those of Werner and Smith (1992) who found that caring adults outside of the immediate family (e.g., grandparents, neighbors, youth leaders, extracurricular leaders, and church members) were significant sources of protection for at-risk children. Similarly, other researchers have shown that caring relationships, high expectations, and opportunities for participation in sports served as protections against daily hassles and depression among at-risk children (Boone & Leadbeater, 2006; Larsen & Birmingham, 2003). With caring and emotionally supportive adults, children often recover from difficult circumstances, acquire the belief that their lives have meaning, and are in more control of their own fate (Larsen & Birmingham, 2003; Werner & Smith, 1992). These studies, along with our own, demonstrate the buffering effects of social support, particularly religiosity/spirituality and social/sports activities, for children exposed to moderate levels of negative or stressful life events. Although children reported that their mothers were the most important source of support, the data suggested that religiosity/spirituality and social/sports activities were, in fact, the most significant types of protection in the face of negative life events.

Summing Up: Protective Factors in Children's Lives

The three studies presented in this chapter focused on mechanisms through which protective factors operate across multiple domains of development, buffering children against potential negative consequences associated with their high-risk status: (a) Howard et al. (in press) found that father presence in the lives of at-risk children protected them from developing both behavioral and academic problems; (b) Carothers et al. (2005) showed that religious involvement fostered positive growth and development in behavioral and socioemotional domains, for both adolescent mothers and their children; and (c) Carothers et al. (in press) found that social supports from community organizations, such as churches and sports leagues, helped children cope with negative or stressful life events. More specifically, we found that

- Surprisingly, 69% of fathers remained involved in their children's lives from birth to age 14, although only 8.5% lived with their children.
- Involved fathers had children who were less aggressive and performed better in reading and math, even when maternal behavioral problems and intelligence were controlled.
- 45% of the mothers were classified as religious: They had significantly higher self-esteem, lower depression scores, less child abuse potential, and higher occupational and educational attainment than mothers classified as nonreligious.
- Children with more religious mothers had fewer internalizing and externalizing problems at age 10, with maternal adjustment mediating this relationship.
- The relationship children had with their parents was the most commonly reported (64%) protective factor in helping them cope with stressful or negative life circumstances, followed by self-esteem (11%).
- Although negative life events were associated with less favorable developmental outcomes, a combination of supports—especially religiosity/spirituality and social groups/sports activities— served as buffers between exposure to negative life events and children's anxiety, internalization, externalization, and maladaptive behaviors.

The overarching theme of this chapter is that support from caring adults, whether within home or community settings, promotes positive development among most at-risk children. In all instances, protection came from important people in their lives who explicitly provided positive support and encouragement. Our findings are consistent with the extant literature on risk and protection showing that close relationships with supportive family members and connections with competent, prosocial adults in the wider community promote resilience during adolescence (Luthar et al., 2000; Masten & Garmezy, 1985; Werner & Smith, 1982; Woolley & Grogan-Kaylor, 2006). In the presence of caring adults, children can recover from and surmount difficult circumstances, often acquiring the belief that their lives have meaning and developing a sense of control regarding their future lives (Larsen & Birmingham, 2003). A good example of the role of support in building resilience in a child's life can be found in the story of Marcus, presented in chapter 10.

The identification of specific protective factors in family, church, and community settings proves useful information for developing community-based prevention and intervention programs. For example, encouraging responsible father involvement has become part of our national agenda. With the development of the National Fatherhood Initiative, the federal government currently supports research and demonstration programs that help fathers connect with their children.

Churches also provide important resources for delivering community-based intervention and prevention programs, such as implementing father initiatives in high crime neighborhoods. Due to their unique position as stable organizations deeply embedded in their communities, churches can provide both opportunities for social support and ideal environments for delivering services. Researchers and service providers will likely do well to partner with local religious organizations, benefitting from their strong connections with community agencies and individuals residing in their neighborhoods.

In short, findings from the NDAPP on the protective factors operating in the lives of children of adolescent mothers point to the benefit of using a strengths-based perspective for understanding resilience and developing intervention programs that focus on building cumulative protections in multiple domains for both children and their immediate families (Maton, Schellenbach, Leadbeater, & Solarz, 2004; Morrison, Brown, D'Incau, O'Farrell, & Furlong, 2006).

OVERCOMING THE ODDS: FUTURE DIRECTIONS

Each of the NDAPP studies presented in this chapter has demonstrated the impact of a single protective factor (i.e., father involvement, religious affiliation, or community support) on children's development. Two of the studies (Carothers et al., 2005; Howard et al., in press) identified family-related protective factors, whereas the final study (Carothers et al., in press) identified protections originating in the surrounding community. The identification of protection in multiple domains can be best understood in the context of Bronfenbrenner's (1986) ecological model. According to this theory, it is important to consider multiple levels of influence acting simultaneously on, and interacting with, children's development. Protection may come from multiple sources, ranging from individual and familial characteristics to those in neighborhoods and cultures. The ecological approach is well-suited for studying protection, highlighting the fact that complex models, which take into account interactions between individuals and their familial and social environments over time, are needed to fully explain the processes at work in child development (cf. Novilla, Barnes, De La Cruz, Williams, & Rogers, 2006).

Unfortunately, most of the extant research on protective processes has examined a single protective factor in isolation from other potential sources of protection. It is imperative that research on risk, protection, and resilience move beyond simple, single-domain explanations of resilience. The joint influences of various protective characteristics and processes present in multiple systems need to be understood if we are to account for children's successful development, despite exposure to stressful environments and personal adversities. New models of cumulative protection will help to identify combinations of patterns that result in the most positive outcomes for at-risk children. Just as risk factors rarely appear in isolation, it is likely that each child experiences protection in more than one area at any given moment of his or her development. It is possible that previous research on isolated protective factors have yielded biased results by failing to account for multiple, interactive sources of protection at work in children's lives that lead to resilience.

Chapter 7 introduced guiding principles for developing cumulative models of risk. These same principles can apply to models of cumulative protection as well. The concept of cumulative protection is defined by the accumulation of a single protective factor over time. We refer to this case as the *chronic cumulative protection model*. Of the studies presented in this chapter, both father involvement and religiosity were measured across time, although longitudinal data were compressed into a single estimate of overall protection (Carothers et al., 2005; Howard et al., in press). The result was *additive protection* in which the same variable (e.g., father presence or religiosity) gathered at different points in time was summed in order to draw conclusions amount the general prevalence of a particular protective factor. In contrast, a cumulative protection model would examine the role of protection by allowing protective factors at each time point to contribute uniquely to overall protection and subsequent child outcomes. Such models provide a framework for truly answering questions about the role of protection in development over time, thereby maximizing the benefits of longitudinal designs.

Cumulative protection can also be conceived of as the accumulation of protection in different domains at any given moment in development (e.g., a *simultaneous cumulative protection* model). For example, a child who has an involved father, ties to a religious institution, an active neighborhood soccer league, rich YMCA programs, and a safe neighborhood would probably receive greater protection than a child with protection in a single domain. Research on cumulative protection across domains is important for identifying the optimal combinations of protective factors that produce resilience. Just as previous research identified that a single supportive adult can buffer children from a host of negative life events (Werner & Smith, 1992), future research on cumulative protection should aim to identify specific sets of protective factors that work best in combination with one another at a given stage of development and in the face of a sequence of specific risks.

Finally, a complete model of cumulative protection needs to include the accumulation of protective factors from multiple domains over time. These models can be tested using longitudinal data sets, such as the NDAPP. Although analytically complex, cumulative models of protection provide a framework for examining processes associated with multiple protective factors occurring over time—a clear "next step" for research on protection. Chapter 9 describes sophisticated longitudinal modeling techniques that can be useful in addressing questions about cumulative risks and protection.

REFERENCES

Amato, P. R., & Gilbreth, J. G. (1999). Nonresident fathers and children's well being: A meta analysis. *Journal of Marriage and the Family, 61*, 557–574.

Ash, C., & Huebner, E. S. (2001). Environmental events and life satisfaction reports of adolescents: A test of cognitive mediation. *School Psychology International, 22*, 320–336.

Benard, B. (1991). *Fostering resiliency in kids: Protective factors in the family, schools, and community*. San Francisco: Western Regional Center for Drug-Free Schools and Communities.

Black, M. M., Papas, M. A., Hussey, J. M., Hunter, W., Dubowitz, H., Kotch, J. B., et al. (2002). Behavior and development of preschool children born to adolescent mothers: Risk and 3-generation households. *Pediatrics, 109*, 573–580.

Boone, E. M., & Leadbeater, B. J. (2006). Game on: Diminishing risks for depressive symptoms in early adolescence through positive involvement in team sports. *Journal of Research on Adolescence, 16*, 79–90.

Brody, G. H., Stoneman, Z., & Flor, D. (1996). Parental religiosity, family processes, and youth competence in rural two parent African American families. *Developmental Psychology, 32*, 696–706.

Bronfenbrenner, U. (1986). Ecology of the family as a context for human development: Research perspectives. *Developmental Psychology, 6*, 723–742.

Brown, B. V., Michelsen, E. A., Halle, T. G., & Moore, K. A. (2001, June). *Fathers' activities with their kids*. Washington, DC: Child Trends.

Cappella, E., & Weinstein, R. S. (2001). Turning around reading: Predictors of high school students' academic resilience. *Journal of Educational Psychology, 93*, 758–771.

Carothers, S. S., Borkowski, J. G., Lefever, J. B., & Whitman, T. L. (2005). Religiosity and the socioemotional and adjustment of adolescent mothers and their children. *Journal of Family Psychology, 19*, 263–275.

Carothers, S. S., Borkowski, J. G., & Whitman, T. L. (in press). Exposure to negative life events among at-risk children: Social support and socioemotional adjustment. *Journal of Clinical Child and Adolescent Psychology*.

Christian, M. D., & Barbarin, O. A. (2001). Cultural resources and psychological adjustment of African American children: Effects of spirituality and racial attribution. *Journal of Black Psychology, 27*, 43–63.

Commerford, M. C., & Reznikoff, M. (1996). Relationship of religion and perceived social support to self-esteem and depression in nursing home residents. *Journal of Psychology, 130,* 35–50.

Cook, K. V. (2000). You have somebody watching your back, and if that's God, then that's mighty big: The church's role in the resilience of inner-city youth. *Adolescence, 35,* 717–730.

Cummings, S. M., Neff, J. A., & Husaini, B. A. (2003). Functional impairment as a predictor of depressive symptomatology: The role of race, religiosity, and social support. *Health and Social Work, 28,* 23–32.

Dekovic, M. (1999). Risk and protective factors in the development of problem behaviors during adolescence. *Journal of Youth and Adolescence, 28,* 667–685.

Dumont, M., & Provost, M. A. (1999). Resilience in adolescents: Protective role of social support, coping strategies, self-esteem, and social activities on experience of stress and depression. *Journal of Youth and Adolescence, 28,* 343–363.

Ellison, C. G. (1993). Religious involvement and self-perception among Black Americans. *Social Forces, 71,* 1027–1055.

Ellison, C. G., Boardman, J. D., Williams, D. R., & Jackson, J. S. (2001). Religious involvement, stress, and mental health: Findings from the 1995 Detroit area study. *Social Forces, 80,* 215–249.

Evans, G. W. (2004). The environment of childhood poverty. *American Psychologist, 59,* 77–92.

Flouri, E., & Buchanan, A. (2001). 'Recovery' after age 7 from 'externalizing' behavior problems: The role of risk and protective clusters. *Children and Youth Services Review, 23,* 899–914.

Ganong, L. H. (1993). Family diversity in a youth organization: Involvement of single-parent families and stepfamilies in 4-H. *Family Relations: Interdisciplinary Journal of Applied Family Studies, 42,* 286–292.

George, S. M., & Dickerson, B. J. (1995). The role of the grandmother in poor single-mother families and households. In E. F. Dickerson (Ed.), *African American single mothers: Understanding their lives and families* (pp. 146–163). Thousand Oaks, CA: Sage Publications.

Halle, T., & Menestrel, S. L. (1999, May). *How do social, economic, and cultural factors influence fathers' involvement with their children?* Washington, DC: Child Trends.

Hammermeister, J., Flint, M., Havens, J., & Peterson, M. (2001). Psychosocial and health-related characteristics of religious well-being. *Psychological Reports, 89,* 589–594.

Hawkins, A. J., & Dollahite, D. C. (1997). Beyond the role inadequacy perspective of fathering. In A. J. Hawkins & D. C. Dollahite (Eds.), *Generative Fathering: Beyond Deficit Perspectives* (pp. 3–16). Thousand Oaks, CA: Sage Publications.

Hess, C. R., Papas, M. A., & Black, M. M. (2002). Resilience among African American adolescent mothers: Predictors of positive parenting in early infancy. *Journal of Pediatric Psychology, 27,* 619–629.

Howard, K. S., Lefever, J. B., J., Borkowski, J. G., & Whitman, T. L. (in press) Fathers' influence in the lives of children with adolescent mothers. *Journal of Family Psychology.*

Jackson, A. P. (1999). The effects of nonresident father involvement on single black mothers and their young children. *Social Work, 44,* 156–166.

Jaffee, S., Caspi, A., Moffitt, T. E., Belsky, J., & Silva, P. (2001). Why are children born to teen mothers at risk for adverse outcomes in young adulthood? Results from a 20-year longitudinal study. *Development and Psychopathology, 13,* 377–397.

Jones, K. (2004). Assessing psychological separation and academic performance in nonresident-father and resident-father adolescent boys. *Child and Adolescent Social Work Journal, 21,* 333–354.

Kim-Cohen, J., Moffitt, T. E., Caspi, A., & Taylor, A. (2004). Genetic and environmental processes in young children's resilience and vulnerability to socioeconomic deprivation. *Child Development, 75,* 651–668.

King, M., & Schafer, W. E. (1992). Religiosity and perceived stress: A community survey. *Sociological Analysis, 53,* 37–47.

Koestner, R., Franz, C., & Weinberger, J. (1990). The family origins of empathic concern: A 26-year longitudinal study. *Journal of Personality and Social Psychology, 58,* 709–717.

Lamb, M. E. (2000). The history of research on father involvement: An overview. *Marriage and Family Review, 29,* 23–42.

Larsen, E. K., & Birmingham, S. M. (2003). Caring relationships as a protective factor for at risk youth: An ethnographic study. *Families in Society: The Journal of Contemporary Human Services, 84,* 240–246.

Leventhal, T., & Brooks-Gunn, J. (2000). The neighborhoods they live in: The effects of neighborhood residence on child and adolescent outcomes. *Psychological Bulletin, 126,* 309–337.

Luthar, S. (Ed.). (2005). *Resilience and vulnerability: Adaptation in the context of childhood adversities.* New York: Cambridge University Press.

Luthar, S. S. (1991). Vulnerability and resilience: A study of high-risk adolescents. *Child Development, 62,* 600–616.

Luthar, S. S., Cicchetti, D., & Becker, B. (2000). The construct of resilience: A critical evaluation and guidelines for future work. *Child Development, 71,* 543–562.

Masten, A. S. (2001). Ordinary magic: Resilience processes in development. *American Psychologist, 56,* 227–238.

Masten, A. S., & Garmezy, N. (1985). Risk, vulnerability, and protective factors in developmental psychopathology. In B. Lahey & A. Kazdin (Eds.), *Advances in clinical child psychology* (Vol. 8, pp. 1–52). New York: Plenum Press.

Maton, K. I., Schellenbach, C. J., Leadbeater, B. J., & Solarz, A. L. (Eds.). (2004). *Investing in children, youth, families, and communities:*

Strengths-based research and policy. Washington, DC: American Psychological Association.

McLoyd, V. C., & Wilson, L. (1990). Maternal behavior, social support, and economic conditions as predictors of distress in children. *New Directions for Child Development, 46,* 49–69.

Menestrel, S. L. (1999, May). *What do fathers contribute to children's well-being?* Washington, DC: Child Trends.

Morrison, G. M., Brown, M., D'Incau, B., O'Farrell, S. L., & Furlong, M. J. (2006). Understanding resilience in educational trajectories: Implications for protective possibilities. *Psychology in the Schools, 43,* 19–31.

Nord, C. W., Brimhall, D., & West, J. (1998). Dad's involvement with their kids' schools. *Education Digest, 63,* 29–36.

Novilla, M. L. B., Barnes, M. D., De La Cruz, N. G., Williams, P. N., & Rogers, J. (2006). Public health perspectives on the family. *Family Community Health, 29,* 28–42.

Paquette, D. (2004). Theorizing the father–child relationship: Mechanisms and developmental outcomes. *Human Development, 47,* 193–219.

Parke, R. D. (2000). Father involvement: A developmental psychological perspective. *Marriage and Family Review, 29,* 43–58.

Pearce, M. J., Jones, S. M., Schwab-Stone, M. E., & Ruchkin, V. (2003). The protective effects of religiousness and parent involvement on the development of conduct problems among youth exposed to violence. *Child Development, 74,* 1682–1696.

Pearce, M. J., Little, T., & Perez, J. E. (2003). Religiousness and depressive symptoms among adolescents. *Journal of Clinical Child and Adolescent Psychology, 32,* 267–276.

Perry-Burney, G. D., & Takhi, B. K. (2002). Self esteem, academic achievement and moral development among adolescent girls. *Journal of Human Behavior in the Social Environment, 5,* 15–28.

Pleck, J. H. (1997). Paternal involvement: Levels, sources, and consequences. In M. E. Lamb (Ed.), *The role of the father in child development* (pp.66–103). New York: John Wiley & Sons, Inc.

Rutter, M. (1987). Psychosocial resilience and protective mechanisms. *American Journal of Orthopsychiatry, 57,* 316–331.

Salem, D. A., Zimmerman, M. A., & Notaro, P. C. (1998). Effects of family structure, family process, and father involvement on psychosocial outcomes among African American adolescents. *Family Relations, 47,* 331–342.

Smith, T. B., McCullough, M. E., & Poll, J. (2003). Religiousness and depression: Evidence for a main effect and the moderating influence of stressful life events. *Psychological Bulletin, 129,* 614–636.

Sobolewski, J. M., & King, V. (2005). The importance of the coparental relationship for nonresident fathers' ties to children. *Journal of Marriage and Family, 67,* 1196–1212.

Tamis-LeMonda, C. S., & Cabrera, N. (Eds.). (2002). *Handbook of father involvement: Multidisciplinary perspectives.* Mahwah, NJ: Lawrence Erlbaum Associates.

Taylor, R. J., & Chatters, L. M. (1991). Nonorganizational religious partici-
pation among elderly Black adults. *Journal of Gerontology, 46,*
S103–S111.
Villarruel, F. A., Keith, J. G., Perkins, D. F., & Borden, L. M. (Eds.). (2003).
Community Youth Development. Thousand Oaks, CA: Sage Publica-
tions.
Werner, E. E., & Smith, R. (1992). *Overcoming the odds: High risk children
from birth to adulthood.* Ithaca, NY: Cornell University Press.
Whitman, T. L., Borkowski, J. G., Keogh, D. A., & Weed, K. (2001). *Interwo-
ven lives: Adolescent mothers and their children.* Mahwah, NJ: Law-
rence Erlbaum Associates.
Woolley, M. E., & Grogan-Kaylor, A. (2006). Protective family factors in the
context of neighborhood: Promoting positive school outcomes. *Family
Relations, 55,* 93–104.

9

Design and Analytic Approaches to Research on Resilience

Shannon S. Carothers
Jaelyn R. Farris
Scott E. Maxwell

There is no single statistical procedure for the analysis of longitudinal data, as different research questions dictate different data structures and, thus, different statistical models and methods.

—Duncan, Duncan, Strycker, Li, and Alpert (1999, p. 1).

Developmental psychologists study a wide variety of processes including sensory, motor, cognitive, language, and socioemotional development. These processes are viewed as continually changing phenomena that are influenced by one another and the surrounding environment. Researchers have sought to examine their stability/instability and continuity/discontinuity over the lifespan as well as document developmental trajectories of change, along with their antecedents and consequences. By studying changes inherent to organisms, as well as those resulting from interactions and transactions with the environment, developmental psychologists have helped shape our current conceptualizations of risk, protection, and resilience. Resilience in the face of adversity can be viewed as a function of exposure to multiple risk and protective factors over time (Cummings, Davies, & Campbell, 2000; Luthar, Cicchetti, & Becker, 2000).

The primary challenge to the study of resilience is to understand the long-term, dynamic processes underlying both continuity and change in patterns of adaptation (Sroufe & Rutter, 1984). The developmental psychopathology perspective that is commonly relied upon in this line of research posits four courses of development: (a) constant positive adaptation, (b) initial positive adaptation followed by negative change toward pathology, (c) constant maladaptation, and (d) initial maladaptation followed by positive change (Sroufe, 1997). Given the variety of pathways, understanding the dynamic processes of behavior and development often necessitates multidomain, multicontextual, longitudinal examinations of the origins and courses of development (Ciccheti & Cohen, 1995), including considerations of interactions and transactions between the individual and his or her surrounding environmental context (Sameroff, 1994).

The study of resilience and vulnerability requires the simultaneous and long-term consideration of individual, family, and environmental processes (Masten & Garmezy, 1985; Werner & Smith, 1982, 1992), together with transactional relationships among these processes (Sameroff, 1994). Although these relationships are often complex, advanced statistical techniques are now available to address these sophisticated, process-oriented issues. In this chapter, we describe designs and analytic techniques that are applicable to the future of research on resilience. When properly applied, these approaches will broaden our understanding of resilience and facilitate the development of effective prevention and intervention programs.

CROSS-SECTIONAL VERSUS LONGITUDINAL DESIGNS

Although cross-sectional designs are often appealing because they allow research to be conducted more quickly and in a cost-efficient manner, they limit the researcher's ability to address developmental issues and make causal inferences about intraindividual change. Several conditions need to be met to infer causality: (a) the presumed cause and effect must be related; (b) the presumed cause must precede the effect in time; and (c) other competing explanations for the observed effect should be ruled out, which ideally involves random assignment (Duncan et al., 1999). In point of fact, the second condition is never met when cross-sectional designs are utilized.

In the social and behavioral sciences, longitudinal designs play a major role in examining natural developmental processes and analyzing change (Boys et al., 2003). In contrast to the "snapshots" of development associated with cross-sectional designs, longitudinal designs allow for repeated assessments over multiple time points. The objectives of longitudinal research are twofold: The first is descriptive and seeks to characterize each person's pattern of change over time (i.e., linear, nonlinear, consistent); the second is relational, examining the association between predictors and the patterns of change (Singer & Willett, 2003). Longitudinal research serves to: (a) identify intraindividual change, (b) identify interindividual differences in intraindividual change, (c) describe interrelationships of change (such as multivariate change), (d) analyze causes of intraindividual change, and (5) describe the direction and magnitude of causal relationships between variables as well as the determinants of interindividual differences in intraindividual change (McArdle, 2005; Menard, 1991; Singer & Willett, 2003). Because resilience is a function of the dynamic interactions and transactions between multiple risk and protective factors, it is essential for research in this area to utilize longitudinal, rather than cross-sectional, designs. Moreover, it is important to measure multiple variables on repeated occasions in order to provide the amount and type of data that is necessary for sophisticated longitudinal modeling techniques.

Although longitudinal designs have often been utilized in the study of resilience, researchers have typically failed to make use of the most appropriate and powerful analytic techniques. As a result, our understanding of the dynamic interactions and transactions that lead to resilience or vulnerability is unclear. For example, the most common practice in assessing the impact of risk has been to measure multiple risk variables at a single point in time, dichotomize the variables based on their "presence" or "absence," sum the dichotomous scores, and use the resulting additive risk index to predict outcomes at a later point in time (cf. chap. 7). There are several drawbacks associated with this approach. First, there is a loss of variability associated with dichotomizing or categorizing variables, which in turn may result in fewer significant findings than may have been evident if continuous variables had been used (MacCallum, Zhang, Preacher, & Rucker, 2002). Next, this approach does not provide information regarding changes in risks over time, ignores the role of protective factors and processes, and inherently conceptualizes resilience as a static outcome variable rather than a dynamic process (cf. chap. 7). Finally, these approaches are often carried out with the use of data editing techniques, such as listwise deletion or mean substitution for missing data, and therefore the results often do not provide the most accurate and powerful representations of the data (Collins, 2006).

Given the dynamic nature of resilience (Luthar et al., 2000), it is important to utilize statistical techniques that examine both within- and between-persons questions about longitudinal change processes. These techniques are used to: (a) model change over time, (b) model latent (i.e., not directly observed) constructs, (c) examine micro-level processes of change, (d) model transitions into and out of particular states and assess predictors of these transitions, and (e) fit more sophisticated mediational and moderational models to the data, providing a more comprehensive picture of developmental trajectories (Singer & Willett, 2003). When these analytic techniques are used in conjunction with longitudinal designs, they allow researchers the opportunity to gain a richer view of the dynamic intraindividual and interindividual processes of change. In the following section we discuss several of the major challenges facing longitudinal research on resilience—including analyses of cumulative risk and protection, timing and consistency of risk and protective factors, and high rates of missing data and attrition—and describe analytic approaches that are appropriate for addressing these issues.

OVERCOMING THE ANALYTIC CHALLENGES FACING RESEARCH ON RESILIENCE

An appropriate developmental model is one that not only describes a single individual's developmental trajectory, but also captures interindividual differences in these trajectories over time (Duncan et al., 1999). A critical aspect of such a model is the ability to study predictors of individual differences in order to answer questions about which variables exert important effects on the rate of development. In addition, the model should be able to capture the vital group statistics in a way that allows the researcher to study development at the group level (Duncan et al., 1999).

The sections that follow describe some of the major considerations and challenges facing research on resilience, including: (a) assessing cumulative risk and protection, as well as changes in resilience over time; (b) assessing the roles of timing and consistency of risk and protection on the development of resilience; and (c) handling the high rates of missing data and attrition that are common in research with high-risk populations. In each case, we suggest advanced analytic techniques that can be used to overcome these challenges. Although there are numerous techniques that could be used to address these challenges, we focus on three approaches: latent growth curve (i.e., "multilevel") models, autoregressive models, and dynamical systems analysis. We contend that these approaches could be readily applied to address the major challenges in this area.

Assessing Cumulative Risk and Protection

Any single risk or protective factor can contribute to children's development. The presence of multiple risk or protective factors, however, is likely to have an even greater impact on outcomes (cf. Masten, Best, & Garmezy, 1990; Sameroff, Seifer, Baldwin, & Baldwin, 1993). Moreover, increases, decreases, or chronicity of exposure to risk and protective factors over time can have important implications for children's development (Appleyard, Egeland, van Dulmen, & Sroufe, 2005). The challenge confronting resilience researchers is to utilize appropriate analytic models that have the capability to assess the impact of cumulative risk and protection. The most commonly used models, which have often been referred to in the literature as cumulative risk models, dichotomize and then sum a variety of risk variables, and then use the resultant risk index to predict children's developmental outcomes (cf. chap. 7). The moderating or mediating role of one or more protective factors or processes is sometimes taken into account, yet it is rare to find studies that describe the long-term impact of multiple and accumulating risk and protective factors over time.

Based on the call for greater consistency in the terminology associated with research on resilience (Luthar et al., 2000), we have proposed distinctions between additive, multiplicative, and cumulative risk and protection (cf. chap. 7). According to our definitions, the most commonly used models in the literature assess multiple risks in an additive or multiplicative, rather than cumulative, fashion. In other words, there are few studies to date that have assessed risk and protection in terms of the accumulation of multiple factors over time in a nonadditive and nonmultiplicative manner. The use of more sophisticated longitudinal models would address process-related questions regarding the accumulation of exposure to multiple risk and protective factors over time.

Three basic types of longitudinal models are of most interest for research on risk and resilience: (a) latent growth curve (i.e., "multilevel") models, (b) autoregressive models, and (c) dynamical systems models. These models, which utilize advanced approaches to handling missing data, can be applied with a variety of software packages (e.g., EQS, HLM, LISREL, Mplus, SAS) to address questions regarding cumulative risk and protection. We will return to the topic of missing data later in the chapter. First, we focus on the applications of these models to the study of risk, resilience, and protection.

Latent Growth Curve Models.   The purpose of latent growth curve analysis is to concurrently examine information about intraindividual change and interindividual differences (Nesselroade, 1991). This is accomplished by estimating individual growth trajectories using repeated measures as indicators of a latent intercept and latent slope (Bollen & Curran, 2006; Duncan et al.,

1999). In this type of model, latent curves are represented by factors and correspond to aspects of change over time. Repeated manifest measures are used as multiple indicators of one or more latent factors (Curran & Willoughby, 2003); thus, repeated measures of the manifest variables are represented as a linear combination of latent variables, such as a latent intercept and a latent slope (McDonald & Ringo Ho, 2002). Change can be characterized in a variety of ways—for example, level, linear, or acceleration—and may be influenced by the inclusion of predictors and/or correlates into the model (McDonald & Ringo Ho, 2002).

In accord with the conceptual scheme described in chapter 7, latent growth curve models can be used to investigate "simultaneous" cumulative risk, in which the impact of several factors at one or more points in time is considered in a nonadditive and nonmultiplicative fashion. These multilevel models can also be used to study "chronic" cumulative risk, with an emphasis on the longitudinal accumulation of one or more factors over time. In both cases, multiple manifest (i.e., observed) risk variables can be used to represent latent (i.e., unobserved) variables and estimate latent trajectories that describe underlying developmental processes (Bollen & Curran, 2006).

In general, the same fundamental approaches to cumulative risk apply to cumulative protection: Latent protective variables can be formed from a combination of multiple manifest protective variables. In the case of protection, however, researchers are typically interested in the moderating or mediating role of the protective variables, in contrast to the direct predictive role of cumulative risk. As a result, the analytic approaches can become more complicated. Findings from these sophisticated models, however, have the potential to dramatically increase our understanding of "cumulative protection," a concept that has been understudied to date. Although the technical details of these approaches are beyond the scope of this chapter, the interested reader is referred to Duncan et al. (1999) for details about testing interaction effects in latent growth models, and Cheong, MacKinnon, and Khoo (2003) and Kenny, Korchmaros, and Bolger (2003) for guidelines on assessing mediational processes in multilevel models.

Just as it is important to consider the effects of multiple changing risk and protective factors, it is also valuable to consider resilience as a composite of development across multiple theoretically-similar adjustment domains (Luthar et al., 2000). For example, high academic achievement is likely to be associated with good behavior in the classroom, and therefore "academic resilience" may be considered as a latent construct rather than as a single manifest variable. Resilience in one domain may influence the likelihood of resilience in other domains, and therefore the outcome variables themselves may become predictors of one another. With multiple latent predictors and outcomes incorporated into the model, it is possible that there may be different pathways for each outcome. Latent growth curve models can be applied to the study of longitudinal changes in resilience across various domains, while simultaneously assessing the influence of multiple risk and protective factors whose values may change over time.

The use of latent growth curve modeling can be illustrated by considering variations in risk, protection, and resilience in the lives of children born to adolescent mothers. Teenage mothers and their children are often confronted with daily stresses and challenges that arise from multiple sources, such as poor maternal resources, family instability, or poverty (Whitman, Borkowski, Keogh, & Weed, 2001). Inconsistencies in parenting practices, composition of the home environment, and neighborhood status can create situations in which children are exposed to periods of turbulence and instability throughout childhood and adolescence (cf. chap. 7). However, protective factors—such as father presence, support from churches, and involvement with social or sports groups (cf. chap. 8)—can often moderate or mediate the impact of exposure to risks, thereby increasing the likelihood of resilience. Given the wide assortment of and sometimes erratic exposure to risk and protective factors, it becomes evident that resilience among children of adolescent mothers must be conceptualized in a multidimensional framework. Although researchers have sometimes utilized "resilience indices" based on categorical scores from multiple outcome variables (e.g., Weed, Keogh, & Borkowski, 2006; Whitman et al., 2001), a more sophisticated approach would be to form latent constructs from the observed variables and assess interrelationships of predictors and outcomes with latent growth curve modeling. This approach would allow for the longitudinal assessment of resilience in various domains—such as educational, socioemotional, and behavioral—rather than as a global construct.

Use of multilevel latent growth models in this area could address questions such as: (a) To what degree is a child's resilience in one domain associated with his or her resilience in other domains?; (b) What is the impact of multiple changing risks on trajectories of resilience in various domains?; and (c) What role do protective factors play in influencing children's trajectories of resilience? Answers to these questions would vastly increase our understanding of the dynamic nature of risk, protection, and resilience on both intraindividual and interindividual levels. The interested reader is referred to Bollen and Curran (2006), Duncan et al. (1999), and Singer and Willett (2003) for details on the technical procedures used to analyze multilevel latent growth curve models.

Autoregressive Models. In another approach to longitudinal modeling, autoregressive models structure the amount of a characteristic or variable at each time point to have a direct impact on the amount of subsequent occasions, typically omitting direct links between nonadjacent measures (Bollen & Curran, 2006). Models of this sort are tested by measuring changes over time, thus necessitating a longitudinal design. It should be noted that, in contrast to the latent growth models described above, autoregressive models focus on interindividual, or between-person, changes in predictor and outcome variables. In other words, these models focus on how individuals change relative to other individuals, in contrast to the combination of intraindividual and interindividual changes that are assessed with latent growth models.

The main focus of autoregressive models, which are sometimes referred to as residual change models, is to explain the pattern of correlations in measures over time (Curran & Bollen, 2001; Duncan et al., 1999). These models rest on the assumption that the effect of a Time 1 measure on the Time 2 measure of the same variable (i.e., the autoregressive effect) is a legitimate explanation for the observed effect at Time 2 (Gollob & Reichardt, 1987). Based on this assumption, it has been argued that time lags and autoregressive effects must be considered before causal inferences can be made about the influence of additional predictor variables.

Autoregressive models are useful for resilience research because they assess the long-term impact that risk and protection, as well as associated *trace* and/or *sleeper* effects, have on the course of development. These models are especially applicable to the study of *chronic* cumulative risk and protection (cf. chap. 7). Moreover, autoregressive models can be used to address issues of change in resilience status over time. Just as with latent growth models, autoregressive models allow for the creation of latent variables and, by taking this approach, researchers can use multiple indicator variables to study changes in resilience across a variety of domains. When utilizing autoregressive models in this area, the chronic occurrence of one or more risk or protective factors is thought to influence resilience. Thus, the defining feature of these models is the chronic presence of negative and/or positive attributes or supports over time. The interested reader is referred to Cole and Maxwell (2003) regarding longitudinal mediation in an autoregressive framework.

When applied to research on resilience, autoregressive models can be used to address questions such as: (a) To what degree is resilience in one domain associated with resilience in other domains?; (b) What is the impact of multiple changing risks on changes in resilience in various domains?; and (c) What role do protective factors play in influencing changes in resilience? In contrast to the results provided by latent growth models, results from autoregressive models focus on interindividual changes in risk, protection, and resilience. Thus, these models address fundamentally different questions than latent growth curve models.

Final Thoughts About Cumulative Risk and Protection.   Regardless of the specific approach that is used, longitudinal modeling techniques are especially applicable to the analysis of cumulative risk and protection. Although the approaches are not as straightforward as the additive and multiplicative risk indexes that are commonly used in research on resilience (cf. chap. 7), they can be worth the extra effort because they provide a greater understanding of the roles of multiple dynamic risk and protective factors in the development of resilience, as well as longitudinal changes in resilience in a variety of domains.

Latent growth curve models are well-suited to address questions regarding *simultaneous* or chronic cumulative risk or protection, and autoregressive models are applicable to questions regarding chronic risk or protection (cf. chap. 7). Although on the surface there appears to be some overlap between the models, it is essential to recognize that latent growth curve and autoregressive models answer different questions. Intraindividual variability is typically of primary interest in the analysis of longitudinal data, because growth is a phenomenon that occurs within the individual (Collins, 2006). In order to fully understand change, the ultimate goal is to abstract general principles about interindividual variability in intraindividual change (Collins, 2006; Curran & Wirth, 2004). Longitudinal growth curve models have the capability to address both intraindividual and interindividual changes, thereby providing greater opportunities to address developmentally sensitive hypotheses (Collins & Shanahan, 1998). As a result, these models are highly applicable to the study of risk, protection, and resilience. Autoregressive models, on the other hand, have received criticism due to their limited focus on changes at the interindividual level (Duncan et al., 1999; Hertzog & Nesselroade, 1987; Rogosa & Willett, 1985), and therefore may be limited in their ability to address the major challenges in the study of resilience.

Timing and Consistency of Risk and Protection

The developmental timing of exposure to risk and protection (e.g., exposure in childhood versus adolescence), as well as the consistency or inconsistency of exposure over time, may lead to variations in the prediction of developmental outcomes (Schulenberg, Sameroff, & Cicchetti, 2004). In order to assess the impact of timing and consistency, it is essential to utilize models that consider the dynamic nature of risk and protective factors over time. In the following sections we discuss the use of a time-varying covariate in multilevel models to address issues of timing and the use of dynamical systems analysis to address issues of consistency.

Assessing Timing Effects Using a Time-Varying Covariate.   R i s k
and/or protective factors may influence resilience to varying degrees
depending on the point of development at which they occur. For example, a recent longitudinal study which assessed risk factors such
as child maltreatment, inter-parental violence, and low socioeconomic status, suggested that the timing of exposure to risks influenced children's development (Appleyard et al., 2005). Specifically,
risks during early childhood were more predictive of adolescent aggression than risks during middle childhood. These types of variations can be assessed in longitudinal growth curve models through
the use of a time-varying covariate.

A time-varying predictor is a variable whose values may change
over time, thereby reflecting differences in status at each measurement occasion (Singer & Willett, 2003). A time-varying covariate can
be used in longitudinal growth curve modeling to address questions
about how changes in an outcome variable can be predicted by
changes in antecedent variables. Moreover, these variables can be included as either predictors or outcomes of growth trajectories,
thereby addressing questions about the antecedents and consequences of development, as well as determining whether development in one domain covaries with development in other domains
over time (Duncan et al., 1999).

Returning to the previous example about risk and protection
among children of adolescent mothers, time-varying covariates
could be used to address questions such as: (a) How do changes in
risk (e.g., cognitive readiness) and/or protective (e.g., father involvement) factors influence children's resilience over time?; (b) Do these
changes have similar or different influences on various domains of
resilience (e.g., educational, socioemotional, and behavioral domains)?; and (c) Do changes in resilience status over time influence
later levels of exposure to risk and protective factors? Answers to
questions such as these would vastly increase our understanding of
the dynamic nature of resilience. Because time-varying covariates are
used in latent growth curve models, results from these analyses will
provide information about change on both intraindividual and
interindividual levels.

Assessing Consistency Effects Using Dynamical Systems Analysis.
The most basic assumption of dynamical systems analysis is that all systems change and evolve. Knowledge of a system's current state gives rise to the prediction of the future state of that system (Nowak & Lowenstein, 1994). *Dynamic systems* are made up of "shifting" variables whose values change over time; in turn, changes in these variables characterize the relevant properties of the system.

Dynamical systems analysis is applicable to research on resilience because it allows for the study of how fluctuations in risk and/or protective factors influence children's development at the intraindividual level. For example, inconsistent parenting practices are common among teenage mothers (Borkowski et al., 2002). We hypothesize that two related variables—the *consistency/inconsistency* and *regularity/irregularity* of instructional approaches to parenting—distinguish adult versus adolescent parents and influence infant and child development (Borkowski et al., 2002). To date, within- and between-day variability in adolescent parenting styles has not been systematically studied. Dynamical systems analysis could help us to identify and describe important inconsistencies and fluctuations in parenting practices across time as well as provide a new theoretical framework for understanding children's development. We predict that greater variability in parenting will occur with adolescent mothers, perhaps associated with the stress, inadequate social supports, depression, or patterns of domestic violence that are often present in their lives, thus compromising children's cognitive and socioemotional development (cf. chaps. 3, 4, 5, and 6). A dynamical systems approach might lead to a better understanding of the causal factors underlying cognitive and socioemotional development by focusing on "consistency" and "variability" as explanatory variables.

A dynamical systems approach to studying inconsistent parenting might explain the role of adolescent parenting on children's diverse developmental problems. For instance, children who have been maltreated and who develop poor self-regulatory skills are often limited by inconsistent and inadequate modeling of self-regulation provided by their caregivers (cf. chap. 5) and are thus constrained by the dynamics of the system in which they are embedded. Alternatively, the development of self-regulation skills allows some children to escape from these constraints. Consistency and regularity in parenting practices may prove to be important causal variables in children's developmental outcomes. Alternatively, fluctuations in adolescent mothers' parenting practices—whether from day-to-day or over longer time periods—are likely associated with inconsistencies in social supports and/or levels of depression, among other maternal characteristics.

Some teens manifest consistent parenting techniques, whereas others display inconsistent parenting because of the nature of their social supports. The former might result from having a grandmother who provides "just the right amount" of support and guidance and the latter due to grandmothers who are intrusive, controlling, and demanding. A "pendulum with friction" model that measures intraindividual disregulation in parenting can be helpful in understanding these differences. For example, the behavior of a teen mother who is consistent in her parenting practices across time may be able to be modeled by a *dampened linear model* (i.e., a pendulum with friction). That is, we would anticipate variability in parenting immediately following birth, which would then decrease over time (see Fig. 9.1a). In contrast, a teen mother who lacks appropriate support from her mother could become neglectful or engage in poor and inconsistent parenting; this behavior would best be described by a *linear oscillatory model* without the dampening parameter (i.e., a pendulum without friction). That is, fluctuations in parenting observed after birth would not decrease with time (see Fig. 9.1b), and perhaps might even increase (see Figure 9.1c).

The equation for the dampened linear oscillator is expressed in a regression model in which the acceleration of the pendulum is the outcome variable and the position and velocity of the pendulum are the predictor variables (Boker, 2001). From a developmental perspective, velocity refers to the linear changes in the system (e.g., changes in a specific parenting behavior or the sum of different measures) and acceleration describes its curvature (e.g., the speed with which behavioral changes occur). Differential equation models can then be used to express effects within a system in terms of their derivatives (i.e., the instantaneous rates of change of the variables) as well as in terms of the values of the variables themselves (Boker & Gra-

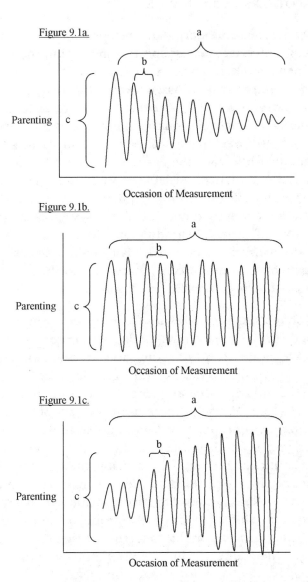

Figure 9.1a. A *dampened* linear oscillator model with three parameters: (a) decay rate, (b) 1/frequency, and (c) amplitude (adapted from Borkowski et al., 2002).

Figure 9.1b. An *undampened* linear oscillator model with three parameters: (a) decay rate, (b) 1/frequency, and (c) amplitude (adapted from Borkowski et al., 2002).

Figure 9.1c. An *increased* linear oscillator model with three parameters: (a) decay rate, (b) 1/frequency, and (c) amplitude (adapted from Borkowski et al., 2002).

ham, 1999). In these models, a distinction is made between *order parameters*, which are macroscopic parameters internal to a system, and *control parameters*, which represent conditions external to the system but determine to a great extent the dynamics observed (Nowak & Lowenstein, 1994). After identifying the order parameters of the system that best represent regularity or irregularity in adolescent parenting, the next step would be to examine factors, or control parameters, that influence the entire system. For instance, mechanisms such as maternal age, social support variables, cognitive readiness, or self-regulation could be used to predict individual differences in the shape or trajectory of the system encompassed by consistent or inconsistent parenting practices. If carried out in this manner, a dynamical systems analysis of daily fluctuations in the parenting practices of adolescent mothers could shed more light on the processes leading to resilience.

Final Thoughts About Timing and Consistency.   In this section we focused on the use of time-varying covariates in longitudinal growth curve models to address questions related to timing of risks and protection, and dynamical systems analysis to address questions related to the influence of consistency and/or variability of risk and protective factors. Although these are only two of numerous approaches to these questions, we contend that these techniques are well-suited to address these issues in a way that would dramatically increase our understanding of the dynamic nature of resilience.

Now that we have described a variety of analytic techniques that can be used to address some of the major challenges facing research on resilience, we shift our focus to the problem of missing data and attrition. This is an important concern in research on resilience, since missing data and attrition are ubiquitous in the longitudinal designs that are necessary for research in this area.

Missing Data and Attrition

There are several reasons for being concerned about missing data: (a) missing data can reduce effective sample size, which results in a loss of statistical power; (b) as sample size decreases, confidence intervals become wider, which results in a loss of precision; (c) if data are missing not at random, the available data may be less representative of the population; and (d) missing data may result in biased conclusions about the size and existence of effects (Little, 1992; Little & Rubin, 2002). For these reasons, missing data can threaten both internal and external validity (Shadish, Cook & Campbell, 2002), due to reduced power to detect differences and because subjects who remain in the study rarely represent the original group or population of interest (Streiner, 2002). These problems often become exacerbated in research on resilience due to the high-risk nature of the samples. Studies of high-risk participants, such as adolescent parents and their children, are notorious for missing data, due to both subject and situational constraints (Letourneau, 2001).

Types of Missing Data.   Several types of "nonresponse" may contribute to the occurrence of missing data (Schafer & Graham, 2002). Unit nonresponse refers to situations in which an entire assessment was not completed, due to situations such as participants not being at home for the scheduled appointment or refusing to participate. In cases of item nonresponse, however, partial data are available. This occurs when individuals participate in the overall assessment but refuse to answer certain items. Finally, wave nonresponse is common in longitudinal studies, in which participants are often present for some, but not all, waves of data collection. Attrition, or dropout, is a special case of wave nonresponse in which a participant leaves the study and never returns.

From an analytic perspective, the pattern of missing data is more important than the amount of missing data (Little & Rubin, 2002; Schafer & Graham, 2002; Tabachnick & Fidell, 2001). Data that are missing independent of all the predictors and dependent variables are termed "missing completely at random" or MCAR (Schafer & Graham, 2002). Missing values of this sort that are scattered randomly through a data matrix pose a less serious problem because the missing data are not related to the outcome variables (Schafer & Graham, 2002; Tabachnick & Fidell, 2001). In this circumstance, available data can be analyzed and unbiased estimates obtained. Even here, however, power and precision will suffer if common methods such as listwise deletion are employed.

Data in which the missingness is random conditional on variables included in the model are referred to as "missing at random" or MAR.

In contrast, nonignorable missingness results when data are "missing not at random" (MNAR; Schafer & Graham, 2002). In this case, data are missing because of the independent or dependent variable. If responses had been observed, they would have turned out to be systematically different from what would be predicted based on variables included in the model. This type of missing data is of great concern and can lead to biased parameter estimates because missingness depends on unseen responses after participants drop out of the study (Schafer & Graham, 2002; Tabachnick & Fidell, 2001).

Handling Missing Data.   Most data analysis procedures were not designed to accommodate nonresponse or attrition (Schafer & Graham, 2002). Lacking resources or even a theoretical framework, researchers and software developers have often resorted to editing the data to lend an appearance of completeness. Depending on the situation, missing data may be addressed in a variety of ways (Little, 1992; Little & Rubin, 2002). Early research employed simple, easy-to-implement methods, such as listwise and pairwise deletion, averaging the available items, mean substitution, reweighting, or regression imputation (Gibson & Olejnik, 2003). Ad hoc edits, however, may inadvertently do more harm than good, producing answers that are biased, inefficient, and unreliable (Schafer & Graham, 2002). Likewise, these approaches may result in biased estimates of parameters or overestimations of the significance of statistical tests (Streiner, 2002).

Although data editing is not an optimal approach, ignoring missing data is also problematic. Advanced analytic approaches often require less stringent assumptions about the pattern of missing data thereby allowing the use of all available data (Maxwell & Delaney, 2004). The choice of which technique to use should be guided in part by the type of missing data. Similar approaches can be taken under missing completely at random (MCAR) and missing at random (MAR) conditions. If the data are missing not at random (MNAR), however, then no technique is guaranteed to produce unbiased estimates (McDonald & Ringo Ho, 2002).

In the following sections we provide suggestions for alternative treatments of missing data under MCAR or MAR conditions. This list is not meant to be exhaustive; rather, we describe two approaches to handling missing data without resorting to data editing techniques: maximum likelihood estimation and multiple imputation. It should be noted that neither of these procedures was created solely for the purposes of the longitudinal models described in this chapter. When used with longitudinal modeling, however, they enable researchers to address questions in ways that are not possible with traditional analytic approaches which require the use of narrower data editing techniques.

Maximum Likelihood Estimation. Assuming multivariate normality, MLE uses the available data to calculate maximum likelihood estimates of the model parameters (Bollen & Curran, 2006). In addition to the parameter estimates themselves, estimated standard errors of the parameter estimates are also obtained. These estimated standard errors then allow for hypothesis testing and the formation of confidence intervals. In this way, MLE makes good use of the available data without resorting to less sophisticated data editing techniques such as listwise deletion or mean substitution. It should be noted, however, that the use of maximum likelihood for estimation when the data are not multivariate normal serves to inflate the value of the chi-square statistic and increase the standard error associated with model parameters (Yuan, Bentler, & Zhang, 2005).

Multiple Imputation. Multiple Imputation (MI), proposed by Rubin (1987), is appropriate for a variety of missing data problems (Schafer & Graham, 2002). To accomplish MI, each missing value is replaced by multiple single values, leading to several alternative versions of the complete data (Little & Rubin, 2002). Each of the datasets is analyzed with a complete-data method, and then the results of all analyses are combined to obtain overall estimates. Although any single imputation will lead to underestimations of the standard errors, the repeated imputation process of this approach leads to increased precision in the estimates.

Final Thoughts About Missing Data.   Maximum likelihood estimation and multiple imputation are only two of a variety of procedures that can be applied to missing data. Although both approaches are becoming more commonly used in psychological research, implementing the methods in practice involves additional considerations. The interested reader is referred to Collins, Schafer, and Kam (2001) for a comparison of different strategies in handling missing data and Schafer and Graham (2002) for a review of available approaches and suggestions for newer methods.

Summing Up: Choosing Appropriate Designs and Analyses

In comparison to first-generation techniques such as regression and analysis of variance, the longitudinal modeling techniques described in this chapter have substantial advantages, in part because of the greater flexibility which they provide for the interplay between theory and data (Chin, 1998). Multilevel, autoregressive, and dynamical systems approaches allow for the examination of relationships among multiple and changing predictor and criterion variables, as well as enable researchers to construct unobservable latent variables; model errors in measurements for observed variables; statistically test a priori substantive, theoretical, and measurement assumptions against empirical data using confirmatory analysis; and employ sophisticated approaches to handling missing data. Latent growth modeling, in particular, has several strengths, including the capacity to (a) test the adequacy of the hypothesized growth form, (b) incorporate time-varying covariates, and (c) develop from the data a common developmental trajectory in an effort to rule out cohort effects (Duncan et al., 1999). Another important advantage of both multilevel and dynamical systems approaches to longitudinal data analysis is the conceptual emphasis on individual growth and the correlates of change as an explicit focus of the study (Francis, Fletcher, Stuebing, Davidson, & Thompson, 1991). Moreover, these longitudinal modeling approaches allow for the examination of group changes as well as individual change (Willett, 1988).

CONCLUSION: CONTRIBUTIONS TO THE STUDY OF RESILIENCE

The advanced longitudinal techniques described in this chapter are more than just an extension of traditional techniques such as regression and analysis of variance. In contrast, these sophisticated longitudinal modeling techniques actually enable researchers to address new questions, in part due to the way that they handle missing data, but also because they allow researchers to study unobservable constructs through the formation of latent variables and to assess the impact of fluctuations in predictor and criterion variables. In contrast to the "snapshots" of development provided by the commonly used approaches to studying resilience, these approaches have the potential to provide a vivid portrait of development that more accurately reflects real life. In other words, when multidomain, multicontextual, longitudinal designs are used, the advanced approaches described in this chapter can vastly increase our understanding of risk, protection, and resilience at both the individual and group levels.

It is important to note that the intention of this chapter was not to present an exhaustive description of longitudinal modeling procedures, but rather to alert developmental psychologists that advanced techniques are available to assess intraindividual and interindividual change over time in the study of risk, protection, and resilience. Regardless of the specific techniques that they choose to employ, developmental researchers should move away from assessing cross-sectional "snapshots" of development and instead focus on understanding the dynamic, longitudinal influence of multiple risk and protective factors in high-risk populations.

REFERENCES

Appleyard, K., Egeland, B., van Dulmen, M. H. M., & Sroufe, L. A. (2005). When more is not better: The role of cumulative risk in child behavior outcomes. *Journal of Child Psychology and Psychiatry, 46*, 235–245.

Boker, S. M. (2001). Differential structural equation modeling of intraindividual variability. In L. Collins & A. Sayer (Eds.), *New methods for the analysis of change* (pp. 3–28). Washington, DC: American Psychological Association.

Boker, S. M., & Graham, J. (1999). A dynamical systems analysis of adolescent substance use. *Multivariate Behavioral Research, 33*, 479–507.

Bollen, K. A., & Curran, P. J. (2006). *Latent curve models: A structural equation perspective.* Hoboken, NJ: Wiley.

Borkowski, J. G., Bisconti, T., Willard, C. C., Keogh, D. A., Whitman, T. L., & Weed, K. (2002). The adolescent as parent: Influences on children's intellectual, academic, and socioemotional development. In J. G. Borkowski, S. L. Ramey, & M. Bristol-Power (Eds.), *Parenting and the child's world: Influences on academic, intellectual, and social–emotional development* (pp. 161–184). Mahwah, NJ: Lawrence Erlbaum Associates.

Boys, A., Marsden, J., Stillwell, G., Hatchings, K., Griffiths, P., & Farrell, M. (2003). Minimizing respondent attrition in longitudinal research: Practical implications from a cohort study of adolescent drinking. *Journal of Adolescence, 26,* 363–373.

Cheong, J. W., MacKinnon, D. P., & Khoo, S. T. (2003). Investigation of mediational processes using parallel process latent growth curve modeling. *Structural Equation Modeling, 10,* 238–262.

Chin, W. W. (March, 1998). Issues and opinions on structural equation modeling. *MIS Quarterly 22,* vii–xvi.

Cicchetti, D. & Cohen, D. J. (1995). Perspectives on developmental psychopathology. In D. Cicchetti & D. J. Cohen (Eds.), *Developmental psychopathology, Vol. I: Theory and methods* (pp. 3–22). New York: John Wiley & Sons, Inc.

Cole, D. A., & Maxwell, S. E. (2003). Testing mediational models with longitudinal data: Questions and tips in the use of structural equation modeling. *Journal of Abnormal Psychology, 112,* 558–577.

Collins, L. M. (2006). Analysis of longitudinal data: The integration of theoretical model, temporal design, and statistical model. *Annual Review of Psychology, 57,* 505–528.

Collins, L. M., Schafer, J. L., & Kam, C. M. (2001). A comparison of inclusive and restrictive strategies in modern missing data procedures. *Psychological Methods, 6,* 330–351.

Collins, L. M. & Shanahan, M. J. (1998). Family-based prevention in developmental perspective: Design, measurement, and analytic issues. In K. E. Etz, E. B. Robertson, & R. S. Ashery (Eds.), *Drug abuse prevention through family intervention.* National Institute on Drug Abuse Research Monograph 177.

Cummings, E. M., Davies, P. T., & Campbell, S. B. (2000). *Developmental psychopathology and family process: Theory, research, and clinical implications.* New York: Guilford Press.

Curran, P. J., & Bollen, K. A. (2001). The best of both worlds: Combining autoregressive and latent curve models. In L. Collins & A. Sayer (Eds.), *New methods for the analysis of change* (pp. 107–135). Washington, DC: American Psychological Association.

Curran, P. J., & Willoughby, M. T. (2003). Implications of latent trajectory models for the study of developmental psychopathology. *Development and Psychopathology*, 15, 581–612.

Curran, P. J., & Wirth, R. J. (2004). Interindividual differences in intraindividual variation: Balancing internal and external validity. *Measurement: Interdisciplinary Research Perspectives*, 2, 219–247.

Duncan, T. E., Duncan, S. C., Strycker, L. A., Li, F., & Alpert. A. (1999). *An introduction to latent variable growth curve modeling: Concepts, issues, and applications*. Mahwah, NJ: Lawrence Erlbaum Associates.

Francis, D. J., Fletcher, J. M., Stuebing, K. K., Davidson, K. C., & Thompson, N. M. (1991). Analysis of change: Modeling individual growth. *Journal of Consulting and Clinical Psychology*, 59, 27–37.

Gibson, N. M., & Olejnik, S. (2003). Treatment of missing data at the second level of Hierarchical Linear Models. *Educational and Psychological Measurement*, 63, 204–238.

Gollob, H. F., & Reichardt, C. S. (1987). Taking account of time lags in causal models. *Child Development*, 58, 80–92.

Hertzog, C., & Nesselroade, J. R. (1987). Beyond autoregressive models: Some implications of the trait–state distinction for the structural modeling of developmental change. *Child Development*, 58, 93–109.

Kenny, D. A., Korchmaros, J. D., & Bolger, N. (2003). Lower level mediation in multilevel models. *Psychological Methods*, 8, 115–128.

Letourneau, N. (2001). Attrition among adolescents and infants involved in a parenting intervention. *Child: Care, Health, and Development*, 27, 183–186.

Little, R. J. A. (1992). Regression with missing X's: A review. *Journal of the American Statistical Association*, 87, 1227–1237.

Little, R. J. A., & Rubin, D. B. (2002). *Statistical analysis with missing data* (2nd ed.). New York, NY: Wiley.

Luthar, S. S., Cicchetti, D., & Becker, B. (2000). The construct of resilience: A critical evaluation and guidelines for future work. *Child Development*, 71, 543–562.

MacCallum, R. C., Zhang, S., Preacher, K. J., & Rucker, D. D. (2002). On the practice of dichotomization of quantitative variables. *Psychological Methods*, 7, 19–40.

Masten, A. S., Best, K. M., & Garmezy, N. (1990). Resilience and development: Contributions from the study of children who overcame adversity. *Development and Psychopathology*, 2, 425–444.

Masten, A., & Garmezy, N. (1985). Risk, vulnerability, and protective factors in developmental psychopathology. In B. Lahey & A. Kazdin (Eds.), *Advances in clinical child psychology* (Vol. 8, pp. 1–52). New York: Plenum Press.

Maxwell, S. E., & Delaney, H. D. (2004). Designing experiments and analyzing data: A model comparison perspective. (2nd ed.). Mahwah, NJ: Lawrence Erlbaum Associates.

McArdle, J. (2005). *Back to school: Longitudinal structural equation modeling in developmental research.* Paper presented at the 18th Biennial Conference on Human Development, Washington, D.C.

McDonald, R. P., & Ringo Ho, M. H. (2002). Principles and practice in reporting structural equation analyses. *Psychological Methods, 7,* 64–82.

Menard, S. (1991). *Longitudinal research.* Newbury Park, CA: Sage Publications, Inc.

Nesselroade, J. R. (1991). Interindividual differences in intraindividual change. In L. A. Collins & J. L. Horn (Eds.), *Best methods for the analysis of change* (pp. 92–106). Washington, DC: American Psychological Association.

Nowak, A., & Lowenstein, M. (1994). Dynamical systems: A tool for social psychology. In R. R. Vallacher & A. Nowak (Eds.), *Dynamical systems in social psychology* (pp. 17–53). San Diego: Academic Press.

Rogosa, D., & Willett, J. B. (1985). Understanding correlates of change by modeling individual differences in growth. *Psychometrika, 50,* 203–228.

Rubin, D. B. (1987). *Multiple imputation for nonresponse in surveys.* New York: Wiley.

Sameroff, A. (1994). Ecological perspectives on longitudinal follow-up studies. In S. L. Friedman & C. H. Haywood (Eds.), Developmental follow-up: Concepts, domains, and methods (pp. 45–64). San Diego, CA, US: Academic Press, Inc.

Sameroff, A. J., Seifer, R., Baldwin, A., & Baldwin, C. (1993). Stability of intelligence from preschool to adolescence: The influence of social and family risk factors. *Child Development, 64,* 80–97.

Schafer, J. L., & Graham, J. W. (2002). Missing data: Our view of the sate of the art. *Psychological Methods, 7,* 147–177.

Schulenberg, J. E., Sameroff, A. J., & Cicchetti, D. (2004). The transition to adulthood as a critical juncture in the course of psychopathology and mental health. *Development and Psychopathology, 16,* 799–806.

Shadish, W. R., Cook, T. D., & Campbell, D. T. (2002). *Experimental and quasi-experimental designs for generalized causal inference.* Boston: Houghton Mifflin.

Singer, J. D., & Willett, J. B. (2003). *Applied longitudinal data analysis: Modeling change and event occurrence.* New York, NY: Oxford University Press.

Sroufe, L. A. (1997). Psychopathology as an outcome of development. *Development and Psychopathology, 9,* 251–268.

Sroufe, L. A., & Rutter, M. (1984). The domain of developmental psychopathology. *Child Development, 55,* 1184–1199.

Streiner, D. L. (2002). The case of the missing data: Methods of dealing with dropouts and other research vagaries. *Canadian Journal of Psychiatry, 47*, 68–75.

Tabachnick, B. G., & Fidell, L. S. (2001). *Using multivariate statistics* (4th ed.). New York: Harper & Row.

Weed, K., Keogh, D., & Borkowski, J. (2006). Stability of resilience in children of adolescent mothers. *Journal of Applied Developmental Psychology, 27*, 60–77.

Werner, E., & Smith, R. (1982). *Vulnerable but invincible: A study of resilient children.* New York: McGraw-Hill.

Werner, E. E., & Smith, R. S. (Eds.). (1992). *Overcoming the odds: High risk children from birth to adulthood.* Ithaca, NY: Cornell University Press.

Whitman, T. L., Borkowski, J. G., Keogh, D. A., & Weed, K. (2001). *Interwoven lives: Adolescent mothers and their children.* Mahwah, NJ: Lawrence Erlbaum Associates.

Willett, J. B. (1988). Questions and answers in the measurement of change. In E. Z. Rothkop (Ed.), *Review of Research in Education, 15*, 345–422.

Yuan, K. H., Bentler, P. M. & Zhang, W. (2005). The effects of skewness and kurtosis on mean and covariance structure analysis: The univariate case and its multivariate implications. *Sociological Methods & Research, 34*, 240–258.

10

Toward Resilience: Designing Effective Prevention Programs

John G. Borkowski
Jaelyn R. Farris
Keri Weed

The term 'resilient' came in not as a simile for competence but as an extension of their competencies despite exposure to significant stressors. That focus was the essence of resilience and that is the way we launched our research efforts.

—Norman Garmezy (Rolf, 1999)

Adolescent motherhood often represents a constellation of risks present in the lives of teenagers from early development to their first pregnancy. These cumulative risks, coupled with an off-timed transition to adulthood, often launch negative life trajectories which spill over to influence children's lives. Opportunities are available at several critical life junctures to transform this developmental scenario, for both teen mothers and their children. An awareness of the risk and protective factors present at each juncture, combined with the delivery of theoretically-driven interventions, will likely reduce the negative consequences to teen mothers, their children, and their involvement with the larger society. In this chapter, we focus on characteristics of prevention and intervention programs aimed at fostering resilience in at-risk mothers and children, such as their timing, comprehensiveness, duration, and curricula orientations.

We draw upon data from the Notre Dame Adolescent Parenting Project (NDAPP) to guide our discussion of new approaches to prevention research, especially as they apply to teenage mothers. First, we summarize the major risk and protective factors that have emerged from 14 years of research with the NDAPP. We highlight the story of Marcus, the child of a teen mother from our project, whose life exemplifies resilience in the context of multiple risks. Next, we present a rationale for the necessity of early intervention, focusing on important developmental transitions as guided by a strengths-based approach to enhancing protective factors. In the final section, we describe a model program that addresses the risks and challenges confronting young mothers and their children and builds upon individual strengths in order to develop unique protective resources in each at-risk mother.

AVOIDING RISKS AND ENHANCING PROTECTION: INSIGHTS FROM THE NDAPP

Although the NDAPP dataset has yielded interesting findings on the transition of adolescent mothers to adulthood, the developmental problems we observed in children and their antecedents are most troublesome, as evidenced by math and reading delays, high rates of achievement-related failures, including increased incidence of mild mental retardation and learning disabilities, elevated rates of ADHD and conduct disorders, and frequent exposure to violence during early adolescence. These findings converge with a recent review by Terry-Humen, Manlove, and Moore (2005) on teen motherhood and children's achievement: After controlling for maternal characteristics prior to birth, age of childbearing was associated with poorer vocabularies among African American and Latino preschoolers and lower math and reading achievement from school onset to age 14 for all children. In the preceding chapters, we have identified some of the major risks associated with similar developmental delays in children of adolescent mothers in the NDAPP as well as important protective factors.

Table 10.1 summarizes major findings from the NDAPP in five important domains of children's development: intelligence, adaptive behavior, language, academic achievement, and socioemotional adjustment. The major risk factors, in order of importance, were low maternal cognitive readiness for parenting, low maternal IQ, abuse and neglect potential, depression, and aggression. In terms of protective factors, father involvement, religiosity, and community-based supports were particularly important, as was children's self-regulation and self esteem.

TABLE 10.1
Risk and Protective Factors in Children's Lives

Domain	Risk Factors	Protective Factors
Intelligence	-Low maternal IQ (Ch. 3) -Low cognitive readiness: i.e., Parenting attitudes, parenting expectations, knowledge of child development (Chs. 3, 5, & 7) -Neighborhood violence (Ch. 8)	
Adaptive Behavior	-Low cognitive readiness (Chs. 3 & 5) -Negative life events (Ch. 8)	-Religiosity (Ch. 8) -Social groups/sports (Ch. 8)
Language	-Low maternal IQ (Ch. 3) -Low cognitive readiness (Chs. 3 & 5)	
Academic Achievement	-Low maternal IQ (Chs. 3 & 7) -Low cognitive readiness (Chs. 3 & 7) -High child abuse potential (Ch. 3) -Maternal internalizing and externalizing (Ch. 3) -Low SES (Ch. 7)	-Self-regulation (Ch. 3) -Father involvement (Ch. 8)
Socioemotional Adjustment	-Low maternal IQ (Ch. 7) -Low cognitive readiness (Ch. 7) -High child abuse potential (Ch. 5) -Exposure to violence (Ch. 6) -Maternal internalizing and externalizing (Ch. 7) -Low SES (Ch. 7) -Negative life events (Ch. 8)	-Self-regulation (Ch. 3) -Father involvement (Ch. 8) -Religiosity (Ch. 8) -Relationship with parents (Ch. 8) -Self-esteem (Ch. 8) -Social groups/sports (Ch. 8)

It is interesting to note that we were able to identify more risk than protective factors in the NDAPP. In reality, however, exposure to multiple risk and protective factors often occurs simultaneously. The extent to which these "competing" factors are present or absent in a child's life can have a substantial impact on establishing resilience. In order to illustrate this notion, we turn to a description of Marcus, a resilient child from the NDAPP. His life experiences point to the importance of building upon individual strengths and protective factors over time, including self-confidence, a positive outlook on the future, and supportive relationships with parents, extended family, and teachers.

An Illustration of Resilience in the Face of Risk

Marcus is the oldest child of Rochelle, an adolescent mother with only a 10th-grade education and few supports from her immediate family. Seven months into her pregnancy, Rochelle moved in to live with Joe, the father of her baby, and his family in hopes that they would provide a more supportive and loving environment for her and her unborn child. Unlike many fathers, Joe shared the early caretaking responsibilities with Rochelle, such as getting up in the middle of the night and feeding their newborn son. Despite a break-up between Joe and Rochelle when Marcus was 18 months old, Marcus's father and paternal grandparents continued to play influential roles in his life. Throughout childhood, Marcus spent half the week with his father and the other half with his mother. After several years, Rochelle married another man, had a second child, earned an associate's degree, moved into a home in a decent neighborhood, and currently works as a full-time supervisor; all of these factors, in combination with the support of Marcus's biological father, have contributed to a stable foundation for his subsequent growth and development.

During his lifetime, Marcus has had many personal experiences, both positive and negative, that he feels have made his life "different from others." He comments often on his success in school and his athletic abilities. During an interview when he was 10, it became obvious that Marcus understood that he had been exposed to a number of adversities, such as exposure to neighborhood violence. Marcus, however, has always chosen to look at the positive aspects of his life experiences as opposed to dwelling on the negative. Specifically, he mentioned that his first 5 years of education were spent in Catholic school. Although he feels that his Catholic school was harder than the neighborhood public school, he believes its strictness made him a "smarter person" by urging high academic achievement. At age 10, he discussed his position as a minority student in the classroom (comprised of 19 European American, 5 African American, and 3 Latino students) as a positive attribute in that he "didn't get sunburned" like other students did when they went on field trips. Nevertheless, Marcus could not mask his sadness, particularly when discussing the death of his grandfather and great-grandparents or the fact that he had only been able to keep two friends longer than 4 years because his family was "always moving around".

When asked about aspects of his life that were most influential in shaping who he was at age 10 and who he wanted to be in the future, several positive themes emerged such as his modesty, sense of realism, and an appreciation for friends and family. A movie about his life would be "based on holidays, not the presents, but the celebration itself," because he considers spending time with his family the most memorable moments of his life.

Although Marcus does not see himself as a very religious person, he acknowledges that religion, or the idea of heaven, is important to him in that he will once again have the chance to see loved ones who have passed away. He attributed much of his success to his parents, particularly his mother's kindness, her willingness to give up everything for him, and her disciplinary practices such as taking away his privileges as opposed to "slapping me for punishment." A trip to Epcot Center in Florida is where Marcus learned "the most he ever has;" it fostered an interest in the human body and the medical field in general. When asked about his future, Marcus mentioned that everyone expects him to be making "big money as a lawyer or doctor;" however, he stated, "I'm not picky ... I just want to be how I am."

At age 17, Marcus continues to be active in school plays, athletic teams, and community programs such as the Urban Youth League. As a senior in high school, he values the relationship that his mother and biological father share with one another. Like most teenagers his age, Marcus reports that he has done things that he is not proud of, such as disobeying his parents, but he believes that he has learned from his mistakes. He attributes much of his success to his family and their financial stability; however, he also acknowledges that the community has provided him with opportunities to volunteer, which have given him greater confidence in himself.

Marcus believes that he "found his calling" as a school teacher through interactions with his teachers and six siblings. He encountered many opportunities as a Cadet Teacher and as president of Project Teach to work with young children. Through the assistance of his high school counselor, Marcus has been accepted to a college preparation program at a major Midwestern university to begin the summer after he graduates from high school. The program will also pay for his 1st year of tuition, books, and fees as well as a supplementary stipend. Marcus is an example of a resilient adolescent, who has matured in the face of challenging life circumstances.

The Need for Research on Parenting Programming

It is a sad fact that Marcus is one of only a handful of adolescents in the NDAPP who has an opportunity for a college education. It seems clear that most of his peers—who did not experience Marcus's supportive home and school environments—would have profited from intense, early intervention programs aimed at stabilizing their mothers' lives, strengthening parenting skills, and helping to find and afford high quality childcare or Early Head Start programs. This suggestion is in line with the conclusions of Terry-Humen et al. (2005) in their excellent review on *Playing Catch-Up*:

> Programs that include an emphasis on academic and employment success may be valuable. These programs not only can reduce the incidence of too-early childbearing, but they also may help improve school-readiness in the next generation by enhancing the economic, educational, and marital status of women before they become mothers. (p.25)

As we have seen in the case of Marcus, a "snapshot" of development at a single point in time cannot provide adequate answers to complex questions about the interaction of risks, protection, and resilience over time. In order to understand the array of multiple risk and protective factors, and their influence on development, it is essential to collect and analyze data within the framework of longitudinal designs. Moreover, it is essential to use multimethod, multi-informant approaches when attempting to understand process-related questions about typical and atypical development (Cummings, Davies, & Campbell, 2000).

We recognize the difficulty of collecting high quality longitudinal data while minimizing missing data and participant attrition, especially with samples of at-risk mothers, fathers, and children. In these situations it is useful to "think outside the box" in terms of data collection approaches. For example, the use of cell phones or laptop computers enables frequent contact with participants and, in turn, allows for the collection of repeated measurements necessary for advanced analytic techniques (cf. chap. 9). In the next section, we set the stage for formulating a model prevention program that builds upon the risk and protective factors identified in the NDAPP dataset. Its design and measurement scheme are in accord with recommendations for conducting high-quality research on resilience (cf. chap. 9).

RETHINKING PREVENTION DESIGNS

Prevention programs have many advantages over intervention programs. For instance, if adolescent pregnancies can be prevented in the first place, then subsequent interventions will not be needed. However, the majority of existing pregnancy prevention programs have focused on commitments to abstinence and/or the promotion of contraceptive methods. These programs have been evaluated elsewhere and, generally, have been found to be ineffective (Klerman, 2004); interested readers are referred to this thorough and important review of the consequences of rapid repeat pregnancies. This section focuses on the multiple risk factors that predispose some adolescents to early pregnancies as well as to the long-term, negative outcomes of an off-timed pregnancy for both mothers and their children.

**Building Comprehensive Prevention Programming:
The Issue of Timing**

In our society, movement toward adulthood is a much anticipated transition in the lives of adolescents. Yet, society provides few clear, unambiguous directions on how to accomplish this transition. The advice that is provided is often unrealistic for many pregnant teenagers, such as encouraging them to obtain a college education that would lead directly to a professional career and stable income. Relatedly, local leaders, pastors, and federal officials often argue strongly for becoming and maintaining two-parent families, a lifestyle not accepted by or available to many adolescent mothers.

As early as middle school, many teens receive negative feedback about the unlikelihood of their meeting society's expectations for academic success. Repeating a grade becomes a red flag, indicating that they are less likely than their peers to meet the educational requirements necessary for "full status" as an adult. For others, symptoms of anxiety, depression, or aggression may cause questions or doubts about their ability to meet societal demands, despite normal educational attainment. If feelings of positive self-efficacy and self-worth are not functional during early adolescence, teens may come to adopt alternative pathways to adulthood, including off-timed pregnancies .

Early Prevention.   An effective prevention program must not only be comprehensive and theory-driven, it should also be tailored to each participant's existing unique strengths and resources (Maton, Schellenbach, Leadbeater, & Solarz, 2004). All individuals and families have strengths that are unique to their personal experiences and cultural and ethnic backgrounds (Dunst, Trivette, & Mott, 1994). By building on existing strengths, prevention programs become more focused on promoting resilience and optimal development, rather than on erasing deficits. This focus empowers mothers, building their self-esteem, strengthening motivation, and fostering independence and success in multiple domains of life (cf. Maton et al., 2004). From this perspective, a mother's failure to display competence in a specific domain can be viewed as a failure of the surrounding systems (or the adequacy of the prevention program) to provide repeated opportunities for achieving success.

The first critical juncture for prevention programming targeting young mothers involves the risk and protective factors that may become apparent during early adolescence, but prior to the first pregnancy. Results of longitudinal research have suggested that adolescent girls from low SES backgrounds sometimes perceive insurmountable barriers along the traditional pathway to adulthood and may, consciously or unconsciously, choose motherhood as their rite of passage (Whitman, Borkowski, Keogh, & Weed, 2001). For instance, grade repetitions and internalizing problems (e.g., depression) have emerged repeatedly in the NDAPP dataset, as well as in other longitudinal projects, as critical risks that lead to adverse developmental outcomes for both mothers and children. Consistent with this assumption, prevention programs need to remove these barriers and provide acceptable alternative pathways.

One problem lies in the fact that preparation for adulthood in the United States has been relegated primarily to institutions of higher learning, leaving non-college bound youth as "The Forgotten Half" (Haggerty, 1989). In point of fact, the path to adulthood by way of a college education often appears blocked for students who struggle academically, to the point of having to repeat grades. Although some federal initiatives have targeted this segment of our under-18 population, most educationally-oriented interventions for disadvantaged youth lack a unifying theoretical model, fail to deliver a useful curriculum for entry into the workforce, and are generally inconsistent in their results. Often, students who choose vocational training over a college education are looked down upon and are, at times, ill-prepared for meaningful employment, with limited advancement possibilities.

Another barrier for many teenagers is their negative feelings of self-worth and their social anxieties. Despite adequate academic skills, some adolescents worry excessively about their ability to succeed, how they appear, or how well they are liked by peers. Others fail to complete the requirements for college admission due to depression, a lack of focus, or unclear views about their "future selves." These problems typically become manifested during the teenage years and are often not addressed by school-based prevention programs.

Early Intervention. Meaningful vocational training programs and school-based therapies provide important starting points for comprehensive community-based models that address the key developmental issues associated with adolescent pregnancy. More targeted approaches, however, are needed for those teens who get pregnant despite school- and community-based prevention efforts. Programs that reduce risks and, in their place, build protective factors promote adolescents' preparation for the critical role transition that lies ahead as they enter adulthood.

A major risk at this juncture is the possibility of an immediate repeat pregnancy. Having a second child within a short time interval after the first has been associated with less optimal developmental outcomes for teen mothers (Klerman, 2004). Although a common sense approach for targeted intervention is to focus on abstinence or contraceptive information in order to prevent additional pregnancies, these approaches are often unrelated to having a second off-timed pregnancy (Klerman, Baker, & Howard, 2003). Since delayed grade placement, poor reading achievement, and school absences are predictive of inter-birth intervals, they could become, during the course of the first pregnancy or the initial phase of parenthood, prevention targets, together with the development of good decision-making skills and a thorough knowledge of contraceptive alternatives.

Klerman (2004) has argued convincingly for a stronger research focus on the problem of repeat pregnancies among teenagers and young adults, since no consistently effective prevention program has been developed. We believe that an adolescent mother who is cognitively and emotionally prepared for parenthood, who embraces her identity as mother, who finishes her education and obtains meaningful employment, and who receives "just the right amount" of support and reinforcement for adopting adult responsibilities may delay a repeat pregnancy on her own, provided she thoroughly understands available contraceptive options. Perhaps the most important preparation is the teen's cognitive readiness for parenting (cf. chaps. 3, 5, and 7; Whitman et al., 2001). Our data consistently suggest that teens need to learn, during pregnancy, how to become effective parents and, in a supportive context, to assume their parenting role during their children's 1st year of life, even in the face of fears, conflicting demands, and emotional stress.

Preparation for the assumption of adult roles involves more than just cognitive readiness for parenting. Adult responsibilities also include the establishment of close, supportive relationships with the infant's father as well as practical issues involved with running a household and "making ends meet" financially, often on a limited and inconsistent income. Residential mobility and unstable intimate relationships emerged in our dataset as additional risk factors (cf. chap. 7), compromising progress toward family stability and personal contentment. In short, prevention programs need to focus not only on parenting preparedness but also on vocational skill acquisition and meaningful jobs; emotional stability and personal safety; high quality childcare and family health care; and understanding how to establish and maintain relationships through improved interpersonal communication, conflict management, and social problem-solving skills.

Prevention programs designed to change parenting practices and to help locate affordable and high-quality daycare are often necessary for at-risk children to reach their full potential prior to the onset of formal education. Social policies need to focus on teaching effective parenting skills and obtaining high-quality early education, as provided by childcare centers and/or Early Head Start programs. In both home and preschool settings, the explicit teaching of emotional self-regulation and early language usage needs to be modeled repeatedly and consistently, since these skills represent the foundation for later academic success.

School entry provides a final juncture for prevention programming, especially for children born to adolescent mothers. Cognitive and socioemotional delays—especially as they relate to the emergence of prereading skills—often go unrecognized within the unstructured and often nonstimulating environments of home and childcare settings. However, the inherent structure of the school day, combined with frequent evaluations and mini-interventions, can reveal and reverse early delays in speech, phonics, and verbal fluency during the pre-kindergarten years.

A final thought about prevention programs concerns the nature of the interactions between educators and young parents. Anecdotal reports of mothers in the NDAPP suggested that they were often estranged from the educational system, were at times patronized by educators who believed that they were unfit to parent, and/or lacked the skills and will necessary to support their children's classroom instruction. From another perspective, our research has shown an association between children's resilience and increasing self-esteem in young mothers. It is imperative for educators to find better ways of working with teen parents, as they become young adults, in order to reinforce positive parenting practices in ways that enhance their self-esteem about parenting so that they can contribute directly to their children's educational advancement through cognitive, emotional, and social skill acquisition in home settings.

We turn now to a model prevention program that addresses many of the risks identified as present in the lives of pregnant teenagers and builds upon the strengths and personal resources that protect at-risk mothers and children in the face of adversity and challenge. Given that neglect, abuse, violence, and harsh and insensitive parenting practices were often prevalent in the lives of adolescent mothers and their children in the NDAPP (cf. chaps. 5, 6, and 7; Whitman et al., 2001), the model project revolves around the prevention of child neglect through direct instruction of active and responsive parenting, minimization of risks (especially maternal depression, substance use, and family violence), and building of cumulative protective factors over time. The prevention program has been designed to provide more functional supports as well as to enhance decision making skills, thereby facilitating positive, consistent relationships between mothers and their infants.

PREVENTING CHILD NEGLECT IN TEEN MOTHERS: A MODEL PROGRAM

Over 2 million cases of child maltreatment are reported each year in the United States. Of these, child neglect is the largest single category; it often co-occurs in homes where abuse is taking place. Cases of neglect and abuse are disproportionately high among adolescent mothers and adult mothers with low levels of education. As mentioned in chapter 9, teen mothers may be at high risk for inconsistent or irregular parenting; these "oscillations" in the quality of parenting over time may constitute low levels of child neglect. The Centers for the Prevention of Child Neglect—made up of scientists from Georgetown University, University of Kansas, University of Texas Health Science Center at Houston, and the University of Notre Dame[1]—have received support from NICHD to conduct a large-scale research and demonstration project that assesses the impact of a highly promising, theory-driven prevention project designed to increase the sense of responsibility, decision-making skills, awareness of the dimensions of neglect, knowledge about child development, and the quality of parenting in at-risk mothers, as they raise their infants and young children over the first 3 years of life.

The intervention is multifaceted and directly informed by a conceptual model of the causes of child maltreatment that considers both proximal and distal supports in the mothers' lives, the emerging developmental needs of infants and toddlers, and their own past histories of depression and maltreatment (cf. Fig. 1.4), among other preexisting maternal risk factors. The measures of program participation, parenting behaviors, and child outcomes are multimethod, multi-informant, and gathered prospectively at frequent intervals over a duration of 2 1/2 years. This intervention program is based on several key assumptions about teen parenting.

- To prevent child maltreatment, at-risk parents—both teen and adult—need to have positive models of responsive parenting. The parenting model must become functional within the child's 1st year of life because the provision of many other parenting activities—such as appropriate health care, responsible caretaking, and language and preliteracy stimulation—flows naturally from a proactive, constructive parenting orientation formed early in parenthood.
- Teen mothers are likely to have incomplete or inappropriate mental models of parenting and may require direct, one-on-one instruction over time to build more positive and ef-

---

[1]The following are principal investigators for this project: Sharon Ramey, Craig Ramey, Bette Keltner, Steven Warren, Judy Carta, Susan Landry, and John Borkowski.

fective models of parenting and acquire positive and responsive (versus negative and harsh) interactional skills.

- In addition to a responsive model of parenting, at-risk mothers would benefit from (a) learning factual information about early child development and (b) receiving direct instruction in parenting skills when their infants are very young. They often need their social support systems strengthened or reorganized.
- The pay-offs for families should be found in less maltreatment, more responsive parenting, improved child development, better personal decision making, and a reduction in costs for the relevant social service and educational systems in the various communities in which the project is embedded.

Project Design

The model prevention project, conducted by the Centers for the Prevention of Child Neglect, was designed to reduce the incidence of child maltreatment, in terms of neglect and abuse, in high-risk mothers by helping them to improve decision making, create mental models of parenting, and develop new parenting styles and practices. In effect, it addresses the major problem we identified in the NDAPP: lack of preparedness for the parenting role prior to childhood and difficulty in adjusting to this transition in the ensuing years.

In the model prevention project, high-risk primiparous women—both pregnant teenage mothers and adult mothers without high school degrees—were recruited and randomly assigned to one of two groups: Treatment Group 1 (T1) received several enhanced services, such as referrals to mental health services for the treatment of depression or job training opportunities. These setting conditions are referred to as "enabling conditions"; in a sense, T1 serves as a "less intense intervention control" for assessing the effects of the more intensive treatment condition (T2) on parenting practices, neglectful behaviors, and children's readiness for school. These enabling conditions focus on major risk factors in the lives of teen mothers both prior to and during the intervention, such as depression, domestic violence, and addiction. We believe these risk factors, if not addressed, would set a limit on treatment effectiveness.

The High Intensity Treatment Conditions.   In addition to the enabling conditions, mothers in group T2 (the main treatment condition), received prevention modules during pregnancy and during the
first 4 months of life on decision making, health and safety, infant massage, and strengthening support networks in the family, church, and
community. The main parenting module, PALS I (Landry, Smith,
Glenn, & Vellet, 2002; Landry, Smith, & Swank, 2006), was designed to
teach responsive parenting to families from low SES backgrounds; it
makes use of extensive "training scripts" and in-home videotapes that
shape responsive and sensitive parenting practices between 6 and 12
months of age. A companion module, PALS II (the Toddler Program),
is introduced at 18 months and continues to 24 months; this module
focuses on language stimulation, play activities, and appropriate
methods of discipline. In the interim between PALS I and II, the "family coaches"—highly trained and experienced professionals—teach
skills such as the promotion of children's play, self-regulatory behaviors, and preliteracy knowledge by increasing the extent of maternal
involvement in home-based instruction.

The main parenting module, PALS I, uses in-home videotapes and
well-developed scripts to teach mothers how to interact, in sensitive
and responsive ways, with their children (Landry et al., 2006). The
importance of positive verbal interactions between mother and child
is repeatedly emphasized and reinforced. In a sense, the main goal of
PALS I, as well as the rest of the modules presented during the 1st
year, is to create a "mental model" of responsive parenting that
prompts and directs the quality and type of interactions with the infant, thus addressing potential problems in parenting knowledge
and style, especially the avoidance of harsh language and physical
discipline. The remaining modules during the 2nd year of life build
upon the "responsive parent model," promoting language stimulation, mother–child play, and appropriate child management and disciplinary techniques. The final part of the 2nd year's curriculum is
PALS II, which promotes the active, responsive parenting style
created during PALS I and also teaches behavioral management
skills.

The effects of the intervention are measured at frequent intervals
across several domains of maternal and child development, especially parenting practices, neglectful–abusive behaviors, maternal

socioemotional adjustment, and substance abuse. In the child, the focus is on socioemotional development, language skills, preliteracy knowledge, intelligence, and various developmental delays. A unique feature of this methodology is the measurement of "low levels" of psychosocial neglect, using a newly constructed phone interview technique as well as more standard measures of parenting incorporating both observational and self-report indicators of maltreatment.

Targeting Risks and Building Protection.   We have outlined in some detail an ongoing intervention program conducted by the Centers for the Prevention of Child Neglect because it targets many of the characteristics identified in this book as risk or protective factors operating in the lives of teenage mothers and their children. For instance, the "enabling conditions" in both T1 and T2 focus on major prenatal risks—such as depression, domestic violence, and the quality and availability of the support systems in participants' families and local communities. In the high-intense treatment condition (T2), the initial module teaches decision-making skills in the context of specific life problems. For instance, if a mother is in an abusive relationship, the focus is on creating a plan to avoid conflict situations, improve communication skills, and/or understand options in the community, including relationship counseling and available women's shelters. The most common referral, however, has been for the treatment of depression, which is first assessed during pregnancy and again after delivery.

Since many at-risk mothers bring their infants to hospital emergency rooms during the 1st year of life (e.g., 20% of all children in the District of Columbia), we focused intently on modules dealing with infant health (e.g., how to handle fever) and safety (e.g., back-to-sleep, car seats, removing dangerous items from the toddler's reach). In each module, mothers role-play and then use their newly learned decision-making strategies to solve hypothetical problems. Another part of the intervention teaches the techniques of "loving touch" and infant massage. The touch module brings the mother and child into close physical contact, thereby increasing bonding and, ideally, secure infant attachment. This training is considered important since teen mothers seldom breastfeed their infants after the first few days of life (Ineichen, Pierce, & Lawrenson, 1997).

In short, the major goal of this rather intense project, conducted by the Centers for the Prevention of Child Neglect, is to develop more sensitive and responsive parents who are fully aware of the importance of enriched home environments and their role in helping children achieve important developmental milestones that are prerequisite for successful entry into Head Start and, subsequently, the formal educational system. All of the goals and activities that are part of the intervention protocol designed by The Centers for the Prevention of Child Neglect were thought to represent the antithesis of maternal neglect. In a sense, they are aimed at enhancing cognitive readiness to parents, helping mothers learn how to control and manage their own lives, and assisting in teaching language and regulation skills to children who might otherwise experience a variety of developmental delays. As part of PALS I and II, mothers also teach their newly learned parenting skills to a significant family member or friend; in this way, they are able to demonstrate their competencies and encourage others to help in the task of childrearing, using a similar approach. This teaching technique was designed to strengthen positive aspects of family support systems. In the final part of the intervention, the focus is on solving mothers' individual needs, such as locating childcare, preschool programs, and job training opportunities, as well as maintaining healthy diets and patterns of daily exercise for both mothers and their children. It should be noted that the repeated assessments of multiple factors over time will lead to the emergence of a dataset with ample opportunities to assess the impact of cumulative risk and protective factors, using the analytic methods described in chapter 9.

CONCLUSION: BUILDING RESILIENCE

Many prevention programs approach treatment from a deficit perspective, with an emphasis on identifying and ameliorating weaknesses assumed to be associated with teen parenting. The major problem here is the rather narrow focus on personal limitations rather than potential strengths. A more subtle problem, however, is the concern for teaching new skills that teen mothers may have difficulty mastering or that have little personal or sociocultural relevance to them. In this sense, the agenda of the prevention researcher may not always be in line with what is meaningful to, and needed by, high-risk parents. As was done in the model prevention project described in the prior section, mothers' needs were always addressed first, through the "enabling conditions" module, and then the prevention program began. The underlying assumption is that for parenting projects to be successful all relevant risk factors—such as abusive environments, mental health or financial problems, or the lack of functional supports—must become integral parts of the comprehensive prevention program. Moreover, the individual strengths and existing protective factors of each participant need to be taken into account and used as a platform upon which to mount the prevention curriculum.

In addition to building on the talents and abilities of at-risk mothers during planning and implementation phases, prevention programs should also incorporate a strengths-based approach in their assessment protocols. Recently, the U.S. Department of Health and Human Services (2004) called for more qualitative, participatory methods of outcome assessments that focus on the measurement of the positive skills and capacities of both mothers and children. These assessments should involve not only the program staff and other essential members of the prevention team but also the participants themselves. By recognizing a vital role for participants in the evaluation and development of prevention programs, their opinions and experiences are heard and valued, thereby leading to more positive relationships with the staff, creating more relevant curricula, producing more optimal outcomes for at-risk mothers and their children, and yielding datasets with minimal missing data and limited attrition.

Comprehensive, well-integrated prevention programs—developed, implemented, and evaluated using a strength-based approach (Maton et al., 2004)—should lead to meaningful and lasting changes in the lives of many adolescent mothers as they move through adulthood and their children enter adolescence. When combined with high-quality childcare, comprehensive parenting programs will likely improve the social, emotional, and academic well-being of children trapped in poverty, who otherwise are at risk for a variety of developmental delays and school-related failures.

REFERENCES

Cummings, E. M., Davies, P. T., & Campbell, S. B. (2000). *Developmental psychopathology and family process: Theory, research, and clinical implications.* New York: The Guilford Press.

Dunst, C. J., Trivette, C. M., & Mott, D. W. (1994). Strengths-based family-centered intervention practices. In C. J. Dunst, C. M Trivette, & A. G. Deal (Eds.), *Supporting & strengthening families: Methods, strategies, and practices* (pp. 115–131). Cambridge, MA: Brookline Books.

Haggerty, R. J. (1989). Youth and America's future: The forgotten half. *Journal of Developmental and Behavioral Pediatrics, 10,* 321–325.

Ineichen, B., Pierce, M., & Lawrenson, R. (1997). Teenage mothers as breastfeeders: Attitudes and behaviour. *Journal of Adolescence, 20,* 505–509.

Klerman, L. V. (2004). *Another chance: Preventing additional births to teen mothers.* Washington, DC: National Campaign to Prevent Teen Pregnancy.

Klerman, L. V., Baker, B. A., & Howard, G. (2003). Second births among teenage mothers: Program results and statistical methods. *Journal of Adolescent Health, 32,* 452–455.

Landry, S. H., Smith, K. E., Glenn, S. M., & Vellet, N. S. (2002). *Joint-attention treatment training manual: The 'PALS' project–1998 revised version for 'My Baby and Me' study.* Houston, TX: University of Texas Health Sciences Center Department of Pediatrics.

Landry, S. H., Smith, K. E., & Swank, P. R. (2006). Responsive parenting: Establishing early foundations for social, communication, and independent problem solving skills. *Developmental Psychology, 42,* 627–642.

Maton, K. I., Schellenbach, C. J., Leadbeater, B. J., & Solarz, A. L. (Eds.). (2004). *Investing in children, youth, families, and communities: Strengths-based research and policy.* Washington, DC: American Psychological Association.

Rolf, J. E. (1999). Resilience: An interview with Norman Garmezy. In M. D. Glantz & J. L. Hohnson (Eds.), *Resilience and development: Positive life adaptations* (pp. 5–14). New York: Kluwer Academic/Plenum Publishers.

Terry-Humen, E., Manlove, J., & Moore, K. (2005). *Playing catch-up: How children of teen mothers fare.* Washington, DC: National Campaign to Prevent Teen Pregnancy.

U.S. Department of Health and Human Services. (2004). *Evaluating your prevention program.* Washington, DC: Author.

Whitman, T. L., Borkowski, J. G., Keogh, D. A., & Weed, K. (2001). *Interwoven lives: Adolescent mothers and their children.* Mahwah, NJ: Lawrence Erlbaum Associates.

Author Index

Subject Index